Workforce Analytics is so much more than a collection of me
those are described very clearly. Readers will welcome th
analyze, and influence) as a comprehensive guide to maki
about the best ways to optimize talent and successfully implement strategic change. Both
academics and practitioners will find a deep reservoir of useful information in this book.

Wayne F. Cascio, *Ph.D. Distinguished Professor Emeritus,*
University of Colorado, The Business School,
University of Colorado Denver

Workforce Analytics offers an invaluable exploration on the use of data to improve decisions
about the workforce. The authors provide both theory and practice ideas, guiding readers
through the history, robust methodologies, ethical considerations, and strategic applications of workforce analytics. It will be an invaluable resource for students, researchers, and
workforce analytics/people analytics practitioners to harness its ACAI model: **A**sk the right
questions, **C**ollect the right data, Conduct the right **A**nalyses, and **I**nfluence the right decisions. Furthermore, it encompasses critical overlapping disciplines such as I/O psychology,
organization behavior, data science and change management, and the invaluable contributions of each.

Lexy Martin, *head of research at Visier from 2016 to 2023*

This book brilliantly bridges theory and practice, offering a comprehensive framework for
building evidence-based and ethical workforce analytics. By challenging conventional wisdom and delivering critical insights, it stands as an essential guide to advancing the discipline.

Salvatore V. Falletta, *Professor, Drexel University; Research Chair,*
The Society for People Analytics; author of Creepy Analytics

Bridging the science-practice divide has never been more critical in workforce analytics.
The authors and contributors to *Workforce Analytics: A Global Perspective* seamlessly integrate
cutting-edge research techniques with real-world applications, making complex concepts
both accessible yet applicable. This resource is as intellectually rigorous as it is practical. I
wouldn't be surprised if this becomes the go-to text for graduate education in workforce
analytics, as well as an engaging read for practitioners looking to stay at the forefront of
the field.

Cole Napper, *VP of Research & Innovation at Lightcast and*
Owner of Directionally Correct Podcast & Newsletter

Workforce Analytics: A Global Perspective is a must-read for anyone looking to harness data
for smarter workforce decisions. This book skillfully bridges science and practice, offering a
clear roadmap—from data and analytic techniques to implementation challenges and ethical
considerations. The ACAI model is a standout feature, providing a practical framework to
maximize the impact of workforce analytics.

Prof. dr. Corine Boon, *Professor of HRM and People Analytics,*
Director of Amsterdam People Analytics Centre (APAC)

Finally, a graduate-level workforce analytics textbook spanning theory and practice, implementation and change, and, most importantly, ethics. This book will inspire and guide the next generation of workforce analytics leaders.

Amit Mohindra, *CEO, People Analytics Success, and*
former global head of people analytics at Apple

The guide I wish I had as the Global Head of People Analytics. This book is a game-changer for anyone navigating the complexities of workforce analytics. With its clear, actionable framework and deep dive into both the strategic and ethical dimensions, it's an invaluable resource for anyone looking to leverage analytics to make smarter decisions that drive organizational performance.

Dr. Serena H. Huang, *Author of* The Inclusion Equation - Leveraging Data
& AI for Organizational Diversity and Wellbeing, *Founder of Data With Serena,*
and former Global Head of People Analytics at PayPal and Kraft Heinz

Human capital is the key to company performance, and this volume gives us the latest and best thinking about how to use the new tools for managing it.

Prof. Peter Cappelli, *Director - Center for Human Resources,*
The Wharton School, University of Pennsylvania

This book provides an amazing insight into the power of data, how to interpret and analyze it and more importantly apply it in organizations with practical behavioural changes, tips and ideas. It is ideal for both people analytics specialists and HR practitioners alike, with an extensive range of models and techniques that are thought provoking and clearly explained. But this book isn't just about statistics and their application, it's about the future of HR and the vital role that people analytics has to play in changing the mindset and perception that exists about the function. It's a must read for anyone who is interested in organizational and people effectiveness.

Dave Millner, *Author and Founder of HR Curator, a People Analytics Training Company*

This book brings you the unique collective perspective of a formidable group of authors with decades of diverse thought leadership in HR analytics. It will help you build an analytics strategy that improves talent decisions, focused on the pivot points that have the greatest strategic impact.

Dr. John Boudreau, *Senior Research Scientist, Center For Effective Organizations, and*
Emeritus Professor of Management and Organization, University of Southern California

This book should be considered required reading for anyone wishing to apply a gold-standard approach to workforce analytics. The book's guiding framework can be used in a myriad of ways, and by many actors in this exciting world. The authors do an outstanding job of focusing on the 'enabling factors', not just the analytical: clear communication and expectation management, product ownership, change management and the accountability to act (or not!). The result is a senior-level practitioner guide, which aims to navigate both the impactful topics, as well as the more nuanced, but supported by five-star quality research, throughout.

Mark Lawrence, *Founder and Executive Consultant, Data Driven HR Ltd*

I have long argued that Workforce Analytics is necessary for effective Strategic Human Resources (HR) and am glad to see this book brings these threads together. There has been a lot written on the topic of workforce analytics over the past decades and this contribution nicely brings together much of this into a compendium of techniques, theories, case studies and a suggested approach to guide the practice of workforce analytics. This is an incredibly rich and varied reference for anyone in HR, particularly if you are working in workforce/people analytics, or as I like to think of it, true strategic HR.

Tony Ashton, *Chief Product Officer, One Model*

Written by leading international experts on workforce analytics, this book demonstrates why it has become central to organizational performance and why it is essential for effective strategic human resource management. The book is highly relevant both for researchers and organizational practitioners as it ranges widely across contemporary analytic techniques, ethical considerations and the contribution of workforce analytics to organizational change. There is even a workforce analytics maturity index to guide practitioners on their path to its effective utilisation. This book should be on the reading list of all advanced human resource management programmes.

David E Guest, Emeritus Professor of Organizational Psychology and Human Resource Management, King's Business School

A powerful and insightful resource for any Workforce Analytics practitioner. This book not only establishes a solid conceptual and ethical framework to guide practice but also inspires possibilities by outlining the latest analytical techniques and how they can be used to progress understanding. It serves as a reminder of why I love my profession, as it highlights that there is always something new to learn and discover in the pursuit of making work and organisations safer, more engaging and productive.

Vaughn Sheahan, *Head of Organisational Development and Analytics, BHP*

From someone who's been deep in the trenches of global workforce analytics, I can confidently say: if you're serious about making a measurable impact with HR data, this is the book you need. Alec, Dana, Mark, and Martin have created a powerhouse of a book, filled with insights from leading experts in our field. This isn't just another theoretical text—it's a practical playbook for anyone looking to start out or scale up in the field of workforce analytics. Their book guides you through the 'what,' the 'how,' and importantly, the 'why' of HR analytics, enabling you to deliver the kind of impactful insights that drive strategic decisions and generate real business value."

Greg Newman, *People Analytics - Human Capital, Deloitte Consulting Pty Ltd*

Workforce Analytics: A Global Perspective provides a comprehensive background and many valuable models for people analytics professionals. As organizations grow in complexity, this type of analysis is now critical to drive growth in the years ahead.

Josh Bersin, *Global Industry Analyst*

I wholeheartedly recommend *Workforce Analytics* to anyone looking to deepen their understanding of using people data to drive business outcomes. This book offers an insightful blend of analytical techniques and change management strategies, making it a wonderful resource for students and practitioners alike. What sets this book apart is its thorough exploration of qualitative analysis and causal modeling. These areas are often overlooked, but critical for understanding the workforce. Plus, the case studies provided throughout demonstrate real world examples that readers can immediately apply. This book provides a framework that blends theory and practice to demonstrate how workforce analytics can deliver organizational value.

Nicole Lettich, *Senior Director of People Analytics in Fintech*

This is *the* book on workforce analytics for the serious practitioners in HR, scholars, and students alike. It brings back the strategic perspective by linking the workforce with how the company creates value and builds competitive edge. Outlining how analytics is properly done, it provides tips and tricks to avoid the pitfalls. Co-authored by some of the most renowned scholars in the field, this is bound to become the reference and standard for strategic work force analytics that add value to business for years to come. I thank the authors for painstakingly putting this together and strongly recommend HR to use it to improve its strategic impact while developing people's ultimate potential.

Jorrit van der Togt, *Executive Vice President Shell Downstream, Renewables and Energy Solutions*

Workforce Analytics: A Global Perspective provides a comprehensive foundation for understanding how data can shape workforce decision-making. With a strong theoretical underpinning, this book is essential for anyone looking to deepen their expertise in the topic, a must-read to build a strong foundation in workforce analytics and data-driven decision-making.

Erik van Vulpen, *Founder, AIHR - Academy to Innovate HR*

If you truly want to understand the power of workforce analytics, this is the book to read. Written by an all-star team of authors, this book provides concrete, concise, and impactful examples of how analytical techniques support decision making within the context of the workforce. The book goes beyond simply describing the phenomenon of workforce analytics and offers a deep and fundamental understanding of applying workforce analytics. A must-read for all interested in workforce analytics.

Patrick Coolen, *Partner at KennedyFitch, and previous head of workforce analytics at ABN AMRO*

In *Workforce Analytics: A Global Perspective*, the authors have created a masterful synthesis of cutting-edge theory and practical application. The book offers a refreshingly holistic approach to the discipline of People/Workforce Analytics, firmly grounded in organisational performance and business strategy. They not only elucidate the complexities of workforce analytics with clarity and rigour, but also provide clear and practical recommendations through the innovative ACAI model. Whether you are a seasoned practitioner, an academic, or a student eager to understand the strategic potential of data-driven decision-making, this book is an indispensable resource. Its global outlook and meticulous scholarship set a new benchmark in the human resource management literature.

Barry Swales, *Managing Director, Tucana, and Founder and curator, People Analytics World*

Workforce Analytics: A Global Perspective is an essential guide for anyone looking to elevate their approach to workforce analytics beyond surface-level metrics and into true strategic impact. What sets this book apart is its insistence on context. Rather than defaulting to generic HR activity metrics that yield little strategic insight, the authors emphasize the importance of applying a research-based lens to workforce analytics. They challenge readers to go beyond data for data's sake and instead focus on understanding which types of work have the greatest impact on firm success and where those critical contributions occur within the organization. For workforce analytics practitioners, HR professionals, and business leaders alike, this book offers not just a roadmap for implementing workforce analytics effectively, but a call to action: to ask the right questions, use the right data, and apply the right analytic techniques to unlock the full potential of the workforce. A must-read for anyone serious about making workforce analytics a true business driver.

Michael M. Moon, *PhD, Director, Organizational Research & Insights, AbbVie*

A great resource for analyst teams to build their project muscle, to focus on the right projects, execute them in an appropriate, research backed way, and present results that compel leaders to act. The authors capture technical detail to support teams to produce high quality analytics to put people analytics at the centre of business. This book will help build connections between people analytics work and business strategy planning and execution.

Jordan Pettman, *Senior Director, Insight222*

Global Perspectives on Workforce Analytics is an essential guide for anyone looking to bridge the gap between the science and practice of workforce analytics. The authors provide a comprehensive exploration of the field—from its historical foundations to cutting-edge methodologies, ethical considerations, and practical implementation strategies. Their global perspective and research-driven insights make this book an invaluable resource for HR leaders, analysts, and executives seeking to deploy workforce analytics for strategic impact. As workforce analytics continues to evolve, this book will serve as a foundational text for organizations looking to unlock sustainable value.

Craig Starbuck, *CEO OrgAcuity*

Workforce Analytics

Workforce Analytics: A Global Perspective provides a comprehensive sweep of key issues facing the evolving discipline of workforce analytics. The editors, all globally recognized in this field, have curated a collection of unique pieces that introduce workforce analytics, discuss its place in the HR sphere, and systematically address the key practical challenges faced by analytics experts working in and with organizations. Drawing on the combined expertise of the editors and a range of practicing expert contributors, the book provides a current, cutting-edge, and multi-perspective survey of workforce analytics. The contributions examine why workforce analytics is important, how it can help contribute to business success, and the considerations businesses need to address to maximize the benefit of this important HR expertise. A breakthrough text in a game-changing emerging discipline, the book is an essential resource for practitioners, students, and researchers in workforce analytics, people analytics, and human resource management more broadly.

Martin R. Edwards is a Professor of Management at the UQ Business School, University of Queensland, Australia. Martin has published widely in the area of Human Resource Management. He is active in the field of HR consultancy, having delivered projects to numerous multinationals; he has also provided bespoke HR Analytics training to global firms.

Dana Minbaeva is a Professor of Strategic Human Capital at King's Business School, King's College London, UK. She also holds a part-time position at Copenhagen Business School, Denmark, and is an affiliate faculty member at London Business School, UK. Professor Minbaeva is a Fellow of the Academy of International Business. She has received several national and international awards for her research achievements, including the prestigious JIBS Decade Award in 2013. Dana is also the founder and director of the Nordic Human Capital Advisory Aps.

Alec Levenson is Senior Research Scientist and Director at the Center for Effective Organizations, Marshall School of Business, University of Southern California. His research has been published in books, academic and business publications, and global media outlets, including the *New York Times*, *Wall Street Journal*, *The Economist*, CNN, Associated Press, *US News and World Report*, National Public Radio, *Los Angeles Times*, *USA Today*, *Marketplace*, and Fox News.

Mark A. Huselid is the Distinguished Professor of Workforce Analytics and director of the Center for Workforce Analytics at the D'Amore-McKim School of Business, Northeastern University. He was the editor of the *Human Resource Management Journal*, and is a current or former member of numerous professional and academic boards. He is a fellow of the National Academy of Human Resources (NAHR), the Society for Industrial and Organizational Psychology (SIOP), and the Association for Psychological Science (APS).

Routledge Global Human Resource Management Series

Edited by David G. Collings, Trinity College Dublin, Ireland, Elaine Farndale, Penn State University, USA, and Fang Lee Cooke, Monash University, Australia

The Global HRM Series has for over a decade been leading the way in advancing our understanding of Global HRM issues. Edited and authored by the leading and highest-profile researchers in the field of human resource management (HRM), this series of books offers students and reflective practitioners accessible, coordinated, and comprehensive textbooks on global HRM. Individually and collectively, these books cover the core areas of the field, including titles on global leadership, global talent management, global careers, and the global HR function, as well as comparative volumes on HR in key global regions.

The series is organized into two distinct strands: the first reflects key issues in managing global HRM and the second comparative perspectives human resource management.

Taking an expert look at an increasingly important area of global business, this well-established series has become the benchmark for serious textbooks on global HRM.

The Publisher and Editors wish to thank the Founding Editors of the series – Randall Schuler, Susan Jackson, Paul Sparrow, and Michael Poole.

Dedication: The late Professor Michael Poole was one of the founding series editors, and the series is dedicated to his memory.

https://www.routledge.com/Global-HRM/book-series/SE0692

Macro Talent Management
A Global Perspective on Managing Talent in Developed Markets
Vlad Vaiman, Paul Sparrow, Randall Schuler and David Collings

Macro Talent Management in Emerging and Emergent markets
A Global Perspective
Vlad Vaiman, Paul Sparrow, Randall Schuler and David Collings

Global Talent Management (second edition)
Edited by David G. Collings, Hugh Scullion and Paula M. Caligiuri

International Human Resource Management (sixth edition)
Policies and Practices for Multinational Enterprises
Ibraiz Tarique, Dennis R. Briscoe and Randall S. Schuler

Performance Management Systems (second edition)
A Global Perspective
Arup Varma, Pawan Budhwar and Angelo DeNisis

Workforce Analytics
A Global Perspective
Edited by Martin R Edwards, Dana Minbaeva, Alec Levenson, and Mark A. Huselid

Workforce Analytics

A Global Perspective

Edited by Martin R. Edwards,
Dana Minbaeva, Alec Levenson,
and Mark A. Huselid

Routledge
Taylor & Francis Group

NEW YORK AND LONDON

Designed cover image: Getty Images

First published 2025
by Routledge
605 Third Avenue, New York, NY 10158

and by Routledge
4 Park Square, Milton Park, Abingdon, Oxon, OX14 4RN

Routledge is an imprint of the Taylor & Francis Group, an informa business

ISBN: 978-1-032-03984-8 (hbk)
ISBN: 978-1-032-02900-9 (pbk)
ISBN: 978-1-003-19009-7 (ebk)

DOI: 10.4324/9781003190097

Typeset in Bembo
by Deanta Global Publishing Services, Chennai, India

Contents

Contributors

Sasa Batistic, Tilburg University, The Netherlands

Matt I. Brown, Human Resources Research Organization (HumRRO)

Andy Charlwood, University of Leeds, UK

Martin R. Edwards, University of Queensland, Australia

Nigel Guenole, Goldsmiths, University of London, UK

Joeri Hofmans, Vrije Universiteit Brussel, Belgium

Mark A. Huselid, Northeastern University, USA

Sarah Kieran, University of Limerick, Ireland

Alec Levenson, University of Southern California, USA

Steven McCartney, University College Dublin, Ireland

Dana Minbaeva, King's College London, UK, and Copenhagen Business School, Denmark

Andrew Pitts, Polinode

Rafael A. Sanchez, Broad Institute of MIT and Harvard, USA

Louise Winton Schreuders, Independent Researcher

Andrew B. Speer, Indiana University, Kelley School of Business

Karen Spilsbury, University of Leeds, UK

Danat Valizade, University of Leeds, UK

Paul van der Laken

Marc van Veldhoven, Tilburg University, The Netherlands

Heather Whiteman, University of Washington Information School, USA

Foreword

For over two decades, the Global HRM Series has been leading the way in advancing our understanding of global human resource management (HRM) issues. Authored by the leading and highest-profile researchers in the field of HRM, this series offers students and reflective practitioners accessible, coordinated, and comprehensive textbooks on global HRM. Individually and collectively, these books cover the field's core areas, including titles on global leadership, global talent management, global careers, and the global HR function, as well as comparative volumes on HRM in key global regions. We now add to this list this important and timely new volume, *Global Perspectives on Workforce Analytics*, co-authored by four leading scholars in the field from across the globe.

This well-established series, which takes an expert look at an increasingly important area of global business, has become the benchmark for serious textbooks on global HRM. The series is organized into two distinct strands: the first reflects key issues in managing global HRM, and the second offers comparative perspectives on human resource management. This book, *Global Perspectives on Workforce Analytics*, adds to the first strand by addressing an increasingly essential part of everyday business in managing global HRM.

The authors unpack the historical roots of the current importance of digital technologies in people management, setting the scene for understanding the practical and theoretical implications of workforce analytics. Overall, the book provides a clear structure for understanding how to effectively and ethically implement workforce analytics by adopting an ACAI (**A**sk, **C**ollect, **A**nalyze, **I**nfluence) model, which can be adopted by researchers and practitioners alike.

Workforce analytics has become an integral part of strategic human resource management. For global firms, this includes managing strategy on a global scale within complex and culturally diverse business environments. This book outlines the role of workforce analytics through different theoretical lenses that can inform

HR analytic practices. Workforce analytics combines the use of both quantitative and qualitative techniques, both of which are addressed in detail here. Scholars and practitioners can learn about appropriate methodologies and the latest techniques to conduct robust analyses of high-quality data. Additionally, the chapters provide insights into how analytics form a fundamental part of change management through sensemaking, and how they are leading to the adaptation of the role of the HR function inside organizations. Using this information, as well as the authors' proposed workforce analytics maturity matrix, will help practitioners better prepare themselves for how workforce analytics can enhance the quality of decisions made inside their organizations.

Throughout the book, the authors encourage the adoption of a critical perspective to ensure only high-quality information is collected and analyzed for organizational decision-making. Importantly, an entire chapter is dedicated to the ethical implications of workforce analytics, exploring issues around data privacy, data quality, and algorithmic bias, resulting in a ten-step framework for ethical workforce analytics that both scholars and practitioners can put into action.

Drawing from the latest research, as well as interviews with practitioners, the book concludes with the shared thoughts of the authors on what lies ahead for workforce analytics. Addressing pressing issues around the future of the workplace and workforce, the closing chapter brings practitioners and scholars closer together regarding the future implementation of workforce analytics.

The Publisher and Editors wish to thank the Founding Editors of the series – Randall Schuler, Susan Jackson, Paul Sparrow, and Michael Poole.

Dedication: The late Professor Michael Poole was one of the founding series editors, and the series is dedicated to his memory.

David Collings, Elaine Farndale, and Fang Lee Cooke,
August 2024

Preface

This book was created over a number of years. Its focus evolved through discussion and collaboration as Dana, Martin, Alec, and Mark shared their interests and passions around the use of workforce analytics.

The idea for this book took root during one of the most transformative periods in recent history. When COVID-19 struck, it disrupted not only our daily lives but also the way we work, collaborate, and connect. As the world went into lockdown, many of our priorities shifted dramatically. In this surreal new reality, the writing of this book became a beacon, reminding us of the old world order where global links and cooperation across geographies were taken for granted. Ironically, it was this very disruption that underscored the potential, enablement, and necessity of global connections in ways we had never fully appreciated before.

From the seclusion of our homes, across continents and time zones, spanning different days, mornings, and nights, we embarked on this ambitious project. The process was both challenging and illuminating. We navigated virtual meetings, often catching glimpses of each other's lives, home offices, and the varied wallpapers on our video calls. These virtual interactions fostered a unique sense of camaraderie and collaboration. We supported each other through varied experiences of COVID-19 lockdowns, border closures, health checks, surgeries, personal ups and downs, and the myriad uncertainties that the pandemic brought into our lives. The first year of writing this book was more than just an academic endeavor; it was a collective journey of sensemaking, as we tried to understand and adapt to the new world order from different global locations.

During this period, we witnessed a profound evolution in the field of workforce analytics. Workforce analytics emerged not just as a tool for efficiency and productivity but as a vital resource for ensuring the well-being and resilience of employees. It became clear that data-driven insights could help organizations adapt to rapid changes, support their workforce through crises, and build more flexible and inclusive workplaces. Advances in digital technologies accelerated workforce analytics to the top of the strategic agenda in companies and organizations worldwide after reopening. This rise provided us with new perspectives and exciting insights, highlighting the next big move on the fast-approaching horizon: machine learning and artificial intelligence.

This book is the product of our shared experiences and insights gained during this tumultuous time across different parts of the globe. It reflects the innovative spirit and collaborative effort of a diverse group of professionals united by a common goal: to explore and elucidate the transformative power of workforce analytics in the modern era. While our individual voices are reflected within the chapters, we collectively stand by every perspective expressed from beginning to end. We hope that our work will provide valuable guidance and inspiration to leaders, managers, and analysts as they navigate the complexities of the post-pandemic world.

As we present this book to you, we extend our deepest gratitude to everyone who contributed to its creation. Your dedication, resilience, and unwavering support have made this journey possible.

Work Force Analytics (WFA)

Introduction and book overview

*Alec Levenson, Dana Minbaeva,
Mark A. Huselid, and Martin R. Edwards*

Introduction

The topic of workforce analytics (WFA) is both new and timeless. While the field has experienced explosive growth in recent years, its origins date back over a century. Despite this lengthy background and considerable progress, many would claim that WFA lacks a theoretical foundation and has vague conceptual boundaries. Some even argue that it should not be considered a discipline, dismissing it as merely a management fad (Rasmussen & Ulrich, 2015). Furthermore, despite the growing attention and the abundance of books, articles, and case studies on WFA applications, there is no overarching view of the field, its gaps, and strategies for enhancing the design, implementation, and outcomes of WFA. Our book is structured to provide just such a view.

Our goal is to take you, the reader, on a journey that mirrors the development of the field of WFA, beginning with its origins and progressing through its development to the current state of the field – and beyond. The four of us, friends and colleagues for many years, offer a global perspective on WFA, integrating both the science and practice of WFA. The book is structured as follows:

- Chapter 1 defines workforce analytics and introduces the overarching framework used to address the topic of global WFA throughout the book.
- Chapter 2 explores the theoretical origins of WFA. Understanding the historical context is crucial for effective WFA system design and implementation. We argue that recognizing and comprehending the field's historical and theoretical origins is essential for addressing the role of WFA in business success and making WFA more actionable and impactful.

DOI: 10.4324/9781003190097-2

- Chapter 3 reviews a variety of approaches to data collection and framing the analysis, including addressing HR and talent processes, as well as the focus and level of aggregation for the analysis (by role, team, business unit, etc.).

- Chapter 4 provides examples of useful statistical techniques and their usage in workforce analytics. It highlights important considerations when deciding on the right choice of analytic approaches to apply to workforce data.

- Chapter 5 addresses implementation challenges for WFA and how to maximize positive impacts on business outcomes. It frames analytics as a change management process and offers insights on initiating sustainable organizational change based on generated insights.

- Chapter 6 reviews important ethical and privacy issues faced when applying WFA and, in doing so, highlights the importance of reflecting on WFA with an ethical lens.

- Chapter 7 discusses the need for a holistic view of WFA maturity, which is crucial for building effective WFA functions in modern organizations. It introduces a new WFA maturity matrix and outlines key elements for building WFA functions, drawn from interviews with leading WFA executives globally.

- The concluding Chapter 8 offers our reflections on the future trajectory of WFA. We contextualize these reflections within the evolving landscape of HR, especially amidst the growing prominence of digital technologies.

We start by describing what we mean by workforce analytics.

Workforce analytics defined

We have chosen the term "workforce analytics" because it directs attention to the collective contributions and combined efforts of employees towards business success or other forms of value creation. Alternatives like "HR analytics," "people analytics," and "talent analytics" have also emerged recently, and they are often used interchangeably in practice, covering similar ground. However, since "HR," "people," "talent," and "workforce" carry different connotations, especially across cultures, the choice among them should be tailored to the audience. "HR analytics" was the first term introduced around 20 years ago, with "talent analytics" emerging subsequently. These terms were used to encapsulate analytics related to HR policies and practices that either enable or impede effective employee contributions. "People analytics" was introduced more recently as an umbrella term, often used by practitioners to denote all activities involving people data. We believe "workforce analytics" transcends the domain of HR practices application and provides a more comprehensive term for assessing the impact of the workforce as human capital on organizational outcomes (Becker et al., 2009; Huselid, 2018).

WFA involves quantitative and qualitative analyses of data or information concerning the individuals employed by an organization – their tasks, roles, relationships, and contributions to organizational outcomes. It explores how individuals engage in their work, the impact their work has on them, and their contributions to job, team, unit, and organizational performance. While there are many ways to manipulate and report data, if such manipulation does not yield actionable insights, we would not include it as an example of (effective) WFA. Actionable insights are generated when appropriate analytics techniques are integrated into sensemaking and purposeful storytelling, showing how variations in human capital – including how it combines together collectively – affect organizational performance. The creation of a dashboard, report, or visualization without that integration and impact is insufficient to be considered true WFA (Becker et al., 2001).

The overarching WFA framework

WFA has the potential to generate new knowledge, leading to improved outcomes at the individual, team, and organizational levels through more effective management of human capital. However, this process requires data, which often needs to be transformed and aggregated to produce actionable insights. Crucially, this process must be grounded in the disciplined application of the scientific method.

Our overall assessment of the current state of WFA as applied internally within organizations and by external consultants and vendors is that the rigorous application of the scientific method is relatively rare. Current WFA practice, in too many instances, consists of analyzing data in search of interesting patterns to exploit rather than starting with the issues to be addressed. Quite similar to the process known as evidence-based management (Barends & Rousseau, 2018), a proper application of the scientific method in WFA begins with defining the fundamental business issues to be addressed, reviewing the research-based evidence on those issues, evaluating which models are best applied, developing hypotheses to test based on those models, collecting the best available data to test the hypotheses, and then conducting the analysis. This process forms the foundation of our approach to WFA and is reflected throughout this book.

There is an old adage about the follies of taking a data-first approach to WFA. As the story goes, a person, we'll call her Jada, leaves a restaurant after dinner and goes to the parking lot next door to retrieve her automobile and drive home. Upon entering the parking lot, she encounters another person, Jo, who is on his hands and knees on the ground, looking for something underneath the sole streetlight in the parking lot. It's clear to Jada that Jo has not found what he is looking for under the light, yet he continues to look in the same place, over and over. Jada asks him, "What are you looking for?" "My car keys," Jo replies. "But they clearly aren't here, so why do you keep searching for them here?" she asks. His response: "Because this is where the light is."

This story, often shared among social scientists, serves as a reminder of the pitfalls of relying solely on readily available data. It underscores the importance of taking the time and effort to examine the situation thoroughly, devise a comprehensive strategy for evaluating the issues at hand, and then implement the strategy in a purposeful and effective way. That is the essence of the scientific method, and it is the journey we hope this book will help enable the field of WFA to navigate better.

We propose that designing and implementing effective WFA requires excelling in four areas, which we present as our ACAI model of WFA implementation:

- Phase 1: **A**sk the right questions.
- Phase 2: **C**ollect the right data.
- Phase 3: Conduct the right **A**nalyses.
- Phase 4: **I**nfluence the right decisions.

We visualize these phases in Figure 1.1 and provide detailed descriptions of each action below. It's important to note that while we number them as sequential phases, effective WFA in practice typically involves multiple feedback loops among these phases.

Phase 1: Ask the right questions. Metrics and measures provide answers to questions. Moving from raw data to actionable insights requires that we ask the right questions about how the workforce contributes to firm success. In our view, data collection and infrastructure are not the biggest challenges in designing and implementing effective WFA systems – knowing what to measure and how to measure it is! So, do not start with the data you have, but rather with the *question* you are attempting to answer.

Developing appropriate questions for the analytics team to focus on requires a clear understanding of the role of human capital in driving the outcomes of interest. In our work, we focus specifically on what we describe as *strategic* work and positions (Huselid, Beatty, et al., 2005). Our view is that not all work or positions are of equal value, so it is critical for managers to gain an understanding of what types of work have the greatest impact on firm success, and where this work is located in the business (Minbaeva & Vardi, 2018).

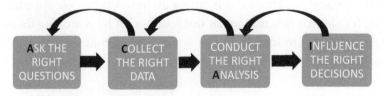

FIGURE 1.1 The ACAI model of workforce analytics.

For example, it might be tempting to argue that the most senior roles are the most important in any business, or perhaps that the most prevalent or customer-facing roles are. Certainly, these jobs are important – all jobs are; otherwise, we wouldn't have them. But we draw the distinction between work that is important and work that is truly strategic. From our perspective, *strategic* jobs and work are both directly linked to the firm's strategy and exhibit considerable variability in individual and/ or team performance (Minbaeva & Collings, 2013). Said differently, a job's or team's impact on strategic success provides the *context for* performance improvement, while the variability in performance provides the *opportunity* for improvement.

Consider the example of the roles on an Olympic basketball team. Each role is undoubtedly important, performance is critical, and losing a team member would certainly be a problem. But, in terms of opportunity for improvement, it is unlikely that coaching and skill development will provide the potential for a 20–30% increase in individual or team performance; the players are already too good! In contrast, consider a team of 8-year-olds playing their first basketball season. Here, coaching and basic skills development could indeed have a substantial impact on performance, because (1) the base rate of player skills is low, and (2) there is a lot of variance among the team members in their level of performance.

We are not saying that coaching doesn't matter for the Olympic team. Rather, our point is that the variance in performance is quite different for Olympic athletes and our 8-year-olds. As a consequence, our expectations for performance enhancement need to be quite different for each of these populations. The key point is that WFA can help managers identify high-impact roles and (team) work, which is done by individuals and groups with considerable variance in their levels of performance. This low-hanging fruit often flies under the radar in many organizations. Here are examples of questions that might be helpful to focus on:

- How do we identify and quantify the organizational capabilities – bundles of information, technology, and people – that drive our strategic success?
- What are our organization's key strategic positions and teams, and how should they be managed?
- How do we identify and quantify the strategic work that has a major impact on value creation in our organization?
- How well is our strategic work currently being performed? What work needs to be added or deleted?
- How do we develop strategic talent inventories – at both the individual and team levels – that help us identify the talent we have versus the talent we need and the actions that will close the gap, including how the talent is configured collectively?
- How do we ensure that our measurement systems enable us to track the impact that our (strategic) management practices have on the workforce, enabling a sophisticated understanding of downstream impact (good or bad)?

■ How do we design and implement measurement systems (HR and workforce scorecards) that ensure managerial accountability for a firm's most important resource – the workforce?

How are these questions different from common views about what WFA is and should be? Historically, WFA has focused on the activities associated with the HR *function*, which are much easier to measure and manage than the business outcomes caused by the *workforce*. This is perhaps not irrational from the perspective of an HR leader because she is more likely to have direct accountability and control over HR-related activities. However, just because these attributes are relatively easy to measure does not make them important. As mentioned above, consider the finding that HR management processes and activities comprise only about 1% of a firm's total expenditure, whereas the total spending on the workforce ranges 50–70% (Huselid, 1995). The most effectively managed HR function cannot create substantial value if it is focused on delivering the wrong talent and/or configuring the talent the wrong way; therefore, it is crucial for the WFA system to be focused on executing the firm's strategic goals.

In sum, we suggest managers and leaders think of the workforce as an investment opportunity and evaluate workforce investments (and accountabilities) with the same level of rigor as they might capital spending or research and development (R&D) expenditures. How do we get started? The process starts with a review of prior research and the development of plausible hypotheses. Once you have (a) formulated the right questions and (b) developed an understanding of the prior research in the relevant area, you will be ready to start the process of designing a data collection and analysis process (Barends & Rousseau, 2018).

Phase 2: Collect the right data. The next step in the process is to collect the requisite data to answer the questions that you have asked. Ironically, more data in this context is not necessarily always a good thing ("quality over quantity"; Minbaeva, 2018). There is a real possibility of data overload, given the prevalence of different software solutions that offer the potential for significantly enhanced data access and reporting. The key issue is that having the right data and analyses hinges on understanding the questions that need to be answered.

It is reasonable to expect organizations to have the data needed to answer many of the most pressing workforce questions, with robust internal data architectures around the workforce. As we described above, workforce costs (e.g., wages, benefits, training) can exceed 70% of total spending in many firms, particularly in service industries. Because the workforce is a key driver of organizational success and spending on the workforce is substantial, would it not be reasonable to assume that we would know a lot about our workforce – both what we spend and, more importantly, where we benefit from these investments? Sadly, the answer is generally no: most data collected in internal accounting and finance systems are unhelpful in answering this question.

As a consequence, one usually has to collect some data, and as we have described, conventional accounting data will not be enough. The important issue is to match the rigor of the data quality and analyses with the importance of the questions being asked. Significant data management discipline is also typically required because the error rates in workforce data are high.

Phase 3: Conduct the right Analyses. As we discuss in greater detail in subsequent chapters, there is a wide range of analytic techniques that a WFA team could draw on in their analytics projects (Edwards & Edwards, 2019; Larsson & Edwards, 2021). Which analytic techniques are considered the "right" techniques is an important question to ask. Importantly, the right technique needs to be the one that can produce output or answers to the right questions that the analyst is asking. The right technique will also match the workforce data that has been collected. The right analysis conducted also doesn't violate assumptions of the technique used (more on this in Chapter 4).

The point that we need to emphasize is that the data analytics framework and approach need to fit the underlying nature of the problem one is trying to solve. Sometimes, this means a complex analysis approach; other times, something simpler may suffice. The impact of talent on business success is both longitudinal and multivariate, and the metrics and analytics deployed to conduct WFA need to reflect these relationships. Investments in the workforce are made today for returns that may be enjoyed sometime in the future, so a net present value approach is essential (Becker et al., 2001). We address these issues in much greater detail beginning in Chapter 3.

Phase 4: Influence the right decisions. Finally, once you have clarified the important workforce management questions and collected, analyzed and interpreted the appropriate data, you have to ensure the results influence the appropriate behaviors and decisions. It is unrealistic to expect that simply presenting data from WFA findings in a meeting with executives will automatically change behavior. Effective change management requires using data for decision-making (for more detailed discussions, see Chapter 5). We advocate for a shift from focusing solely on data collection and measuring everything to prioritizing high-quality, evidence-based decision-making needed for deriving competitive advantage from human capital. In short, design WFA with implementation and action in mind (Levenson, 2015, 2018).

When, and where, will WFA make a difference?

Let us finish this introductory chapter with another adage. One day, Alice came to a fork in the road and saw a Cheshire cat in a tree. "Which road do I take?" she asked. "Where do you want to go?" was his response. "I don't know," Alice replied. "Then," said the cat, "it doesn't matter."

Where do you want to go with WFA? Are you doing this because it is fashionable (e.g., analytics as a management fad; Rasmussen & Ulrich, 2015) or because it is rational (e.g., analytics as a way to do "more for less"; Huselid & Becker, 2005)? Aligning WFA with business strategy might appear straightforward at first glance, but achieving this alignment necessitates deeper clarity and communication. It involves more than just acknowledging the importance of analytics within the context of organizational goals; it requires a deliberate effort to articulate how WFA initiatives directly support and enable the overarching business strategy.

Furthermore, explicit articulation involves ensuring that all stakeholders within the organization are aligned and on board with the strategic importance of WFA (see Chapters 5 and 7 for further discussion). This may entail educating leadership and decision-makers on the value proposition of analytics and fostering a culture that prioritizes data-driven decision-making. In essence, aligning WFA with business strategy requires a concerted effort to articulate and integrate analytics initiatives into the fabric of the organization (Minbaeva, 2018, 2021).

And one more thing: As we have described above, WFA matters most when there is substantial variance in talent and talent-related outcomes (at the individual and/or team levels) and when this variance is directly linked to core business outcomes. But, if talent doesn't make a difference in your organization, then neither will analyzing it.

Overview of the book

Chapter 2. This chapter takes a broad overview reflecting on WFA, including considering different disciplinary perspectives in **A**sking the right questions. It carefully considers how different disciplinary approaches may bring their own lens to the field of WFA and demonstrates the different and varying perspectives of actors in the WFA field. Different perspectives bring different questions and different approaches to answering these questions.

Chapter 3. This chapter addresses the challenges of **C**ollecting the right data and conducting the right **A**nalyses. Specific issues addressed include (a) the importance of both quantitative and qualitative data, (b) quantifying attitudinal and subjective data, (c) the importance of using multivariate behavioral models, (d) addressing correlation versus causation, (e) data mining, (f) hypothesis testing, (g) collecting new data, (h) the value of analysis that can show return on improved performance (ROIP), (i) collecting survey and other types of static data, (j) conducting interviews and dynamic ways of collecting new data, (k) preparing the data for analysis, (l) addressing data outliers, weaknesses and limitations, (m) combining quantitative and qualitative data in the same analysis, (n) quantitative versus qualitative data analysis approaches, and (o) applying the scientific method.

Chapter 4. This chapter takes the reader on a journey through a range of interesting techniques and applications. In doing so, it helps us begin to reflect on what factors may determine whether a WFA project conducts the right **A**nalyses when trying to **A**sk the right questions. The techniques are applied to very different questions, using very different types of data. The chapter starts with a technical section considering an analytics technique (DAG) used to consider questions that may provide information about causality. It then presents examples from a range of experts who present different applications of particular techniques. These include person-centered profile analyses, natural language processing, decision trees, organizational network analyses, machine learning, and macro-micro multi-level analyses.

Chapter 5. Every analytics project serves as a stepping stone for strategic change by **I**nfluencing the right decisions. However, although data can be analyzed meticulously and accurate predictions made about actions needed to initiate a change, uncertainties persist. Organizational change is not deterministic; deviations from intended goals are common, even when steps are clearly outlined and supported by evidence. This chapter addresses how to use WFA projects to help drive strategic change by applying a sensemaking approach consisting of three phases: leaders envision, managers execute, and employees adapt. Integrating WFA throughout each phase can provide the insights, tools, and platforms necessary to facilitate and expedite this sensemaking process, acting as a catalyst for meaningful and sustainable strategic change.

Chapter 6. Every business decision involves an ethical component. As WFA grows as a discipline, its ability to address ethical issues also needs to grow. This chapter details a range of ethical considerations that a WFA team needs to be able to address when carrying out a WFA project. The ACAI framework for conducting WFA argues that there is an inherently "right" way to effectively implement WFA. In Chapter 6, we show how ethical considerations must be addressed at each stage: deciding the right questions to **A**sk, the right data to **C**ollect, the right **A**nalyses to conduct, and the right decisions to **I**mpact (ACAI).

Chapter 7. Despite the widespread adoption of WFA, guidance is still needed on attaining the right level of WFA maturity and establishing a robust WFA function. This chapter addresses the missing elements by introducing a novel WFA maturity matrix. In doing so, we challenge the common view of WFA maturity as a linear process that evolves predictably from low-level operational reporting to highly sophisticated advanced analytics. Instead, we argue that the equilibrium between "push" and "pull" factors defines the desired level of WFA maturity. Chapter 7 also offers an overview of the components essential for constructing effective WFA functions, including team compositions, along with the components' respective merits and drawbacks.

Chapter 8. The final chapter summarizes the key takeaways from the book and provides concluding thoughts on applying the ACAI model to the field. It further reflects on the future of WFA: the changing nature of work that WFA experts, who will be expected to support navigation through such changes, will be faced with. Changes will likely include varying forms of impermanence – of work, workers, and organizations. The chapter also highlights the importance of understanding the complexities of the field, ranging from varied actor perspectives to data and analytic demands to answer the right questions.

References

Barends, E., & Rousseau, D. M. (2018). *Evidence-based management: Making better organizational decisions*. Kogan Page.

Becker, B. E., Huselid, M. A., & Beatty, R. W. (2009). *The differentiated workforce: Translating talent into strategic impact*. Harvard Business Press.

Becker, B. E., Huselid, M. A., & Ulrich, D. (2001). *The HR scorecard: Linking people, strategy, and performance*. Harvard Business Press.

Edwards, M. R., & Edwards, K. (2019). *Predictive HR analytics: Mastering the HR metric*. Kogan Page.

Huselid, M. A. (1995). The impact of human resource management practices on turnover, productivity, and corporate financial performance. *Academy of Management Journal, 38*(3), 635–672.

Huselid, M. A. (2018). The science and practice of workforce analytics: Introduction to the HRM special issue. *Human Resource Management, 57*(3), 679–684. https://doi.org/10.1002/hrm.21916

Huselid, M. A., Beatty, R. W., & Becker, B. E. (2005). "A" players or "A" positions? The strategic logic of workforce management. *Harvard Business Review, 83*(12), 110–117.

Huselid, M. A., Becker, B. E., & Beatty, D. (2005). *The workforce scorecard: Managing human capital to execute strategy*. Harvard Business Press.

Larsson, A. S., & Edwards, M. R. (2021). Insider econometrics meets people analytics and strategic human resource management. *The International Journal of Human Resource Management, 33*(2), 1–47. https://doi.org/10.1080/09585192.2020.1847166

Levenson, A. (2015). *Strategic analytics: Advancing strategy execution and organizational effectiveness*. Berrett-Koehler.

Levenson, A. (2018). Using workforce analytics to improve strategy execution. *Human Resource Management, 57*(3), 685–700. https://doi.org/10.1002/hrm.21850

Minbaeva, D. B. (2018). Building credible human capital analytics for organizational competitive advantage. *Human Resource Management, 57*(3), 701–713. https://doi.org/10.1002/hrm.21848

Minbaeva, D. B. (2021). Disrupted HR? *Human Resource Management Review, 31*(4), 1–8. https7/doi.org/101016/jhrmr.2020ti00820

Minbaeva, D. B., & Collings, D. (2013). Seven myths of global talent management. *International Journal of Human Resource Management, 24*(9), 1762–1776.

Minbaeva, D. B., & Vardi, S. (2018). Global talent analytics. In D. G. Collings, H. Scullion, & P. M. Caligiuri (Eds.), *Global talent management* (2nd ed., pp. 197–217). Routledge.

Rasmussen, T., & Ulrich, D. (2015). Learning from practice: How HR analytics avoids being a management fad. *Organizational Dynamics, 44*(3), 236–242.

Theoretical frameworks for workforce analytics

Mark A. Huselid

Introduction

As we described in Chapter 1, the field of workforce analytics (WFA) is growing rapidly, and many professionals assume that the origins of the field are relatively recent. However, measuring and managing workforce contributions to organizational success have been topics of study for many years. In fact, the history of WFA is long and varied, and designing and implementing effective WFA systems requires incorporating many of the conceptual underpinnings of the field. As a consequence, we believe that recognizing and understanding the historical and theoretical origins of the field are essential. However, this is not as easy as it might seem because numerous disciplines have addressed these issues, focusing on different aspects along different timelines and with different constituencies.

Why do we believe that understanding the historical context is so important? Consider the challenges that a senior vice president of human resources (HR) at a large Fortune 500 corporation faces. She understands the importance of effective workforce management and measurement for both implementing her current strategy and designing an effective strategy going forward in her industry. However, similar to most other firms in her highly dynamic industry, her current workforce measurement system is limited, and there is not a single person or group who "owns" the entire process.

So, having read the literature and received coaching from her peers in the industry, she assembled an interdisciplinary team of capable managers to do the work. During the project launch meeting, she described the nature of the business and competitive pressures and the role that she hoped an analytics project could play in executing strategy. Then, she asked the team if they had any questions. Here is how they responded:

DOI: 10.4324/9781003190097-3

An executive with an MBA, responsible for helping develop and implement the firm's strategy, asked the following:

- How do we create value for our very best current and potential customers through the workforce?
- Do we understand how value is created at the level of the individual, group, and organization?
- Do our analyses and conclusions influence customer purchasing behavior?

A line manager trained in economics and finance asked the following:

- Can we afford to implement our strategy through the workforce?
- Can we link our workforce data with important firm-level outcomes?
- Have we made the right investments in the workforce?

A senior HR leader with a background in HR strategy asked the following:

- What system of HR management practices is needed to execute our strategy?
- To what extent have we implemented this system effectively?
- Have we placed our top talent in our most important strategic positions?

An industrial and organizational (I/O) psychologist asked the following:

- How do we measure the key constructs in our model linking talent with customer and shareholder outcomes?
- What are the reliability and validity of the important measures in our model?
- Are our data designed to be persuasive so as to influence managerial decisions?

A senior leader with a PhD in organizational behavior (OB) asked the following:

- At the *individual* level, do our measures and analyses drive the right behaviors?
- At the *group* level, do our measures and analyses drive the right behaviors?
- At the *organizational* level, do our measures and analyses drive the right behaviors?

A statistician with a background in psychometrics and econometrics asked the following:

- Does the variance in our measurements match the variance in the phenomenon we are measuring?
- Are we using an appropriate multivariate, multiple-period model?
- Have we audited our data collection and analysis processes?

A data scientist with a strong background in statistics and management asked the following:

- Do our data scientists understand the problems we are trying to solve?
- Do we understand how to collect the required data?
- Does the data architecture allow managers to understand data outcomes?

An organizational development (OD) and change management consultant asked the following:

- How will we use the data once we have it?
- How do we address managerial concerns about our data and conclusions?
- What are the most important decisions we need to influence? Are we making progress?

The chief human resources officer (CHRO) was overwhelmed by the breadth of the questions (many of which the team could not answer) as well as the breadth of the conceptual frameworks that they used to approach the problem. What are we to make of all these questions? Who was right? We believe that each of the questions is helpful but incomplete. In addition, depending on the stage of development, each of the queries will be more or less relevant and important. In short, the answer is "it depends"—but on *what*?

Why do we see the level of confusion and uncertainty in the workforce management process that we might not see from our colleagues in finance, accounting, or marketing? We believe it is because the nature of the problem to be solved—how to measure and manage the contribution of the workforce to firm success—is as interdisciplinary and varied as the people who are drawn to solve it. No one person is likely to know and understand the whole story to make these systems and programs a success.

Each of us brings our training and disciplinary focus with us when we approach problems to be solved at work, and we tend to align the interventions we propose with our own training and background. This makes sense. However, just as a great surgeon would not be much help if you really need a dentist, you need to align your firm's WFA capabilities to the nature of the problem you are trying to solve—an issue we address in detail in Chapter 7. WFA needs to focus on the whole, not the parts, and doing so requires a team with diverse expertise and thorough training (Levenson, 2011, 2015).

For example, if your firm is worried about turnover in high-potential R&D staff, then you would need to understand that there is extensive relevant literature on this topic in HR. Or, if you think you need to measure job involvement in the sales staff, you need to understand not only the literature in this area but also the literature associated with item analysis and scale construction and validation. Meanwhile, if you need to connect your job involvement measures to organizational outcomes that unfold over time, econometrics becomes critical. The data need to come from somewhere, so data collection and integration, as well as computer programming expertise (more broadly, data science), are essential. Finally, none of these data and analyses will be of much use unless you can generate the buy-in and acceptance of your process and results throughout the organization. Therefore, understanding OD and change management becomes critical (see Chapter 5).

In this chapter, we take a broad and somewhat conceptual approach to help the reader develop their own approach to the design and implementation of effective workforce management systems and to address the specific issues that we described above. We start with a historical overview of the elements that drive the design and implementation of WFA systems and then describe how conceptual and theoretical thinking and analysis can help throughout the process.

The history of workforce analytics

Consider this description of the challenges that leaders and managers face on a large construction project:

> The systematic classification by division, phyle, gang, and crew would have made it possible for the administrators to monitor labourers both spatially and temporally. Each gang was allocated a particular space on a project. Workmen were expected to comply with certain control measures, while working on projects, and their work progress was reported upon and monitored by the scribes. The control measures included: (i) output control forms, showing for each workman his location, number of stones requested, number delivered, and the remaining balance for every working day; (ii) control notes which provided information about dates, procedures for transporting stones and the workmen involved; (iii) team marks (which identified the specific division, phyle, and gang); and (iv) setting marks intended to ensure that the stones were assembled in the right order. Each division had a specific name, and belonged to a specific phyle, which in turn was classified under a particular gang making it easy for those in charge to trace responsibility to individual workmen, to check their absence or presence and to rotate them either individually or in groups ... Work targets were set for divisions or individual workmen and were monitored daily by the scribes using a variety of accounting techniques, such as time–volume ratios and conversion ratios.
>
> *Ezzamel (2004)*

What was the context for this management (and WFA) challenge? Perhaps it describes a project in the 1970s or 80s, as the management of HR was becoming more important? Actually, it describes the construction practices of ancient Egypt's

"Middle Kingdom" era (2050–1780 BC; Ezzamel, 2004, p. 507). Ancient scribes were the equivalents of today's WFA professionals, grappling some 4,000 years ago with similar challenges to those faced by their modern counterparts.

WFA draws on a long and rich history in the applied social sciences. Indeed, management science has "done" WFA for over a century (Levenson 2015). Key milestones in its development include Frederick Taylor (1913) and Henry Ford's analysis of work design and worker capabilities to create the first modern manufacturing lines (1913), the Hawthorne Studies on worker productivity and fatigue in production lines conducted by Roethlisberger and Dickson (1939), and Deming's work a half-century later on quality management and self-managing teams (Deming, et al., 2013).

What distinguishes these classic examples of WFA is that they were part of a larger series of inquiries addressing important business issues of their time. Taylor and Ford aimed to establish the first modern manufacturing lines, enabling the production of complex machinery using a pool of mostly unskilled labor. Mayo and others focused on the human element and worker productivity in the growing use of production lines, while Deming addressed the second generation of manufacturing, when quality became a top strategic priority.

More recent examples include analyzing how the advent and evolution of the internet enabled the global distribution of knowledge work to lower-cost locations and the proliferation of virtual/distributed work within organizations (OECD, 2023). This essentially is a form of labor arbitrage. The growth of contingent work, which started with part-time and temp work to make labor costs more flexible and on demand, has recently evolved into gig work managed both externally and internally (Kalleberg, 2018; Katz & Krueger, 2019; OECD, 2023). WFA has played a central role in analyzing how workers have received these new forms of work, and evaluating the pros and cons of including them as part of comprehensive labor strategies supporting business models. Recently, this analysis has extended to understanding the impacts of the COVID-19 pandemic on organizations and employees, including effects on retention and productivity, and the ongoing challenges with remote and hybrid work (Minbaeva & Navrbjerg, 2023).

Over the past century, the fields of management research, I/O psychology, and labor economics have developed robust models and tools for analyzing workforce issues within organizations. What may have changed over the past couple of decades is that more and more insiders are taking the lead on defining the WFA analytics agenda and conducting WFA work. This period has seen a rapid and significant increase in both the internal capabilities for WFA within organizations and the overall activity in this field.

The point we are trying to make is that while the field of WFA has received substantial recent attention, measuring and managing workforce contributions has been a topic of study (and managerial concern) for much, much longer. Consequently, there are many conceptual frameworks that can be used to aid in problem-solving and decision-making with WFA. However, sustaining conceptual clarity is essential for meaningful progress. Here, we highlight eight broad domains to help you develop and maintain an appropriate level of focus.

The impact of theory on workforce analytics

As we highlighted in Chapter 1, effective WFA requires at least four broad elements, which we describe as the *ACAI model*:

- **A**sking the right questions
- **C**ollecting the right data
- **A**nalyzing data in the right way
- **I**nfluencing the right decisions and workforce outcomes.

In this section, we argue that understanding the history of WFA requires learning about the various conceptual frameworks and models that drive firm-level outcomes. Learning WFA demands patience, as you will need to understand the basic elements associated with the theoretical background in the field. Why is theory important? Consider the following (fairly famous) quotes:

- "Nothing so practical as a good theory" (Lewin, 1943).
- "Every good regulator of that system must be a model of that system" (Conant & Ashby, 1970).

Our point is that people are trained with a wide variety of disciplinary perspectives. That can be a strength—but only if they understand one another's perspectives. Said differently, it is important to have a point of view about how talent makes a difference in your organization (Lewin, 1943), and it is also very important that your measurement system captures and represents the key dimensions of this viewpoint (Conant & Ashby, 1970).

The differences in disciplinary foci partly stem from varying levels of analysis. For example, economists have often taken a more macro or large-scale approach, although this is certainly changing with the development of "insider econometrics" (Larsson & Edwards, 2021). In contrast, I/O psychologists tend to be more micro in their focus. However, there are several other conceptual frameworks relevant to WFA as well. We believe that the most important theoretical domains with implications for WFA are as follows:

- Strategic management
- Economics
- Strategic human resource management (HRM)

- I/O psychology
- Organizational behavior
- Psychometrics and econometrics
- Data science
- OD and change management.

In the following sections, we provide an overview of each of these domains and their implications for WFA.

Strategic management

The field of strategic management integrates insights from management, economics, marketing, and the behavioral sciences. The overall objective is to *design* and *implement* a comprehensive plan that outlines how an organization will achieve its goals and sustain a competitive advantage in the market (Barney et al., 2011).

The academic and practitioner disciplines of business strategy are multifaceted and draw from several disciplines to guide decision-making and resource allocation for long-term success. However, there is a consensus that a carefully developed and effectively implemented business strategy is crucial for long-term success and decision-making (Rothaermel, 2023). Types of business strategy (levels of analysis) include:

- Corporate strategy: This concerns decisions that affect the organization as a whole, such as mergers, acquisitions, and portfolio management.
- Business unit strategy: This focuses on how a specific business unit or department should compete within its market.
- Functional strategy: This addresses specific functions within a business, such as HR, marketing, or production, and aims to align them with the overall business and corporate strategy.

There are two broad domains that are important to consider in this area (Rothaermel, 2023). The first is *strategy formulation*, which asks the following question: Where do we compete? The second is *strategy implementation*, and the question shifts to: How can we win? WFA has much to add to both of these elements. Although strategic management has always been an important determinant of firm success, a number of factors in the external business environment have made this element even more important:

- Globalization: Managing strategy on a global scale requires dealing with complexity and cultural diversity.

■ Digital transformation: The rise of digital technologies has disrupted traditional business models.

■ Sustainability: Increasing focus on social and environmental factors is a component of strategic planning.

■ Agility: With fast-changing markets and technologies, strategies need to be flexible and adaptable.

■ Data-driven decision-making: The role of big data and analytics shapes and informs business strategy.

Key elements of business strategy include:

■ Vision and mission: Both articulate the long-term direction and purpose of the organization. Vision provides a long-term picture of what the firm wants to become, and the mission spells out its fundamental purpose beyond just making money.

■ Objectives and goals: These are specific, measurable outcomes the company aims to achieve within a certain time frame.

■ Competitive advantage: This is a unique advantage that allows a business to outperform its competitors. It stems from various sources like unique technology, superior customer service, cost advantage, brand reputation, and more.

■ Core competencies: These are unique capabilities or resources that a company possesses, giving it a competitive edge in the market.

■ Resource-based view: This focuses on leveraging unique internal resources, like human capital, to gain a competitive advantage.

■ Innovation strategy: Clayton Christensen's influential work, including the book *The Innovators' Dilemma*, has made the point that when businesses focus on meeting the current needs of current customers through continuous improvement, they often miss the potential for industry disruption through new products and services for new customers. Examples include Amazon, Apple, cryptocurrency, Uber, and streaming media, all of which disrupted old industry standards and created new (and profitable) ecosystems.

The key point to understand is that workforce data—not only on costs but also on competencies and capabilities—are essential components of both the formulation and implementation processes. A clear understanding of the firm's current and intended business strategy is an important element of a well-crafted WFA system.

Economics

The field of economics focuses on developing an understanding of how individuals, organizations, and societies manage and allocate their scarce resources (Mankiw,

2023). Its goal is to understand and explain how markets work, how people make choices, and how economies function at both micro and macro levels. Economic analysis can be applied to a wide range of issues, including individuals' choices, markets, business practices, public policy, and international relations. Economics often overlaps with other disciplines such as political science, sociology, psychology, and history.

Microeconomics focuses on the individual level of analysis, while macroeconomics examines the economy as a whole, including issues like inflation, unemployment, economic growth, and monetary and fiscal policy. The fields of cost accounting and supply chain management draw heavily on microeconomics. Personnel economics applies economic and mathematical tools to traditional HR topics, including compensation, hiring practices, pay and incentive structures, teamwork, and worker empowerment and motivation.

Microeconomics, and especially labor economics, is an integral contributor to several other disciplines that provide important perspectives for WFA, including industrial and organizational psychology and organizational behavior (see the following sections in this chapter). Labor economics provides frameworks for understanding how jobs and careers evolve across the life cycle as people transition from entering the labor market through retirement. It also contributes to understanding how human capital is rewarded through compensation and promotions in both internal and external markets.

The insights provided by labor economics are particularly useful for understanding external job opportunities in the broader labor market in terms of availability (via the unemployment rate) and remuneration (comparable wage distributions). These data and reference points contribute to understanding how employees evaluate their alternative job opportunities and how compensation policies are set within the organization.

Strategic human resource management

Strategic HRM (or, more broadly, HR strategy) is a comprehensive framework that outlines how an organization's people practices, programs, and policies will support and drive its business goals and objectives (Noe et al., 2022). It bridges the broader corporate strategy and HR management practices, focusing on aligning a firm's talent strategy with the overall goals and objectives of the organization. The overall goal is to ensure that the organization has the right skills, competencies, and behaviors required to meet current and future challenges. This strategy serves as a guide for HR activities such as recruitment, retention, training, compensation, and employee relations (Becker & Huselid, 1998).

The literature on HR strategy has grown rapidly since the beginning of the 1980s. In contrast to earlier work that tended to focus on individual policies and practices, the HR strategy literature focuses on (a) systems of integrated HR practices and

(b) the impact of these HR practices on important firm-level outcomes, such as employee turnover, productivity, and overall firm performance (Huselid, 1995).

One of the key conceptual challenges in HR strategy with direct relevance to WFA (and a key debate in the literature) is the debate between best practices and best fit. The essential question is whether there is one best way to manage (and subsequently measure) a firm's workforce, or whether the optimal workforce management strategy will vary as a function of firm strategy, goals, or other contextual factors (Becker & Huselid, 1998; 2006). In essence, this literature has evolved from asking, "Do investments in more effective HR management practices and systems impact important firm-level outcomes?" (Becker & Huselid, 1998; Combs et al., 2006; Huselid, 1995) to the more recent focus on "How are investments in HR management systems most effectively managed and measured?" (Becker et al., 2009).

Out of this literature has evolved the concept of *strategic positions*, which are those roles that offer the greatest potential for improvement, given their direct impact on the firm's business success associated with relatively low average levels of current performance (Huselid et al., 2005; Huselid, 2018, 2023). In contrast to conventional HR management and measurement systems that predominantly focus on the most senior (or, at times, the most common) organizational roles, a focus on strategic positions encourages workforce analysts to "follow the variance" and focus their measurement efforts on roles that 1) exhibit considerable variability, and 2) are most likely to impact firm success. And, in keeping with our whole systems perspective on WFA in this book, we would also extend those questions to the team level.

Industrial and organizational psychology

I/O psychology is a subfield of psychology that applies psychological theories, principles, and research methods to the workplace. This interdisciplinary field borrows theories and methods from psychology, sociology, economics, and management studies, among others. Its primary goal is to improve the well-being and performance of both employees and organizations (Dipboye, 2018; Spector, 2021).

The following are key domains within I/O psychology—each of which is potentially an important focus of WFA systems.

- Job analysis: This involves a detailed study of the tasks, responsibilities, and skills required for particular jobs. The information gleaned is often used to create job descriptions, select appropriate candidates, and identify training needs. Job analysis data can be a primary source of information when selecting workforce metrics.

- Personnel selection: One of the primary roles of I/O psychologists is to design and validate selection systems to help organizations hire and promote the most suitable candidates for a given job. This often involves creating aptitude and skills tests, personality inventories, work sample tests, and structured interviews.

■ Talent management: This term is often used to describe the overall process of recruiting, developing, and retaining the talent required for the strategy to succeed. This involves performance assessments, succession planning, skill development, and internal promotions.

■ Performance appraisal: As a subset of talent management, I/O psychologists create tools and metrics for accurate performance measurement. They also explore the most effective feedback methods to motivate and support employees.

■ Workforce planning: This ensures organizations have the right number of employees with the necessary skills to execute their business strategies.

■ Compensation and benefits: This involves designing reward systems to attract, motivate, and retain employees, requiring market research, salary benchmarks, and benefits packages. There is a significant overlap with the talent management and performance appraisal processes here, in that understanding the drivers of employee motivation is key to improving performance and job satisfaction.

■ Training and development: I/O psychologists create and evaluate programs to train employees in new skills, ranging from technical proficiencies to soft skills like leadership and communication.

■ Organizational culture and design: This involves cultivating a work environment that aligns with the company's mission and values, influencing employee engagement, retention, and productivity.

■ Legal compliance: This ensures that organizational HR policies adhere to legal and ethical standards, including workplace safety, equal opportunities, and employment law compliance.

■ Employee relations: This involves managing employer–employee relationships and conflict resolution to foster a productive and harmonious work environment.

■ Diversity and inclusion: I/O psychologists study how different cultural backgrounds and identities impact workplace dynamics and help formulate policies to encourage diversity and inclusion. As organizations become increasingly diverse, understanding how to create an inclusive environment is crucial. Organizations must research best practices for creating diverse and inclusive workplaces and understand the benefits and challenges of diverse teams.

■ Occupational health and well-being: I/O psychologists help identify causes of workplace stress or accidents and recommend measures to improve health and safety.

■ Work–life balance: Recognizing the importance of employee well-being, I/O psychologists examine how work impacts life outside the office and vice versa. They develop strategies to promote balance and reduce workplace stress.

Organizational behavior

OB is an interdisciplinary field that explores individuals, groups, and structural behaviors within organizations (Griffin & Phillips, 2023). OB professionals aim to understand, predict, and improve organizational efficiency and effectiveness by studying how people interact at work. Drawing from various disciplines like psychology, sociology, anthropology, economics, and political science, OB provides a comprehensive framework for understanding complex human dynamics. There is significant conceptual overlap between the fields of I/O psychology and OB.

OB is both a theoretical and applied discipline. OB professionals employ rigorous research methods to develop theories about human behavior in organizations and then use these theories to guide management practices. The ultimate goal is to enhance the performance and well-being of organizations and their members.

Levels of analysis

- The individual level focuses on personal attitudes and behaviors; topics include personality, perception, motivation, and individual decision-making.
- The group level investigates group and team processes and performance; topics include communication, conflict, and negotiation.
- The organizational level examines organizational culture, structure, and strategies.

Understanding how workforce outcomes vary across these levels is important for designing and implementing effective workforce measurement systems. Some scholars refer to these distinctions as *micro*, *meso*, and *macro* (Cappelli & Sherer, 1991).

Psychometrics and econometrics

Psychometrics is the field of study concerned with the theory and technique of psychological measurement, which includes the measurement of knowledge, abilities, attitudes, personality traits, and educational achievement (Price, 2011). The aim of psychometrics is to produce quantitative scales of measurement that are both valid (i.e., they measure what they are supposed to measure) and reliable (i.e., they are consistent in their measurement).

Psychometrics focuses on objectively measuring latent constructs—attributes that cannot be directly observed, such as intelligence, introversion, mental disorders, educational achievement, and, in an organizational context, job performance (Price, 2011). Psychometrics encompasses a wide variety of measures:

- Aptitude tests measure the potential to learn or acquire a new skill.
- Achievement tests measure what one has already learned or acquired.

- Personality tests aim to assess typical patterns of behavior, thoughts, and emotions.

- Attitude scales measure feelings or beliefs about a particular topic.

- Performance appraisals can reflect a combination of both performance and potential.

Econometrics applies statistical methods to economic data to give empirical content to economic relationships (Wooldridge, 2019). This interdisciplinary field combines economic theory, mathematics, and statistical methods to analyze and interpret economic data to quantify the relationships among economic variables so that they can be used for forecasting trends, evaluating policy, and testing theories. Econometricians develop and apply statistical models to explore complex relationships and to identify causal links among economic variables.

Contrasting psychometrics and econometrics

Econometrics and psychometrics are both subfields of applied statistics, each with its unique area of application and focus. Psychometrics is often linked to I/O psychology, whereas econometrics is more closely linked to the field of economics. Each uses models, estimation techniques, and hypothesis testing to analyze and interpret data. However, they differ in several key respects, such as their primary subject matter, methodologies, and applications.

Psychometrics is focused on the measurement of psychological attributes, including personality traits, intelligence, attitudes, and abilities. As we described above, it aims to create valid and reliable tests and questionnaires for measuring these variables. Meanwhile, econometrics focuses on the empirical analysis of economic data. It aims to quantify economic relationships, test economic theories, and predict economic outcomes. Subjects can include everything from labor markets and international trade to finance and macroeconomic policy.

Although both fields employ statistical techniques and emphasize the importance of measurement and empirical validation, they differ considerably in their objectives, applications, challenges, and theoretical foundations. In comparing psychometrics and econometrics, the question is not to choose one or the other; rather, both can usefully contribute to the development of effective WFA. However, professionals tend to be trained in one or the other, so it's important to be cautious of missing an important part of the discussion.

Data science

Data science is a relatively new and integrative field that enables the use of theoretical, mathematical, computational, and other practical methods to study, evaluate, and model data. It is geared toward helping individuals and organizations make well-informed decisions from stored, consumed, and managed data. This broad and rapidly evolving field encompasses the collective processes, theories, concepts, tools, and technologies that enable the review, analysis, and extraction of valuable knowledge and hidden information from raw data (Hastie et al., 2009).

Because data often relates to individuals, ethical considerations are paramount. These include issues like data privacy, fairness in algorithms, transparency in decision-making, and ensuring that data and models do not reinforce biases or unfair practices. We discuss these ethical issues in detail in Chapter 6.

Organizational development and change management

Organizational development and change management are two distinct but interrelated disciplines within the domain of the study and practice of managing organizations (Cummings & Worley, 2018). Although closely related and often intersecting, they are distinct in terms of their focus, foundational concepts, and applications. Both provide frameworks for understanding how organizations operate and evolve, but they differ in focus, scope, methodologies, and objectives.

Overview of the field of organizational development

OD is a multidisciplinary field that studies how organizations can initiate and manage change to enhance adaptability and efficacy (Cummings & Worley, 2018). OD interventions are designed to diagnose organizational problems and culture, facilitate change initiatives, and enhance organizational performance and employee well-being. It incorporates perspectives from psychology, sociology, economics, management science, and even anthropology.

The levels of analysis are individual, team, and organization, with a systemic focus. Evaluation tools generally include organizational diagnosis, action planning, implementation of interventions, and evaluation of outcomes. Common interventions include team building, leadership development, change management, organizational culture change, and process improvement initiatives. The ultimate goal of OD is to create a more productive, responsive, and resilient organization that can better respond to both competitors and environmental shocks and changes.

OD emerged as a field in the mid-20th century, drawing on various disciplines and intellectual traditions. Its origins were drawn from contributions of the human relations movement (in the 1930s and 1940s), Kurt Lewin and the action research methodology (Lewin is often referred to as the "father of OD"), T-group training (in Europe in the 1940s and 1950s), systems theory, and a broad range of management consulting firms that further refined and applied these concepts.

Overview of the field of change management

Change management focuses on the processes, tools, and techniques to manage the people side of change to achieve required business outcomes (Hayes, 2021). Its main focus is on transitioning individuals, teams, and organizations from a current state to a desired future state. Similar to OD, change management is a multidisciplinary field that guides how organizations, teams, and individuals transition from their current state to a desired future state. It is often necessary because changes in strategy, operations, technology, and culture can be disruptive if not managed properly. The goal of change management is to ensure that changes are implemented smoothly and with minimal resistance to increase the likelihood of success and achieve desired outcomes.

Contrasting organizational development and change management

Although distinct, it is important to note that insights from OD can greatly inform change management practices. Understanding the underlying structure, culture, and behavior of an organization can provide valuable insights for planning and implementing change successfully. Similarly, experiences and data gathered during change management initiatives can offer empirical material for OD. In essence, OD seeks to explain the "why" and "how" behind organizational structures, behaviors, and interactions, whereas change management is more prescriptive, offering the "what" and "how" to effectively implement change. We revisit the topics of OD and change management in greater detail in Chapters 5 and 7.

Integrating questions and domains into workforce analytics

We have argued that various disciplines make important contributions to the design and implementation of effective WFA systems. There is no "one best way," but we believe that there is "one best process." World-class WFA systems draw from a broad range of conceptual frameworks and, above all, are rooted in the execution of firm strategy. This process is the focus of our book. In this section, we integrate these ideas and show how different disciplines can be used to develop questions (and answers) in each area. We summarize these concepts in Table 2.1.

Summary

In this chapter, we make the point that the field of WFA has a long and diverse history and that world-class analytics systems will draw on an understanding of

TABLE 2.1 The intersection of questions and concepts in workforce analytics in the ACAI model

The problem to be solved vs. conceptual framework	Strategic management	Economics	Strategic HRM	I/O psychology	Organizational behavior	Psychometrics/ econometrics	Data science	Organizational development/ change management
Phase 1: Asking the right questions	How do we create value for our very best current and potential customers through the workforce? Do we understand how value is created at the level of the individual, group, and organization?	Can we afford to implement our strategy through the workforce?	What system of HRM practices is needed to execute our strategy?	How do we measure the key constructs in our model?	At the individual level, do our measures and analyses drive the right behaviors?	Does the variance in our measurements match the variance in the phenomenon we are measuring?	Do our data scientists understand the problems we are trying to solve?	How will we use the data once we have it?

(Continued)

TABLE 2.1 (Continued)

The problem to be solved vs. conceptual framework	Strategic management	Economics	Strategic HRM	I/O psychology	Organizational behavior	Psychometrics/econometrics	Data science	Organizational development/change management
Phase 2: Collecting the right data	Have we collected longitudinal data on the performance of our key products and services?	Can we link our workforce data with important firm-level or organizational unit level outcomes?	Have we collected data or metrics that help provide an understanding of the extent of employee strategic goal alignment?	Have we collected psychometric data at employee and team level? Have we assessed the reliability and validity of the important measures in our model?	Have we collected psychometric data at the level of the group or team? Have we assessed the reliability and validity of the important measures in our model?	Have we carefully assessed our survey measures and data? Is our scale construction appropriate? Are we using the appropriate econometric estimation models?	Have we carefully integrated data across organization levels and units? Do we have a data audit procedure in place?	Have we collected cross-sectional and longitudinal level data that provides information on the success and impact of our change initiatives?
Phase 3: Analyzing data in the right way	Are we using an appropriate multivariate, multiple period estimation model?	Are we using an appropriate multivariate, multiple period estimation model?	Are we using an appropriate multivariate, multiple period estimation model?	Are we using an appropriate multivariate, multiple period estimation model?	Are we using an appropriate multivariate, multiple period estimation model?	Are we using an appropriate multivariate, multiple period estimation model?	Are we using an appropriate multivariate, multiple period estimation model?	Have we collected and analyzed data that follows outcomes of the change management process over time?

(Continued)

TABLE 2.1 (Continued)

The problem to be solved vs. conceptual framework	Strategic management	Economics	Strategic HRM	I/O psychology	Organizational behavior	Psychometrics/econometrics	Data science	Organizational development/change management
Phase 4: Influencing the right decisions	Do our analyses and conclusions influence customer purchasing behavior?	Have we made the right investments in the workforce?	Have we placed our top talent in our most important strategic positions?	Is our data analytics process designed to influence managerial decisions? Are we persuasive in helping to drive change?	At the group and organizational level, do our measures and analyses drive the right behaviors?	Have we audited our data collection and analysis processes?	Does the data architecture allow managers to understand data outcomes?	What are the most important decisions we need to influence? Are we making progress?

this diversity. We are not making the point that any single conceptual domain is the most important; rather, we stress that we need to match the type of question and the theoretical or conceptual domain to the problem being solved. There is no "one size fits all" solution to designing and implementing effective WFA systems. In summary, we have made the following broad points:

- WFA is a broad and diverse field with many complex elements. It also has a long history—much richer and longer than is typically represented in the current WFA literature. Effectively designing and implementing WFA systems means appreciating and staffing for these different elements.

- As we have described in our ACAI framework, leading effective WFA requires, first, asking the right questions; second, collecting the right data; third, analyzing data the right way; and fourth, influencing the right decisions and workforce outcomes.

- It is important to align the type of analysis with the importance and complexity of the problem being addressed.

- Understanding the breadth and complexity of the issues that influence WFA is foundational to doing WFA the right way (which is the focus of this chapter).

Examples and further details on these points are the focus of our subsequent chapters.

References

Barney, J. B., Ketchen, D. J., Wright, M., & Foss, N. J. (2011). Invited editorial: Why micro-foundations for resource-based theory are needed and what they may look like. *Journal of Management, 37*(5), 1413–1428. https://doi.org/10.1177/0149206310390218

Becker, B. E., & Huselid, M. A. (1998). High performance work systems and firm performance: A synthesis of research and managerial implications. *Research in Personnel and Human Resource Management, 16*, 53–101.

Becker, B. E., & Huselid, M. A. (2006). Strategic human resource management: Where do we go from here? *Journal of Management, 32*, 898–925.

Becker, B. E., Huselid, M. A., & Beatty, R. W. (2009). *The differentiated workforce: Transforming talent into strategic impact.* Harvard Business Press.

Cappelli, P., & Sherer, P. (1991). The missing role of context in OB: The need for a meso-level approach. *Research in Organizational Behavior, 13,* 55–110.

Combs, J., Liu, Y., Hall, A., & Ketchen, D. (2006). How much do high-performance work practices matter? A meta-analysis of their effects on organizational performance. *Personnel Psychology, 59*(3), 501–528.

Conant, R. C., & Ashby, R. W. (1970). Every good regulator of a system must be a model of that system. *International Journal of Systems Science, 1*(2), 89–97. https://doi.org/10.1080/00207727008920220

Cummings, T. G., & Worley, C. G. (2018). *Organization development and change* (11th ed.). Cengage Learning.

Deming, W. E., Orsini, J., & Cahill, D. D. (2013). *The essential deming: Leadership principles from the Father of quality.* McGraw-Hill Companies, Inc.

Dipboye, R. L. (2018). A history of I/O psychology. In *The emerald review of industrial and organizational psychology* (pp. 1–49). Emerald Publishing Limited. https://doi.org/10.1108/978-1-78743-785-220181004

Ezzamel, M. (2004). Work organization in the middle kingdom, ancient Egypt. *Organization, 11*(4), 497–537. https://doi.org/10.1177/1350508404044060

Griffin, R. W., & Phillips, J. M. (2023). *Organizational behavior: Managing people and organizations* (14th ed.). Cengage Learning.

Hastie, T., Tibshirani, R., & Friedman, J. (2009). *The elements of statistical learning: Data mining, inference, and prediction* (2nd ed.). Springer.

Hayes, J. (2021). *The theory and practice of change management* (6th ed.). Bloomsbury Academic.

Huselid, M. A. (1995). The impact of human resource management practices on turnover, productivity, and corporate financial performance. *Academy of Management Journal, 38*(3), 635–672.

Huselid, M. A. (2018). The science and practice of workforce analytics: Introduction to the HRM special issue. *Human Resource Management, 57*(3), 679–684. https://doi.org/10.1002/hrm.21916

Huselid, M. A. (2023). Integrating utility analysis and workforce strategy research: Suggestions for future work. *International Journal of Human Resource Management, 34*(13), 2620–2635. https://doi.org/10.1080/09585192.2023.2225281

Huselid, M. A., Beatty, R. W., & Becker, B. E. (2005). "A" players or "A" positions? The strategic logic of workforce management. *Harvard Business Review, 83*(12), 110–117.

Kalleberg, A. L. (2018). *Precarious lives: Job insecurity and well-being in rich democracies*. John Wiley & Sons.

Katz, L. F., & Krueger, A. B. (2019). The rise and nature of alternative work arrangements in the United States, 1995–2015. *ILR Review, 72*(2), 382–416.

Larsson, A. S., & Edwards, M. R. (2021). Insider econometrics meets people analytics and strategic human resource management. *The International Journal of Human Resource Management, 33*(2), 1–47. https://doi.org/10.1080/09585192.2020.1847166

Levenson, A. (2011). Using targeted analytics to improve talent decisions. *People and Strategy, 34*(2), 11.

Levenson, A. (2015). *Strategic analytics: Advancing strategy execution and organizational effectiveness*. Berrett-Koehler.

Lewin, K. (1943). Psychology and the process of group living. *Journal of Social Psychology, 17*, 113–131.

Mankiw, N. G. (2023). *Principles of economics* (10th ed.). Cengage Learning.

Minbaeva, D., & Navrbjerg, S. (2023). Strategic HRM: The Covid-19 test? *Human Resource Management, 62*(6), 811–832.

Noe, R., Hollenbeck, J., Gerhart, G., & Wright, P. (2022). *Human resource management: Gaining a competitive advantage* (13th ed.). McGraw-Hill.

OECD. (2023). *OECD employment Outlook 2023: Artificial intelligence and the labour market*. OECD Publishing. https://doi.org/10.1787/08785bba-en

Price, L. R. (2011). *Psychometric methods: Theory into practice* (1st ed.). The Guilford Press.

Roethlisberger, F. J., & Dickson, W. J. (1939). *Management and the worker: An account of a research program conducted by the Western electric company, Hawthorne works, chicago*, Harvard University Press.

Rothaermel, F. (2023). *Strategic management* (6th ed.). McGraw-Hill.

Spector, P. (2021). *Industrial and organizational psychology: Research and practice* (8th ed.). Wiley.

Taylor, F. (1913). *Principles of scientific management*. Harper.

Wooldridge, J. M. (2019). *Introductory econometrics: A modern approach* (7th ed.). Cengage Learning.

Data collection and analysis

Alec Levenson

Introduction

The amount and variety of data available for workforce analytics (WFA), and the software programs and tools to analyze that data, keep growing. This expansion creates increasing opportunities for data-based insights while simultaneously increasing the risk of analysis paralysis and pursuing dead ends that do not yield actionable insights. With those increased potential rewards and risks in mind, this chapter addresses the importance of **C**ollecting the right data and selecting the right **A**nalysis to conduct.

The chapter covers a lot of ground. Specific topics addressed include:

(a) The importance of analyzing quantitative and qualitative data and information

(b) Developing and using Likert scale data the right way

(c) Prioritizing which issues to address—where there will be the largest return on investment (ROI)

(d) Expanding data collection beyond readily available sources

(e) Understanding and addressing data limitations

(f) Preparing the data for analysis, including cleaning and dealing with outliers

(g) Building and testing multivariate models based on evidence from social science research

(h) Addressing correlation versus causation

(i) Using demographic data appropriately

(j) Analyzing data statistically

(k) Data mining versus hypothesis testing

DOI: 10.4324/9781003190097-4

(l)   Conducting analysis at the appropriate organizational levels (role, team, business unit/business process, region/geography, and/or enterprise)

(m) Applying the scientific method to balance the roles of qualitative and quantitative data in an analysis.

This chapter complements other sections of the book, particularly Chapter 2, which focuses on building models based on existing research about how businesses succeed at the individual, team, and organizational levels, and Chapter 5, which emphasizes the importance of engaging stakeholders and senior decision-makers early and often in the analysis process to maximize organizational learning and insight implementation.

The importance of both quantitative and qualitative data

The data needed for analysis and sense-making are at the heart of any WFA project. When most people think of data, they immediately focus on statistics and statistical analysis, and the quantitative data required for those tasks. Yet qualitative data, which cannot be statistically analyzed in the classic sense, is usually equally important in addressing the big challenges WFA needs to help solve (Levenson, 2015).

Although numerical data often seems more precise and scientific, it can be difficult to interpret without the appropriate context. Explanations of "what the numbers mean" are essential to turn data into information, and qualitative data (information) is often required for this task, making it an essential part of any robust WFA project.

There are many potential sources of qualitative information within an organization. New qualitative data can come from text responses collected during interviews, focus groups, surveys, and recorded chat conversations. Archival—or "existing"—qualitative data includes organizational narratives found in company documents, reports, and documented histories. Other sources include oral histories about the company's origins and culture, including the "accepted wisdom" of how things happened in the past and why things happen the way they do in the organization today. The topics covered include team and leadership behaviors, as well as expectations for what will happen in the future, especially in relation to anticipated organizational changes and transformation initiatives.

Quantifying attitudinal and subjective data

Psychology, economics, and other social science disciplines have a long history of creating quantitative measurements from qualitative data, especially attitudinal data and observations of behaviors. The famous Likert (1932) scale was pioneered to enable statistical analysis of responses to questions such as "How much do you agree with the following statement?" and "To what extent does ＿＿ happen in your organization?" Responses usually range from "strongly disagree" to "strongly agree" or "not at all" to "a great extent."

While the Likert scale is a foundational tool for collecting attitudinal responses and classifying them into a form that can be numerically analyzed, it has some limitations that may not be fully appreciated outside the realm of psychometric experts. Given the prevalence of data science skills and a large underrepresentation of behavioral science skills in WFA functions, several challenges and risks associated with Likert scale data are common in organizations and threaten the quality of analysis and insights. These include (a) overly relying on analyzing single-item Likert scale measures rather than constructing valid and reliable scales, and (b) not constructing and evaluating multivariate behavioral models.

Problem #1: Overreliance on analyzing single-item Likert scale measures rather than multi-item scales

Converting a series of five or seven response options into numerical values (e.g., one to five or one to seven) is an entirely artificial process that does not reflect the true meaning behind each response.

Assigning numerical values to the responses implies that the difference between adjacent responses is the same because the numerical difference is the same, which is often not the case. For example, a classic five-point agree/disagree scale is "strongly disagree (1); disagree (2); neither agree nor disagree (3); agree (4); strongly agree (5)." Yet, what does it mean to say that the "distance" between "strongly agree" and "agree" is the same as between "neither agree nor disagree" and "agree"? The answer: we do not have a logical basis for reaching that conclusion, especially considering that respondents can have idiosyncratic ways of interpreting these options. Thus, the actual "distance" between the responses, in a numerical sense, varies significantly from one person to another.

A second related issue is that we cannot be certain that two people mean the exact same thing when they say they "agree" or "slightly disagree" with a statement. In fact, there often are systematic biases across individuals. Some people always reply more positively, whereas others reply more negatively across most or all items on a survey. These kinds of differences are called general affect differences.

Because of these limitations, psychologists strongly advise against using single items for measurement and drawing conclusions. Yet, this practice remains common in organizations and among consulting groups that collect and provide employee survey data across multiple organizations. These services are sold as a type of benchmarking, and WFA practitioners widely embrace them as essential for HR and business leaders to understand what is going on with employees.

What does this look like in practice? The reporting, sense-making, and actions that follow many annual employee surveys in organizations are illuminating. The norm for many surveys run by external vendors is to focus on single items and compare them to either benchmark data from other organizations or to a desired response level, such as 90% or more "agree" or "strongly agree." And, taken at face value, focusing on single items this way can seem reasonable for the following reasons:

■ It is much easier to benchmark "percent agree" for single items than to create a comparable benchmark for a Likert scale that averages multiple items.

■ People are used to being graded on a 0–100 scale, especially in school; as a result, having an objective of achieving what can seem like a "passing grade" of 85% or 90% "agree" can feel like the right thing to do.

Yet, despite the apparent reasonableness of focusing on single items, this is a classic case of perception not aligning with reality. In a small number of cases, such as when measuring job satisfaction (Scarpello & Campbell, 1983), there is sufficient evidence to allow for using single items instead of a validated scale. In all other cases, it is unwise to use single items rather than scales that have been validated and shown to have sufficient reliability (Levenson, 2014a).

The argument for comparing individual survey items across organizations—benchmarking—is similarly suspect because context matters. It is nearly impossible to draw actionable insights by comparing individual survey items across organizations (Levenson, 2015). For example, what does it mean if the employees of one organization are less likely to say that decision-making happens in a timely fashion than at other organizations that operate in the same industry? Does that mean the organization's leaders are too slow in their decision-making? It may. However, it may also signal that slower, more deliberate decision-making is preferred given the history and circumstances in which that organization and its leadership are operating. Examples could include recent operational or reputational problems that created the need to be more deliberate in decision-making.

The other problem with organization-wide benchmarking for a question like this is that it obscures critical differences across departments and units. Decisions that are the purview of specific departments and leaders usually are not best evaluated by asking everyone in the organization for their opinion. Some examples include decisions dealing with issues of quality and integrity, and the speed of decisions about developing new products.

While benchmarking "percent agree" for individual survey items against specific thresholds, such as 85% or 90%, is common, it lacks a strong scientific foundation. Generally speaking, it is perfectly fine to use responses to individual survey items to get a sense of how things are trending in the organization. If, from one year to the next, people become much more negative about some items, that could be a good sign that something needs to be addressed. However, what often happens is that huge attention is paid to relatively small variations in responses from year to year: if the percent agree goes up slightly, it is viewed as positive; if it stays the same, that is neutral; and if it goes down, that is taken as a negative sign.

However, normal measurement error means that some of the year-to-year variation is due to nothing more than noise and should not be taken as a sign of anything positive or negative. Further complicating the issue: once the percent agree approaches or exceeds 90%, which is quite common, leaders often maintain an expectation that further improvements should still be possible, where they assume that, say, 91% agree is objectively worse than 93% agree. However, there are two legitimate reasons to question such a view.

The first problem is that, at a certain point, there will be diminishing marginal returns to improving scores on any one survey item. If people are generally happy along a particular dimension, indicated by a percent agree of 85–90% or higher, it is not clear that there would be any additional benefit to increasing that metric. Rather than focusing on individual survey items that already score so high, a better ROI is likely to be found by looking at other issues to address. If all items on the employee survey score so high, it is quite likely that other new dimensions should be addressed in future surveys that are in greater need of attention than what is currently included.

To address the limitations of using single survey items, psychologists develop scales (or constructs) that consist of multiple Likert survey items. The scale is an average of the numerical values assigned to the responses for the individual survey items. Once constructed, there are well-established ways to evaluate the validity and reliability of scales to ensure they measure what was intended (Cronbach & Meehl, 1955; Clark & Watson, 1995). Yet, WFA practitioners seldom follow these standard research practices, risking inaccurate and misleading data collection.

The second problem regards creating more nuanced, systemic views of what is happening with the employees and managers who fill out the survey. Rather than focusing on a set of single items or even individual constructs that measure only one thing, organizations should focus greater time and energy on developing and testing multivariate behavioral models.

Problem #2: Insufficient use of multivariate behavioral models

Before diving into multivariate model construction, it is worth spending a bit more time addressing the use of Likert scale data. Despite the limitations of Likert scale data, the answer is not to reject it entirely but to understand the pros and cons and how to best leverage it.

Attitudinal data represent how people feel about an issue at a specific point in time. These subjective measures can be influenced by various factors, including recent events both at work and outside of it. Moreover, individuals have different tendencies to be more positive or negative in general, which can directly affect how they respond to the questions; what "agree" means can vary greatly from one person to the next.

Because attitudinal data are subjective, the first essential step is to put the responses into context. If a group of employees appears unhappy about a particular subject, based on their responses to a series of questions, the immediate questions that should be asked are:

- What does it mean that they are happy (or unhappy) about the issue? Does it matter for the experiences the employees have?

- Are there direct or indirect implications for business performance in the short or long term?

- What more do we need to know to understand the full context? What types of responses might the organization take, and will those responses have the intended effect?

Note that the answers to these questions partly depend on whether the person asking them believes that organizations should inherently care about their employees' welfare. Extensive research has shown strong correlations between employee attitudes and performance on the job. So, one can argue that organizations *should* care about how their employees feel about various issues because their attitudes *could* ultimately affect the bottom line.

Yet the link between employee attitudes and organizational performance is not necessarily immediate or direct. The way consulting groups such as Gallup tell the story, it seems that changes in employee attitudes—especially "engagement"—always precede changes in organizational performance. Although a compelling story can be told along those lines, the opposite is equally true (Levenson, 2014a):

- Engagement leads to performance: When people are unhappy, they disengage from the work, and their individual and team performance suffers, which affects the organization's performance.

- Performance leads to engagement: When things are not going well in the business, employees become demotivated because they can see they will not be earning bonuses, raises, and promotions that depend on organizational performance. Additionally, the conditions under which they work become less inviting and harsher (resources are cut back, managers are stretched thin, etc.).

In reality, engagement and performance are mutually codependent, feeding off each other in what Edward Lawler called a "virtuous spiral." When people are engaged, they perform better, leading to greater feedback, rewards, and camaraderie, which in turn improves engagement. If the two can feed off each other on the way up, the same is true in reverse: when things are going poorly on one front, the feedback effects on the other can pull both down in mutually reinforcing ways. As a result, measuring employee attitudes such as engagement could be an important avenue for examining the complex relationship between attitudes and performance, which is just one among many potential uses for employee attitudinal data.

Even if we accept the importance of attitudinal data, the challenges of impermanence and subjectivity remain. Collecting repeated measures of the same thing under various contexts and over time addresses the impermanence of responses to get a better sense of durability versus the transitory nature of feelings about the topic. This is the origin of pulse survey techniques, which recognize the importance of measuring the same concepts repeatedly over a relatively short time rather than once a year, which is often the default in organizations. Yet, it is not practical to do such repeated measurements in most cases due to cost issues and the downsides of over-surveying the people in your organization.

The standard way to address the nuances of understanding the story attitudinal data tell is to construct multivariate models. A multivariate model consists of the dependent variable—the outcome one wants to understand—and a group of independent variables—explanatory and control variables. The explanatory variables represent the factors (or hypotheses) that may drive or relate to the outcome—the factors to test to see if they are strongly related to or cause the outcome. The control variables are demographics and other factors that help explain variation in the outcome and that need to be "held constant"—that is, their effect on the outcome needs to be removed so one can more purely test the relationship between the explanatory variables and the outcome.

An example will help illustrate this. Consider employees' happiness with the work, as measured either by their commitment to the organization, job satisfaction, or their intention to leave for a job elsewhere. Factors that could affect how they feel about the work include their relationship with their supervisor, how they feel about their compensation, their relationships with their coworkers or teammates, work–life balance (or job stress), and opportunities for advancement. We can use these factors to construct a multivariate model as follows:

- Outcome (Y): commitment; job satisfaction; or intention to leave (only one can be analyzed in a specific model or analysis)
- Explanatory variables: relationship with supervisor ($X1$); pay satisfaction ($X2$); relationship with teammates ($X3$); work–life balance ($X4$); opportunities for advancement ($X5$)
- Control variables: gender ($Z1$); race ($Z2$); age ($Z3$); tenure with the organization ($Z4$)
- Model: $Y = f(X1, X2, X3, X4, X5; Z1, Z2, Z3, Z4)$, where "$f()$" is the particular model—and accompanying statistical technique—used to test the relationships between the outcome (Y) and the set of explanatory ($X1$–$X5$) and control

(Z1–Z4) variables. Examples of statistical techniques that could be applied to estimate such a model include regression, ANOVA, discrete choice (binomial; multinomial), simultaneous equations, maximum likelihood, and many more. The choice of which technique to apply is dictated by best practices from social science research methods. Examples of some cutting-edge practices are provided in Chapter 4.

Providing a detailed explanation of how to run multivariate models is beyond the scope of this chapter and book. Those who want to learn how to do so can take advantage of social science research methods courses. For everyone else, what matters is understanding that (a) models are complex and (b) multivariate models need to be constructed and run properly to ensure reliable insights are derived.

Before concluding this section, one key point will help tie together some of the earlier discussion points about using attitudinal data and Likert scale constructs. This point is important for people in WFA who are technically trained well enough to run multivariate models but may lack extensive experience constructing, estimating, and interpreting such models.

The issue is that attitudinal data can vary systematically from one person to the next, as discussed above. "General affect" differences like these make it hard to know for sure what is being measured when comparing responses to individual measurement items across people. The power of multivariate models is that they can be employed to get around some of the challenges of general affect differences across people.

One solution that addresses the challenges of general affect differences uses models where (a) the outcome variable is attitudinal and (b) two or more of the explanatory variables are also attitudinal. This maximizes the likelihood that the measured relationship between the outcome variable and each of the attitudinal explanatory variables reflects the marginal correlation with the outcome variable. When that is the case, the output from the multivariate model can be legitimately viewed as testing the importance of the different (attitudinal) explanatory variables relative to each other. However, if only one attitudinal explanatory variable is used in a model where another attitudinal variable is the outcome, general affect differences across people will cause a highly spurious correlation between them, making it much harder to identify the real relationship.

For example, suppose one wants to understand the drivers of turnover intention. If a multivariate model is run with only one attitudinal explanatory variable, such as work–life balance, the results will generally show an extremely strong negative relationship between good work–life balance and turnover intention. Yet, if another attitudinal explanatory variable is added, such as pay satisfaction, the measured relationship between work–life balance and turnover intention will become much weaker and could become statistically insignificant. Having a second attitudinal explanatory variable present in the model and analysis means one can better isolate the real relationship between work–life balance and turnover intention.

Thus, one key feature and benefit of multivariate models is their power to overcome measurement and interpretation challenges with attitudinal variables.

Data mining versus hypothesis testing

Until recently, calling an analysis "data mining" was typically viewed as negative criticism. It meant the analyst was aimlessly poking around in the data without a clear purpose or way of understanding the statistical relationships that might emerge. Social scientists also call this "dust bowl empiricism." The epitome of this approach is illustrated quite vividly and humorously in Vigen's website and book (2015) on spurious correlations.

Yet the massive increase in computing power and the ability to mine ever-larger databases in recent years has created a positive image around the notion of "big data" analysis (Levenson, 2014b). At its core, however, big data analysis is simply data mining. So, how can we reconcile traditional negative views of data mining with the recent hype and activity?

In traditional social science research, data exploration plays an important role. It is often the discovery of an interesting relationship in data that kicks off a research inquiry. Thus, data mining often plays an important role in unearthing interesting patterns that *could* warrant further investigation.

A second role for data exploration is during the model testing phase of a research inquiry. Any good model has to be built on a solid foundation of what is known about the issue being studied, based on the existing literature, which dictates the types of variables to be included or excluded from the model. Yet, just because past research might indicate a variable should be included, that does not guarantee the data collected for the current analysis will conform to expectations for the actual empirical relationships among the variables in the data. So, exploratory data analysis is a key first step in model testing, where the properties of each variable (range, standard deviation, etc.) are examined, and the bivariate relationships among all the model's variables are also explored through correlation tables or matrices.

Both types of data exploration are important for helping advance knowledge of human behavior in organizations, which is the real goal of WFA. Yet they are not the final stage of analysis but rather a means to an end. The ultimate goal is developing and testing hypotheses about human behavior that come from both the pressing business needs and observed relationships in the data.

Correlation versus causation

The discussions in the previous two sections touch on one of the most fundamental challenges in WFA: identifying correlation versus causation. The challenge is that there is a big gap between the concept of causation and the ability to prove that it exists in any WFA analysis. For example, putting a variable on the left-hand side of a multivariate model (calling it the outcome variable) means there is good reason to believe that it is caused by the explanatory variables in the model. Yet, even if the model is run and the results seem reasonable, that does not prove that the model—and the causal story—has been proven correct.

An easy way to see this challenge is to switch places for the outcome variable and one of the explanatory variables. In the example of engagement and performance from above, it would look like the following:

- The initial model tested proposes that performance is a function of engagement and other variables. Performance is the outcome variable, and engagement is one of the explanatory variables.

- The alternative model would switch the roles of those two variables: treat engagement as the outcome variable and use performance as one of the explanatory variables while keeping all the other explanatory variables in the model.

Because of multicollinearity (correlation), if the first model produces reasonable-looking results, the second model almost always will as well.

Being able to specify models the right way (ask the right questions) is complicated greatly by the challenge of differentiating causation from correlation. Knowledge of existing research (Chapter 2) is one essential part of specifying the right model to test. The other is knowing how to apply statistical methods that can help tease out this difference (Chapter 4).

Collecting new data

When it comes to the types of data that can and should be included in a WFA project, what is readily available is only a fraction of the potential data that could be collected and analyzed. Therefore, one also has to consider what is currently in hand, the cost-benefit tradeoff of collecting more data, and whether what should be collected is quantitative data, qualitative data, or both.

Is there enough time to collect new data?

With enough time and energy, anything can be measured, but the ROI for doing so often is not there. The reason why "analysis paralysis" is such a common phrase is that it is a real thing. Extensive time can easily be spent adding more and more data and analyses. Yet, these additional data and analytics need to improve the insights produced. Otherwise, these additions likely waste time and detract from stakeholders' confidence in the analytics team and the results. In the context of organizations and WFA, this crops up often because of the critical importance of making decisions in a limited time frame.

What most people in organizations often fail to recognize, however, is the value of collecting and analyzing data over longer time horizons than the initial decision-making process requires. Many of the more pressing topics in WFA that affect organizational performance are what Levenson (2015) calls "perennial problems" because they come up repeatedly. This happens because they are usually challenging to solve, such as lower-than-desired productivity in a team or work unit, low morale, or quality of hires. When previous attempts to address the issue have fallen short, a new team or expert is called in to try and fix what previously was not fully solved. Yet, the new team or experts are given very little time to collect and analyze new data to thoroughly address the issues at hand.

If the new team/expert (a) does not construct a proper causal model, (b) is not provided enough time and resources to collect and analyze the necessary data to test the model, and (c) is unable to convince leadership to take appropriate actions following the analysis, it is highly likely that the issue will come up in the future yet again. If a WFA team finds itself in a time crunch situation like this—which is quite likely—Levenson (2015) advocates for working backward from the next decision-making cycle.

Start with whatever "quick and dirty" analysis can be done with the data and information on hand for the current too-short decision-making cycle. This shows responsiveness to the need for a quick decision. At the same time, emphasize that the recommendations provided are tentative and cannot be relied on with great confidence because of the lack of time or resources to do a proper analysis. Following the delivery of those recommendations, determine what kinds of data and analysis are needed to produce a truly thorough assessment of the issues, make a plan for doing the additional work, and launch the work "under the radar" of high-level leadership.

This means enlisting key stakeholders who recognize the importance of getting to the right answer and who are skeptical that the quick and dirty analysis was sufficient to find the root causes that need to be addressed. Partnering with these stakeholders, one can take the time to do a more thorough assessment, including collecting new data and information at a more relaxed pace and conducting the analysis well before the next decision-making cycle. For example, this approach was deployed quite successfully by Levenson and Faber (2009).

What is the value of collecting and analyzing new data? Where is the greatest ROI?

Two sets of authors—Becker, Huselid, and Beatty (Becker & Huselid, 1998; Becker et al., 2009; Huselid et al., 2005; Huselid, 2018) and Boudreau and Ramstad (2006, 2007)—have noted that some roles are often much more "important" than others in a statistical sense. Improving performance in those roles could have a much larger effect on the bottom line than focusing on other roles. This means concentrating efforts on those roles and the work groups in which they are embedded could yield a higher ROI than working on challenges facing other roles and work groups. This can help improve the credibility of the WFA team, yielding support for future projects.

A key aspect of the framework that both sets of authors use to highlight these key roles is that they benefit from a high potential return on improved performance (ROIP). This is quite different from the "average" value a role provides to the organization and is often a product of a role being relatively neglected in the past in terms of status and perceptions of how much it contributes to organizational performance. In calculus terms, this is the difference between the average value produced by a role and the marginal value created by a change in performance (first derivative).

Two examples from Boudreau and Ramstad's pivotal role framework illustrate the point. The first (Boudreau & Ramstad, 2006) comes from package delivery companies such as FedEx, DHL, and UPS. These companies have pilots who fly planes and drivers who pick up and deliver packages. On average, pilots can be viewed as "more important" because they transport thousands and thousands of packages every time they fly, whereas a driver transports at most a few hundred packages each day. Yet, the organizational systems built and optimized for the pilot role ensure very little variation in performance. Really bad performance for a pilot would mean the plane crashes and all packages are destroyed. Yet, this type of bad performance is virtually completely engineered out of the system. Among the drivers, in contrast, there is a very wide variation in performance. Consequently, these companies typically yield much greater ROI from investing in improving performance differences among their drivers than among their airplane pilots.

A second example (Boudreau & Ramstad, 2007) comes from the Walt Disney Company and the potential ROIP from the role of the characters versus street sweepers. The characters—the people who play Mickey Mouse, Minnie Mouse, Goofy, Donald Duck, Jack Sparrow, Mulan, etc.—are the essential employees in the parks because they are the number one reason most families with children come to the parks in the first place. Without the characters, Disney's competitive advantage over other amusement parks would be substantially lower. Because of the extremely high value of the characters, the company invests enormous time, energy, and resources in ensuring all aspects of the job are performed as flawlessly as possible, to the point where there arguably is little to no room for improved performance in the role, even if more resources were invested.

The role of the street sweeper is a different story. In other amusement parks, street sweepers have only one role: sanitation. At Disney's parks, however, the street sweeper is viewed as an ambassador for the customer experience, including breaking out into what seems like spontaneous song and dance routines. New customers who have never visited the parks come expecting the high-quality character experience but not the street sweeper experience. As a result, street sweepers have the potential to improve the customer experience and make the difference between a magical versus a more ordinary experience. Thus, the company must optimize the allocation of investment between deploying street sweepers solely for sanitation duties versus entertainment duties, creating a much greater potential ROIP for the sweepers than the characters.

Applying the principles of these examples to a more general topic universal across all organizations, consider the potential ROIP from leadership development for more senior roles in the company versus training or on-the-job learning for lower-hierarchy roles. At most companies, much greater time, energy, and resources are invested per capita in leadership roles than in frontline and lower-level supervisory roles. The justification for this disproportionate investment in developing leaders is usually the argument that if a leader fails, they can have huge negative effects across an entire business unit or business process, creating major repercussions for the organization's bottom line. This is an argument about the average impact or productivity of senior leaders compared to lower-level employees.

Yet, much like the potential ROIP for the FedEx pilots and the Disney characters, this heavy emphasis on leadership means that most "low hanging fruit" gains from improved leadership performance have already been optimized out of the system. There is a low ROIP from additional investments in leadership development; in calculus terms, the second derivative of performance is extremely low or even zero. In contrast, the much lower per capita levels of investment in development for many frontline roles and lower-level supervisory roles mean there are substantial potential gains to be realized from investing the next set of funds in developing those people rather than leadership.

Now consider the question of where to invest precious time and budget in collecting new data to analyze and improve organizational performance. Stakeholders who manage "high value" roles will always argue that their issues should receive top priority for evaluation, analysis, and new data collection because of the high average contributions of those roles to organizational performance. Yet, rather than always responding to those requests by prioritizing them over all others, the right approach for the shareholders of the company is to take a step back, assess the ROIP of different roles and business processes, and prioritize collecting and analyzing new data based on the potential ROIP.

Note that the analysis needed to determine ROIP for different roles is not statistical. What is required is a type of case study analysis. One collects the information needed to understand the potential upsides of improving performance, which comes from interviewing stakeholders with expert knowledge of each role. Additional insights can come from reviewing previous job analyses and attempts to improve performance in the role.

Furthermore, even if leadership in the organization invests in new data collection and analysis for roles that traditionally have been relatively starved for attention, one should not ignore the highest profile roles that traditionally have gotten disproportionate investments. The best strategy is "both/and." Monitoring processes are needed for all roles that play an important part in creating the organization's competitive advantage. Otherwise, whichever roles go for extended periods without being analyzed for potential improvements will likely become the ones with the greatest potential ROIP.

Surveys and other "static" ways of collecting new information

The first thing that comes to mind when one hears "collect more data" is often a survey. Surveys are one of the most traditional ways of collecting new data in organizations and the social sciences. A survey is a set of preselected questions with either preset answer choices or open-ended options where the respondents provide their own answers.

A second common data collection approach is to access existing stores of information that may not be immediately accessible to the analyst. This includes data collected systematically for purposes other than WFA, which could yield important insights if incorporated into a WFA model. Examples include business-process outcomes such as customer reviews and complaints, quality, uptime, and other operational metrics. In recent decades, the rollout of data warehouses, enterprise resource planning systems such as SAP and Oracle, and other systematic ways of collecting and linking data from different parts of the organization has greatly expanded the available data for potential use in WFA.

More recently, applications and platforms developed specifically for managing workforce processes and data, such as Workday, SAP SuccessFactors, and Oracle Cloud (HCM), have focused on bringing together the information most likely to be useful for analyzing the workforce. However, they often do not automatically include survey data and other "sensing" data collected by internal analytics groups or outside vendors. These data must be manually linked to be included in analyses combining data from both sources.

Many sources of archival data on WFA issues come from HR data. Yet they often require substantial time and effort to transform into data that can address central WFA issues. The main source of the problem is that most HR information systems (HRIS) were historically built on an accounting platform designed to report real-time information on the roles but not the people in the roles. So, a historical look-up could easily describe how the compensation for a role changed over time but would struggle to track a specific individual's compensation over time or their career trajectory across different roles.

In the early days of WFA, these data structure issues were substantial barriers to conducting meaningful analysis on topics such as career paths and internal labor mobility within the organization. Over time, the situation has improved dramatically, first with the creation of data warehouses that enable the linking of all records associated with an employee's identification (ID) number, and later by building

HRIS systems around an employee view of workforce data or robust global data warehouse platforms that combine data from a wide variety of sources in the business, including HR—often called "data lakes."

In recent years, increased computing power and more sophisticated data warehousing systems using relational databases have made historical views on an employee basis much more ubiquitous. Yet the legacy of how the systems evolved and the primacy of the finance view of organizations, which cares only about the costs of each role and not the people in the role, means that the people-centric data view will likely always be treated as an add-on or something to be addressed in parallel HRIS systems. As a result, WFA may always need to invest substantial time and resources in transforming the data generated by the business into usable forms for the most insightful WFA models. And anytime data are drawn from a source that was not designed explicitly with WFA in mind, including privacy and other considerations, there are potential ethical issues that need to be addressed before using such data (see the discussion in Chapter 6).

A third source of new information is individual-level or team-level evaluations such as 360-degree appraisals, performance reviews, and team assessments, which are designed to address issues central to WFA but are often collected and stored separately from the main data used for WFA. Related sources include information produced by succession planning processes, training and development programs, individual development planning meetings, and exit surveys.

Interviews and other "dynamic" ways of collecting new information

Talking to people is one of the oldest methods of collecting new information, dating back to the dawn of human civilization. The classic approaches include one-on-one interviews and focus groups where multiple people answer questions and discuss topics among themselves and with the interviewer (facilitator).

Yet, despite the widespread use of interviews by researchers, HR professionals, and consultants, many WFA practitioners appear to have little to no interest in engaging with this rich source of information and sense-making. The main reason for this is the strong bias toward using existing and new sources of quantitative information, especially among WFA practitioners who come from a strict data science background.

Another likely reason is the ever-growing supply of data that can be analyzed using data science techniques. The sources of this data include surveys, employees' online activities, matching and analysis of historical data in existing HRIS and other organizational data warehouses, and more. With such a large and growing supply of data to analyze, some might question why a WFA practitioner would need to look for more information to collect and process, especially if it is unstructured and much harder to analyze. However, relying on quantitative data alone severely limits the insights into the drivers of organizational performance and strategy execution that can be derived from the analysis. Used correctly, interviews and other qualitative data are an essential part of any quantitative analysis.

Collecting new data from other sources

Advances in technology, computing power, and the internet have made it much easier to collect data about employee and organizational behavior in new ways. Three examples include (a) information on the internet, (b) "digital exhaust," and (c) aggregating qualitative data and information via technology.

Information on the internet can take many forms, but generally can be broken into two main categories: information about people as consumers (meaning in their role as non-employees or potential customers or clients of the organization) and information about people as employees. When companies collect information on people's browsing behavior, their responses to information on social media, and their interactions with digital ads, the purpose is largely to understand consumer behaviors. When the information is about what people do and how they act in their work lives, it can be used to generate insights about employee behaviors. The latter is a more recent development and can be leveraged for important insights about external labor markets and the experiences of current and future employees.

For example, LinkedIn has become a "go-to" source for information about job postings, searches, and more. In addition, because people keep their professional information reliably up to date on LinkedIn, it can be an easy way to learn about the past work histories of current or prospective employees, or the subsequent work histories of those who leave. Combining such data with internal information can enable more robust analyses of career dynamics, talent pools, and the labor markets in which the organization competes.

Digital exhaust refers to data generated by people communicating and working electronically. The most common applications include collecting patterns of communication and interaction based on who sends and receives emails and texts and on who meets with whom based on calendar information. Microsoft recently developed an entire suite of productivity tools that use such data. Other applications include analyzing patterns of communication among individuals and between groups within and across organizations; for example, analyzing whether the people and groups that are expected to be collaborating intensively actually are. This last application is an example of organizational network analysis, which is discussed in detail in Chapter 4.

Several qualitative data sources are becoming increasingly important for WFA's ability to analyze. For example, qualitative comments drawn from surveys (rather than Likert responses) are increasingly being included in the data available to WFA teams: technology enables the coding and analysis of open-ended comments, which can be aggregated at the team or business-process level. Transcripts of video interviews can be analyzed with natural language processing and included in statistical models. The same techniques can be applied to narratives generated by performance appraisals and to matching the text in job applicants' resumes to job requirements. Chapter 4 provides further discussion on collecting and analyzing qualitative data aided by technology.

Preparing the data for analysis

Cleaning and exploratory analysis of the data are foundational activities of an effective WFA function: if the data are inconsistently defined or full of errors, it is hard to use them to derive useful insights. Workforce data are often quite error-ridden because numerous people create the data, including through employee and manager self-service data entry. Decisions on how to deal with such errors have important implications for both the meaning derived from the analysis (and subsequent decision-making about people and processes), as well as potential ethical concerns (see Chapter 6).

A second set of data challenges comes from differences in how measures are defined. Calculating tenure and turnover should be straightforward. Yet, in practice, establishing a "single source of truth" for both is exceedingly difficult. Some of the many reasons include:

(a) Multiple dates are associated with someone being hired (date when their record is created in the system, first day of work, date of first salary or wage payment, etc.).

(b) Tenure in a role differs from organizational tenure—internal transfers or promotions may be coded in ways that make it unclear to the analyst what happened.

(c) Some people leave the organization and return later, including common scenarios like interns or various leaves of absence, creating potential confusion between the date of first hire or payment versus their most recent stint working with the organization, or some calculated date representing cumulative service.

(d) Company transactions like transfers between divisions, mergers, acquisitions, and divestitures may include multiple "start" dates or partial credit for tenure as part of a different legal entity.

Some of these are data governance decisions, while others may be governed by labor contracts or similar legal agreements. Additionally, different tenure calculations may be used for different purposes within the same organization. For example, a rehired employee may be able to use cumulative service across both the original and new periods of employment for identifying their step on a pay scale or vacation eligibility, but have to restart their vesting schedule for company 401(k) matches (for employees based in the United States), effectively counting only their new term of service. Determining which of those two calculations to use in reporting average tenure in a particular role or average tenure at termination then becomes more complex. These data definition and quality issues are theoretically surmountable. Yet, it often takes considerable time and resources to resolve them, delaying when the analyses can be done or creating a barrier to doing the analyses at all.

The flip side to the challenges of data cleaning is that one can spend too much time getting the data ready for analysis, hunting down minor discrepancies in the data that likely would not make a meaningful difference in the analysis results. Experienced analysts can determine when diminishing returns to further data cleaning set in. Those with less experience working with a particular organization's data need to seek out internal experts—both analysts and subject matter experts—for direction on how far to take data cleaning and the decisions to be made on data definition.

WFA datasets usually also have missing data in key variables used for the analysis. As discussed in detail in Chapter 6, decisions must be made about whether to exclude the records from the analysis, which reduces the representativeness of the data and insights, or to impute values for the missing data, which risks introducing biases that are not clear. Both options present considerable challenges that need to be addressed by the analyst and communicated to the recipients of the results so they are aware of the risks. Chapter 6 presents a thorough treatment of the need for data transparency.

Accounting for outliers in the data

The presence of outliers can also significantly impact the results and interpretation of a WFA project, so their potential role needs to be thoroughly vetted and accounted for in the analysis. For example, analyses that use age (or organizational tenure) as an explanatory variable need to check for the influence of outliers. In the case of age, it is highly likely that the group under study could have members that range from people in their 20s through 50s. If the vast majority of group members are clustered in their 20s and 30s, with a much smaller number in their 40s and only a few in their 50s, the latter two groups will dominate the "age effect" in the data—perhaps inappropriately. In such cases, the analyst can try removing the oldest people from the analysis to see how the results change, try including indicator (dummy) variables for wide age ranges (e.g., 20s versus 30s versus 40s versus 50s), or consider a model that explicitly addresses life cycle differences.

Another example is compensation, which is highly skewed in organizations. Any model that includes the most highly compensated people in the same analysis as the less highly compensated should explore options such as using a log transformation of income to reduce the undue influence of the highest earners. Other options include using job level—or compensation band—as the explanatory variable, which would have a similar effect as log transforming compensation.

Using demographic information to understand the data and appropriately estimate the models

Demographic data is usually an important part of any WFA analysis. Demographic information includes characteristics such as age, gender identity, sexual identity, race, ethnicity, national origin, native language (language spoken from birth), and whether the person has a physical disability. Demographic data can be important for two reasons: as a primary focus of the analysis, and as a moderator or mediator. Consequently, properly using demographic data is essential to correctly specifying and analyzing most WFA models.

Demographic information should always be examined to understand how the data vary based on observed characteristics. In all societies, position in the organizational hierarchy and career success are correlated with demographic characteristics. As a consequence, controlling for demographic characteristics in an analysis must be done with care: since demographic characteristics frequently are correlated with role, status, and compensation, there are substantial challenges in establishing causality. Yet ignoring demographic characteristics is equally problematic for the same reason: the potential presence of discrimination and/or self-selection into a role or career path should be acknowledged, even if that is not the main focus of the analysis.

The bottom line: the role of demographics in any WFA analysis is often complex and must be handled with care and diligent attention to detail.

Data weaknesses and limitations

It is essential to understand the limitations of certain types of data that are commonly used for understanding and managing performance and employee engagement. Just because it seems reasonable to use data for a particular purpose does not mean that it should be.

A prominent example is using employee engagement data for the performance management of individual managers. Given the positive relationship between employee engagement and performance, many organizations try to hold managers accountable for maintaining or improving employee engagement scores. Yet doing so can quickly contaminate the source data on employee engagement: once managers are held accountable for achieving specific numerical targets, they can easily be tempted to act in ways that could lead to better survey scores, yet do not measurably improve employee engagement itself. For example, they might strike side deals where they reward their team members for higher scores on the survey.

This same critique has been voiced for years about the pros and cons of using 360-degree evaluations for feedback versus performance management purposes. The research is clear that using such data for feedback can be very helpful for managers who have gaps in their capabilities. Yet, once such data are used for performance management (London, 2001, 2003) or incorporated into a managerial competency model that is tied to performance management (Levenson, 2021), there is a substantial risk that the quality of the data itself can be degraded, as managers "teach to the (performance management) test" rather than focus on improving their behaviors or competencies because it is the right thing to do for their careers and the organization.

Performance management ratings also suffer from quality issues related to how they are created. The widespread usage of forced distribution rankings means that managers are forced to differentiate among team members in ways that are not related to actual performance (Lawler, 2002). When WFA includes performance ratings in analyses, great care needs to be taken to understand the source of variance within and across teams or reporting units. Rather than taking low ratings as indicating "pure" measures of performance, WFA practitioners must directly account for the very prevalent sources of non-performance-related variation, even in systems where forced distributions are not a design feature. Examples of such sources include having team members take turns receiving lower ratings to "spread the pain," using higher ratings and providing greater salary increases to lower-paid members (low relative to their external job opportunities, not necessarily relative to their peers at the organization), and discriminating or playing favorites. (See also the discussion of challenges with performance ratings in Chapter 6.)

Combining quantitative and qualitative data in an analysis

Qualitative data plays two central roles in partnership with quantitative analysis. It is a complementary, essential element for conducting robust quantitative analysis. Additionally, qualitative data can sometimes substitute for quantitative analysis when addressing many of the most important questions about organizational performance, business model effectiveness, and business-process optimization.

First, consider the complementarity. In social science research, interviews are essential for setting up a quantitative analysis and providing the sense-making needed to understand the results. At the beginning of an analytics inquiry, interviews are used to identify the initial hypotheses to be developed. They also help determine which data to analyze and which to exclude.

Conducting interviews initially is necessary because statistical models are limited in the number of potential factors that can be included without reducing the quality of the analysis. Typically, no more than ten factors can be included because there is only so much variation in the outcome variable. Adding additional potential explanatory variables after a certain point does not further increase the percentage of variation explained (the R squared). Also, each additional variable often introduces unwanted multicollinearity with the other variables already in the model.

The initial interviews allow the exploration of which potential explanatory variables to include and which to exclude based on what the key players and knowledge about the work system reveal. For example, consider three different work systems where turnover is a concern:

- At the first site, initial interviews might reveal a toxic environment and great mistrust between management and frontline employees, where employees complain about a lack of managerial support, poor communication, arbitrary rewards and performance management processes, and limited information on opportunities for advancement.
- At the second site, initial interviews generally reveal positive relations between management and the frontline in terms of communication and feedback, but major concerns about frontline compensation and benefits relative to other opportunities in the market. Employees voice concerns about commuting long distances because they cannot afford to live in the expensive area where they work. Parents also indicate they struggle with work–life balance and finding affordable childcare options.
- At the third site, the interviews reveal a focus on the work itself. The work environment is very fast-paced, and employees struggle to meet quotas. Additionally, HR processes focus on finding replacement hires rather than making it easier and more humane to get the work done. The work system seems designed only for a top echelon of highly motivated and productive employees. Yet, the company struggles to find enough people who fit that profile for their jobs. Employees express frustration with how little they are paid for the work they do, and it is unclear if paying more would address the turnover issues or whether the work design itself might need to be altered to decrease turnover.

Some of the information needed to better understand what is happening at each site is likely available from sources such as prior employee surveys. Yet existing data is never comprehensive enough to paint the full picture, which is why initial interviews are needed. As discussed earlier, there are fairly strict limits on the number of explanatory variables that can be included in a model, which means that for each of the three sites under consideration here, a different model is likely needed. The initial interviews help identify which hypotheses are to be tested (building the model) and help determine which data to include in the analysis (to test the hypotheses).

As the analysis is conducted, the results from the initial interviews are also important for making sense of the findings. The pictures painted about the work system from the interviews provide critical details about the context and the work system that are essential for understanding the results of any statistical analysis. Thus, the initial interviews are an integral complement to data collection and analysis for model building and testing.

In addition to their complementary role, interviews are often a substitute for quantitative analysis. This happens when the issues that need to be addressed are focused on higher-level aggregates, such as organizational performance or business model and business–process optimization.

For statistical reasons, multivariate analysis can only be applied to questions about variation in performance among individuals or teams. The reason is that statistics can be calculated, and multivariate models can be estimated reliably using data, only where many members of the "population" are being analyzed, such as salespeople, call center employees, customer service teams, software programming units, or retail outlets. The statistical condition that has to be satisfied is that the members of the population be sufficiently "homogeneous" (similar) so that the comparison is "apples-to-apples." In addition, there need to be a lot of them: typically at least 50 or more in order for most parsimonious multivariate models to be statistically identified (enough "degrees of freedom" to conduct the analysis reliably); for bigger and more complex models, the required number of observations is much higher.

Therefore, the first instance in which interviews and qualitative analysis substitute for quantitative analysis is when the population being analyzed is homogeneous, but there are not enough members of the population for statistical reliability. Having only one hundred or fewer people in a role, or in teams, or retail outlets, etc., typically means no multivariate statistics or models can be applied, and the only option is qualitative analysis.

The second instance is all data that comes from "higher levels" of aggregation: anything that measures or describes the work or organization above the team or work-group level. Examples include departments, geographies, functions, and business units. For the vast majority of these types of populations, there simply are not enough of them to meet the criteria of 50 or more population members to enable multivariate analysis. Just as important: these populations always violate the "homogeneity" assumption because they are too dissimilar from each other to enable mostly context-free analysis, which is the essence of multivariate models. Context-specific analysis almost always requires at least some type of qualitative analysis.

For example, even if a company operates in hundreds of regions around the world, the differences in local labor market characteristics, local customer demand characteristics, and local supply chain and vendor characteristics mean that regions are not homogeneous enough to be directly analyzed by multivariate models. (Technically, they could be if sufficient variables measuring the differences in those local characteristics are included as control or explanatory variables in the multivariate model; however, practically speaking, the number of variables that would need to be included would likely overwhelm the degrees of freedom available to estimate such a model.) In contrast, if those regions each had the exact same type of teams or roles in them, doing the exact same type of work, there often are enough degrees of freedom to estimate an appropriately specified multivariate model. As discussed earlier, the details behind this are part of standard advanced social science knowledge about how to build and estimate multivariate models, which requires advanced training in such methods, not just data science expertise.

Thus, for analysis of any question that requires looking at or comparing the performance of departments, functions, business units, or the entire enterprise, only qualitative analysis can be applied, not quantitative—and interviews are a foundational part of such analysis.

Analyzing data statistically

Providing a detailed primer on where and how to conduct different types of statistical analysis is beyond what we can accomplish in this chapter. However, the challenges and limitations of different types of statistical analysis create real restrictions on what can be learned in any context. The differences among different types of analysis are important enough to require a short review here.

Statistical versus qualitative analysis

In general, statistical analysis can only be applied to data derived from homogeneous populations. For example, conducting a survey of everyone who works for an organization and reporting the results only in the aggregate, regardless of individual roles, is nearly useless for understanding the challenges leaders face in terms of employee engagement and performance. This is why results are typically broken down into many different sub-populations of the entire workforce for reporting and sense-making.

The most basic types of statistical analysis are univariate and bivariate. Univariate analyses included calculating means (averages), reporting minimum and maximum values, and plotting a single data series over time. Bivariate analyses involve creating correlations between two variables or plotting two different data series on the same graph or bar chart. These types of analyses account for the overwhelming majority of WFA statistical analyses conducted in most organizations. Yet, on their own, they rarely provide enough information to make reliable conclusions about what should be acted on or changed; integrating qualitative analysis of the context, culture, history, and more is essential for reaching actionable conclusions.

As previously discussed, multivariate statistical analysis can only be conducted on homogeneous samples, which means primarily individuals in the same role. Statistical analysis can also be conducted on team-level data, but only if they are doing the exact same kind of work. For everything else, something other than traditional statistics has to be used, and that requires a different kind of orientation toward answering the right questions, including using the correct frameworks addressed in Chapter 2.

Qualitative analysis at the unit level (team, business unit, function, department, geography, or enterprise) generally consists of two complementary types: case studies and logic models. Case studies are carefully constructed narratives of what happened. Logic models are carefully constructed narratives of why it happened. In both cases, initial interviews with organizational members and key stakeholders help to establish the facts (or perceived facts). Subsequent interviews and sense-making sessions with key stakeholders help vet the conclusions for validity and explanations of what happened and why.

Among WFA practitioners today, "storytelling" is perceived as a required element of effective WFA implementation. Done correctly, storytelling often encompasses both case studies and logic models. This includes laying out a persuasive case for why the outcomes happened the way they did, and why alternative explanations do not appear to do a better job of explaining the outcomes. Done incorrectly, the storytelling will sound overly simple and focus on too few drivers of the outcomes.

Consider the example of the three sites. The following are summaries of the case studies and what was happening:

- **First site:** toxic environment; great mistrust between management and frontline employees; employees complain about a lack of managerial support, poor communication, arbitrary rewards, and performance management processes; there is little information on opportunities for advancement.

- **Second site:** positive relations between management and the frontline in terms of communication and feedback; major concerns about frontline compensation and benefits relative to other opportunities in the market; employees concerned about commuting long distances because they cannot afford to live in the expensive area where they work; parents struggle with work–life balance and finding affordable childcare options.

- **Third site:** very fast-paced work environment; employees struggle to meet quotas; HR processes focus on finding replacement hires rather than making it easier and more humane to get the work done; work system seems designed only for a top echelon of highly motivated and productive employees; the company struggles to find enough people who fit that profile for their jobs; employees express frustration with how little they are paid for the work they do.

The complementary logic models accompanying the case studies need to address the range of potential causal factors for high turnover in each case and propose potential solutions. Starting examples for each are:

- **First site:** The quality of management appears to be a significant potential contributor to turnover. Why the poor management? Is there a history of management-employee strife? Are the problems recent? Are the management ranks dominated by inexperienced people? Are there aspects of the job design that make it hard for the company to attract motivated and qualified candidates—such as low pay and/or excessive job demands?

- **Second site:** How much the jobs pay appears to be a significant potential contributor to turnover. How long has this been an issue? Is it longstanding or recent? Has the job design—what the employees have to do—changed? Is the company now demanding more work for the same or only slightly higher pay? Has the work gotten harder to perform, requiring higher skill levels? Have conditions shifted in the local labor market, making it harder to attract quality candidates?

- **Third site:** The job demands appear to be a major potential contributor to turnover. Has this been an issue for a long time, or only recently? What has been going on recently and over the longer term? If the job demands have increased, why? Why haven't employee competencies increased correspondingly, either through training incumbent job holders or hiring new people? Have work demands exceeded reasonable expectations for most people? Are there sources of potential hires that have not been fully explored?

In most cases, qualitative analysis of the interviews means reading through them or using technology/artificial intelligence solutions to identify common themes and consistent patterns. Different stakeholders and participants in the work (employees, managers, coworkers) will have different perspectives on potential causes and solutions. The analysis should use these perspectives to paint a multifaceted picture of what is going on, rather than just looking for the most commonly cited explanations.

For example, people with extensive experience working at other companies will understand how similar issues might have been caused and addressed elsewhere. Complementing that perspective, long-tenured employees and managers will know the company culture best and have insights into why things could be different than at other organizations. Both sets of perspectives are important for creating an accurate case study and logic model, even if the number of internal "experts" (long-tenured people) is very high while the number of external "experts" (who have worked elsewhere extensively) could be quite low. The quality of the insights matters most, to the point where even just one external expert could have important insights that balance or outweigh what many people who have only ever worked at the company feel to be the case.

In addition to these types of qualitative analysis, quantitative analysis of qualitative information can be included:

- Counting the number of times a word or phrase appears in text responses
- Using machine learning to analyze text responses and identify themes

Such quantification of qualitative information can help provide more systematic examples or numerical summaries of the importance of themes, helping tell the story.

Table 3.1 summarizes many, but not all, types of quantitative and qualitative methods typically applied to data and information collected at different organizational levels: role/job, team or group, business process or unit, and the entire organization. "Exploratory" analysis refers to the initial stages of an inquiry, when learning about the context of the issue is the primary objective. "Diagnostic" analysis refers to the later stages of an inquiry, when hypotheses have been identified and the requisite data to answer the hypotheses have been collected.

Note that survey data about business-process (unit) and organization-level issues can be used for exploratory purposes, but not for making accurate diagnoses or identifying appropriate solutions. Standard statistical methods applied to large quantitative datasets are most appropriate for issues that exclusively or predominantly involve the work of frontline employees in specific roles, such as manufacturing

TABLE 3.1 Quantitative and Qualitative methods with WFA

	Quantitative methods	Qualitative methods
Role/job level	■ **Archival data** on the individual performance and demographics: *exploratory only* ■ **Surveys** to differentiate among people in the roles: *exploratory and diagnostic*	■ **Interviews and coding of qualitative data** from incumbents, peers, managers, and stakeholders: *exploratory and diagnostic* ■ **Focus groups** with incumbents: *exploratory and diagnostic*
Team/group level	■ **Archival data** on team performance and member demographics: *exploratory only* ■ **Surveys** to differentiate between groups and teams: *exploratory and diagnostic* ■ **Surveys** to measure within-team issues: *exploratory & diagnostic*	■ **Interviews and coding of qualitative data** from team members and the people they work with: *exploratory and diagnostic* ■ **Data** from team-based interventions: ongoing performance assessments, post-action reviews, etc. (*exploratory and diagnostic*)
Business-process/ business-unit level	■ **Surveys** to gauge individual sentiment: *exploratory only*	■ **Interviews and coding of qualitative data** from people at all levels: *exploratory and diagnostic* ■ **Case study analysis**: assessing system alignment, cross-functional issues (*diagnostic*)
Organizational level	■ **Surveys** to gauge individual sentiment: *exploratory only*	■ **Interviews and coding of qualitative data** from people at all levels: *exploratory and diagnostic* ■ **Case study analysis**: assessing system alignment, cross-functional issues (*diagnostic*)

machinery operators, customer service representatives, software programmers, sales-people, and truck drivers. For the analysis to be confined only to such frontline roles, the sources of organizational performance issues must come almost entirely from variation in performance across people in those roles, rather than from how those roles interact interdependently as contributors to team performance.

Mixed quantitative and qualitative methods are usually needed for issues that manifest at the team level. If there are enough homogeneous teams—such as customer service teams, R&D teams, or sales teams—that are designed similarly and share common objectives, then statistical analysis can be applied to compare differences among those teams. However, statistical analysis alone is rarely sufficient to provide the full range of insights needed to make the best decisions about areas for improvement, and qualitative data and methods are almost always needed to make final decisions on the best course of action.

Qualitative and case study methods are not necessarily the only ways to address issues at the enterprise-wide or business-process levels. In those cases, if data can be collected from many companies in the same industry, standard statistical tools can be applied to understand what drives differences in organizational performance across companies. That is why academic researchers, financial market analysts, and management consultants use industry-level analytics extensively. Yet, except in extremely rare cases, internal WFA practitioners do not have access to such data nor the time and resources to collect it anew. This highlights the importance of relying on a mixed strategy of reviewing existing evidence from such studies and applying qualitative and case study methods to internally collected data and information.

An example can help illustrate how quantitative and qualitative data are usually combined in a robust analysis. If the turnover rate for a site is calculated to be 40%, the question that follows is always, is that a good or bad number?

Initial quantitative analysis to help answer the question probes deeper and puts it into context using variations of the same information or different ways of calculating and comparing turnover rates. These are called "univariate analyses" because they involve the same type of data: turnover rates. Probing deeper includes breaking down the turnover rate into different demographic or other categories, such as (a) differences by role; (b) differences by gender, race, etc.; and (c) how much of the 40% turnover represents "regrettable" turnover (high performers) or "non-regrettable" turnover (low performers).

A second line of inquiry examines benchmark sites: other locations in the organization or elsewhere in the industry or economy where similar work is done, such as call centers, research laboratories, manufacturing sites, and sales offices. A third common quantitative question is how the current turnover rate compares to the history at the site. Pursuing those quantitative comparisons and drilling into the details of the 40% turnover rate is standard practice for initial sense-making in WFA.

Equally important are the contextual (qualitative) details that cannot be addressed solely through additional data analysis, as indicated in the example above of the three sites. Candidate hypotheses at this point include: What are the potential reasons turnover is as high (or low) as it is? How important is turnover relative to other measures for providing the insights needed to improve workforce engagement? And does this level of turnover create a significant negative impact on the business?

Use the scientific method to strike the right balance between collecting and using quantitative and qualitative data

One of the most significant developments in WFA in recent years has been the explosion of people working in data scientist roles. On the one hand, this is a very positive development because it indicates that data and analytics have "come into their own" as central players in how organizations everywhere make sense of the large and growing amounts of data available to learn about their products, services, and processes. That message has been particularly strongly touted by authors such as Davenport and Harris (2007), Davenport et al. (2010), and Provost and Fawcett (2013), who have championed the ever-expanding role of analytics in daily business decision-making.

On the other hand, the downside of the explosion of data science approaches to analyze business issues is that, too often, they are data-led or methods-led rather than theory-led. The subtitle of Provost and Fawcett's *Data Science for Business* (2013) is emblematic of the challenge: "What You Need to Know About Data mining and Data-Analytic Thinking." Data mining is the classic term used by statisticians to describe atheoretical analyses of data that look for patterns of interest that could potentially yield useful insights. It is the opposite of starting with the right theoretical approach, as outlined in Chapter 2.

Data mining has an essential role in data analysis, especially at the beginning of an analysis, where basic characteristics of the data and patterns among potential variables are explored. The output of initial data mining can be essential for identifying which variables are worth including in a model from a purely statistical sense (do they have enough variance, what type of distribution do they most closely resemble, etc.) and to help identify whether prospective independent and dependent variables that might be included in a model have a strong enough relationship in the first place.

The problem today is that exploring patterns in the data has become not just a first step on the journey to building theoretically grounded models but, too often, an end in and of itself. The most prominent example of an atheoretical, data-mining approach in business today is almost everything done under the heading of "big data." Usage of the term "big data" has exploded in recent years. The origins of the term trace back to the mid-1990s and early 2000s with the rapid increase in the volume, velocity, and variety of data (Diebold, 2021; Kitchin & McArdle, 2016).

The big data challenges facing businesses should not be discounted. There are real technical and statistical problems to be solved when processing increasingly large datasets that can tax the physical limitations of modern computer systems. Yet the danger of finding interesting patterns in data that appear to be actionable but instead represent only spurious or nonsensical correlations increases with each passing day of growing data volume, velocity, and variance. The challenge for organizations is to take advantage of the technological advances that allow for quicker and more complex data manipulation and analyses, while not allowing those activities to overwhelm the time and resources needed to build and test models explaining organizational and human behavior.

The answer lies in applying the scientific method, which dates back over 400 years. The steps are broadly:

(1) State the problem

(2) Formulate hypotheses

(3) Design the experiment

(4) Collect data

(5) Analyze data

(6) Draw conclusions.

Data mining belongs in step five (analyze data) and thus should never be conducted without also addressing the first four steps.

As detailed in Levenson (2015) and many other critiques of WFA in recent years, steps one and two are the most important, often requiring that the underlying business issues be clearly stated upfront to ensure the right challenges are addressed by the analysis. Step three is more appropriate for actual scientific experiments where conditions can be varied carefully. Yet, there is a direct analog for WFA: defining the analysis to be conducted to ensure the right amount of variation in the data can be analyzed to properly test the hypotheses. Options include cross-sectional analysis and longitudinal analysis, along with designing actual work design experiments—commonly called pilots or beta tests. Steps four, five, and six are straightforward and need no further discussion here.

What differentiates the scientific method applied to WFA from the classic laboratory setting is the use of qualitative information and analysis in steps one and two. When working with a complex organizational system, initial interviews with key stakeholders and system participants (employees, managers, and leaders) and qualitative analysis of other sources of information, along the lines described earlier in this chapter, are essential for defining the issues that need to be addressed and the hypotheses to be tested.

An analogy from medicine can help illustrate this. When a patient goes to their doctor with a fever or elevated heart rate, these symptoms are treated as starting points for understanding what could be going on in the person's body. The doctor must determine the full range of symptoms and potential causes; this is a combination of steps one and two. Potential treatments are then prescribed (step three), the results are monitored for their impact (steps four and five), and conclusions are drawn about their efficacy (step six).

In the WFA context, if the presenting problem is high employee turnover, low productivity, or disharmony among team members, the WFA practitioner needs to be just as methodical. First, determine the real business issues (step one). Second, formulate the hypotheses to be tested (step two). Then, design (step three) and collect (step four) the data needed to evaluate the hypotheses. Next, conduct the analysis and interpret the results (step five), and finally, assess the feasibility of potential work design or organizational changes, and make recommendations (step six).

Conclusion

This chapter addressed a broad spectrum of issues that have to be addressed for WFA to provide meaningful, scientifically valid, and evidence-based insights. Specific topics included:

(a) The importance of analyzing quantitative and qualitative data and information

(b) Developing and using Likert scale data the right way

(c) Prioritizing issues to address based on potential ROI

(d) Going beyond readily available data to collect new data and sources

(e) Understanding data limitations

(f) Preparing data for analysis, including cleaning and dealing with outliers

(g) Building and testing multivariate models based on evidence from social science research

(h) Addressing correlation versus causation

(i) Using demographic data appropriately

(j) Analyzing data statistically

(k) Data mining versus hypothesis testing

(l) Analyzing at appropriate organizational levels: role, team, business unit/process, region/geography, and/or enterprise

(m) Applying the scientific method to balance the roles of qualitative and quantitative data in an analysis.

As discussed in Chapter 5, many, if not most, WFA projects fail to produce actionable insights that lead to meaningful change. Part of the problem lies in WFA projects that do not follow the recommendations detailed in this chapter.

Following these recommendations often requires more time, resources, and persistence than is often afforded to most WFA practitioners. This is why WFA, in practice, so often falls short of having meaningful impacts on organizations. Yet, this does not remove the responsibility of WFA practitioners to follow these guidelines. Taking the time to build their own and their team's capacity to collect the right kinds of data and apply the right kinds of analysis will yield extraordinary benefits for the organization's success and bottom line.

References

Becker, B. E., & Huselid, M. A. (1998). High performance work systems and firm performance: A synthesis of research and managerial implications. *Research in Personnel and Human Resource Management, 16*, 53–101.

Becker, B. E., Huselid, M. A., & Beatty, R. W. (2009). *The differentiated workforce: Transforming talent into strategic impact.* Harvard Business Press.

Boudreau, J. W., & Ramstad, P. M. (2006). Talentship and HR measurement and analysis: From ROI to strategic organizational change. *Human Resource Planning, 29*(1), 25. https://link.gale.com/apps/doc/A144869296/AONE?u=googlescholar&sid=bookmark-AONE&xid=477cbe43.

Boudreau, J. W., & Ramstad, P. M. (2007). *Beyond HR: The new science of human capital.* Harvard Business School Press.

Clark, L. A., & Watson, D. (1995). Constructing validity: Basic issues in objective scale development. *Psychological Assessment, 7*(3), 309–319.

Cronbach, L. J., & Meehl, P. E. (1955). Construct validity in psychological tests. *Psychological Bulletin, 52*(4), 281–302.

Davenport, T. H., & Harris, J. G. (2007). *Competing on analytics: The new science of winning.* Harvard Business Review Press.

Davenport, T. H., Harris, J. G., & Morison, R. (2010). *Analytics at work: Smarter decisions, better results.* Harvard Business Review Press.

Diebold, F. X. (2021). What's the big idea? "Big data" and its origins. *Significance, 18*(1), 36–37.

Huselid, M. A. (2018). The science and practice of workforce analytics: Introduction to the HRM special issue. *Human Resource Management, 57*(3), 679–684.

Huselid, M. A., Beatty, R. W., & Becker, B. E. (2005). "A" players or "A" positions? The strategic logic of workforce management. *Harvard Business Review, 83*(12), 110–117.

Kitchin, R., & McArdle, G. (2016). What makes big data, big data? Exploring the ontological characteristics of 26 datasets. *Big Data & Society, 3*(1), 1–10.

Lawler, E. E. (2002, January). *Getting rid of the bottom 10% sound good but ...* (Working Paper #G02-2(411)). Center for Effective Organizations.

Levenson, A. (2014a). *Employee surveys that work: Improving design, use and organizational impact.* Berrett-Koehler.

Levenson, A. (2014b). The promise of big data for HR. *People & Strategy, 36*(4), 22–26.

Levenson, A. (2015). *Strategic analytics: Advancing strategy execution and organizational effectiveness.* Berrett-Koehler.

Levenson, A. (2021). Competencies in an era of digitalized talent management. In S. Wiblen (Ed.), *Digitalized talent management: Navigating the human-technology interface.* Routledge, pp. 51–78.

Levenson, A. and Faber, T. (2009) Count on Productivity Gains. *HRMagazine*; Vol. 54, Iss. 6, (Jun 2009):67–70,72,74.

Likert, R. (1932). A technique for the measurement of attitudes, *Archives of Psychology, 140*, 1–55.

London, M. (2001). The great debate: Should multisource feedback be used for administration or development only? In D. W. Bracken, C. W. Timmreck, and A. H. Church (Eds.), *The handbook of multisource feedback: The comprehensive resource for designing and implementing MSF processes* (pp. 368–385). Jossey-Bass.

London, M. (2003). *Job feedback: Giving, seeking, and using feedback for performance improvement* (2nd ed.). Lawrence Erlbaum Associates.

Provost, F., & Fawcett, T. (2013). *Data science for business: What you need to know about data mining and data-analytic thinking.* O'Reilly Media, Inc.

Scarpello, V., & Campbell, J. P. (1983). Job satisfaction: Are all the parts there? *Personnel Psychology, 36*(3), 577–600.

Vigen, T. (2015). *Spurious correlations: Correlation does not equal causation.* Hachette Books.

Analytic techniques

4.0

Considering techniques in workforce analytics

Martin R. Edwards

Introduction

In our discussion of what to include in a book on workforce analytics (WFA), the author team wanted to include some more technical material that may be useful for readers. Obviously, there is a multitude of different analytic techniques that an analyst can utilize, ranging from correlations, ANOVA, OLS regression, and machine learning to much more complex econometric and data science tools. Here, we draw on a number of useful examples of different techniques (with explanations and examples) that may be useful but are not generally presented in introductory WFA texts (e.g., Edwards & Edwards, 2019).

Effective workforce analytics implementation: Conducting the right analyses

As discussed in the introductory chapters of the book, two key steps in the four-phase ACAI approach to implementing effective WFA include Collecting the right data and conducting the right Analyses. In Chapter 3, we discuss data collection and analyses. This discussion includes reflecting on the use of different types of data, including, for example, survey questions, in WFA. We also discuss data mining, hypothesis testing, and approaches to examining different types of data (qualitative versus quantitative). We also discuss applying the scientific method as an approach. The points made in Chapter 3 are important foundational considerations when considering the four-step ACAI approach to implementing WFA. Of course, using the "right analyses" when approaching WFA implementation depends on selecting the right data. The right choice of analysis approach will always depend on what data has been collected.

DOI: 10.4324/9781003190097-6

Building on the discussion in Chapter 3, we designed the current chapter to present a selection of useful analytic techniques, some of which use very different types of data, spanning qualitative, longitudinal, and multilevel data structures. Here, a range of researchers have contributed to the book, providing illuminating examples of important and interesting analytic technique choices. The examples help highlight the utility of each particular analytic technique: each contributor has provided an example relevant to WFA. Importantly, the researchers who contributed to each chapter carefully consider what the right analyses are for their particular analytic or business question. Making the right decision on which analytic technique to use is sometimes straightforward and obvious. Yet, other times, a judgment call is needed on what analytic or statistical procedure can and should be utilized, with no clear-cut answer; in those situations, the analyst should consider implementing multiple approaches and comparing the results and insights generated.

Data science or social science techniques?

As discussed elsewhere in the book (Chapter 2), variations in disciplinary norms mean that the analytic techniques used when conducting data analyses vary considerably; a choice of techniques used by an analyst in the HR field may be partly driven by the discipline in which the analyst was trained. Even if the analytic project starts with trying to answer a particular problem, different analysts with the same data available may use completely different techniques to shed light on the data in an attempt to answer the business (or research) question. The analysts' selection of techniques may be restricted by their familiarity with favorite techniques: all researchers are likely to have their go-to techniques. To help ensure that a WFA team has the highest likelihood of providing insight and answering the right business question at hand with the appropriate amount of (scientific or data-analytic) rigor, having a broad understanding of techniques is important, so there is always room to consider different approaches.

Considering causality

Concerns about causality in WFA are often of paramount importance. Often, an analyst conducts analyses to try to understand what features of the workplace environment predict or explain a particular outcome. A simple example might be analyzing aspects of the employees' employment experience to understand what might be predicting or influencing levels of engagement or performance for more on the relationship between engagement and performance, see the discussion in Chapter 3).

Understanding predictors of key HR outcomes can be particularly important for businesses if they want to use analytics as a source of evidence to justify making a particular investment in an HR practice. If an organization wants to improve line manager competencies, for example, what data, evidence, and analytic techniques can be drawn on to (a) justify a potential significant HR intervention (such as line management training), (b) identify what the training should look like (that should be effective), and (c) follow and track any impact that the training may have to ensure that the intervention achieves the required outcomes. To explore these issues, a workforce analyst can trawl through existing available HR records to see what training activities may have had some success in the past; however, analyzing available observational data will have some limitations (see Chapter 3).

A good example of this kind of analytic project would be the Google Oxygen project, where the analyst team tried to show that "managers matter" and that it was worth investing in line manager training (see Garvin, 2013: HBR). This team used a combination of existing data to try to show that good managers seemed to make a difference (with team member performance and retention). They also collected more data, with interviews at the beginning of the process (a recommended practice in Chapter 3). So, they didn't restrict themselves to available observational HR data. One of the key things that their analytic team did was to show that there was a difference in retention and attitude scores between employees with high versus low-rated managers. Of course, using this as evidence of causality remained a challenge as, without randomized intervention, they were only ever able to show that there was a correlation between manager ratings and subordinate outcomes of retention and other features. However, gathering observational data and showing relationships between the data's features is a key HR analytic activity that helps with the evidence collection one might need before making an investment decision based on a presumed causal relationship.

Once available data is identified for an HR analytic project, a choice of analytic techniques will then be made, and some analyses will be conducted to show potential evidence for "predictors" of particular outcomes (such as engagement, turnover, performance, or the success of a training program). Such analyses, however, may involve the analyst making some (possibly flawed) assumptions about causality. For example, where there is evidence that previous training provision (to line managers) may be followed by positive outcomes (such as subordinate performance increases or an increase in team member employee engagement scores following the training), an analyst may be tempted to draw causal inferences. However, the ability to draw causal inferences from (existing workforce) observational data will be limited regardless of the analytic techniques used.

Most WFA techniques that hope to identify information about causality draw on correlation and covariance techniques in some way; this includes the application of predictive models where patterns from past available observed HR-linked data can be identified to point toward potential "predictors" of future behavior or expected outcomes. Ultimately, the analyses of available observational data that can be drawn on by a workforce analyst will have their limitations in terms of the researcher drawing "confident" causal inferences, even when applying the most rigorous contemporary statistical or data science techniques (see Hernán et al., 2019). With the right data and sophisticated analytics techniques, a high level of prediction accuracy may be achieved. However, successful prediction is different from being "sure" about making causal inferences, which may require randomized and experimental techniques to be utilized to obtain a higher degree of certainty around causality.

In Chapter 4.1, Guenole and Charlwood discuss a unique technique that can be used as a method or framework to begin to explicitly expose some of the issues and assumptions that an analyst may be making around causality. This technique utilizes a method that can help add a greater degree of confidence linked to possible evidence supporting causal relationship claims. The method uses Directed Acyclic Graphs (DAG) as a structured analytic method (originally proposed by Pearl, 1995) to explicate assumptions in the data framework. This is a useful approach to use when concerned about whether the relationships identified in an analytic project are (more or less) likely to represent causal links.

While this method won't necessarily solve all challenges and concerns around whether the data and relationships between variables represent causal relationships, the DAG technique is a very useful methodology that can help the analyst become more competent at considering what relationships may or may not reasonably be considered to represent causal relationships.

Person-centered analyses versus variable-centered analyses

Chapter 4.2 uses a person-centered approach that contrasts with the main variable-centered correlation/covariance approach used in most branches of social science as a norm, including WFA. Variable-centered approaches explore covariance and relationships between variables collected in a dataset, using correlational and regression techniques as a key part of their toolkit. These techniques often make some assumptions about homogeneity in the population and, generally speaking, explore broad trends (and relationships) from data that is expected to represent patterns in a broader population. For example, a company may explore team engagement scores and show that they are correlated with team performance.

A person-centered approach, in contrast, uses a technique that is particularly useful when the population of interest is heterogeneous in nature, or when there should be substantively different groups, classes, or clusters of people who may share particular features or responses to the workplace environment. In many settings, it is reasonable to expect that the workforce is not made up of a relatively homogeneous population with similar reactions, responses, or interests across the organization. Thus, in WFA, we may want to explore the dataset to see whether the workforce separates or clusters into different groupings. A useful paper by Zyphur (2009) highlights broad mindsets that analysts may apply when conducting analyses: he makes a distinction between variable-centered analyses and person-centered analyses.

Interestingly, the norms of using variable-centered versus person-centered approaches vary depending on the discipline of an analyst's training. Some disciplines—for example, psychology—rely heavily on the deductive (scientific) method and use variable-centered analytic approaches as a go-to form of analysis and have only recently started to utilize person-centered (more exploratory and data-driven) techniques more frequently. In the data science discipline, exploratory techniques are the norm and therefore person-centered analyses in particular forms are much more prevalent. In the data science field, there is no real focus on looking for evidence that supports (or not) a theoretically derived hypothesis (see the discussion in Chapter 2); thus, techniques that explore the data field for interesting (and often complex or non-linear) patterns are often used. In the social sciences, exploratory analyses are not only less common, but they are also frowned upon by many (e.g., the management and OB field) due to their unscientific nature. However, in some branches, for example, marketing and health sciences, the tendency to use analytic techniques that explore features, differences, and groupings in the population is more common. Latent profile analyses are one form of person-centered analyses that have increased in prevalence across the social science fields; below in Chapter 4.2, Joeri Hoffmans discusses the use of latent class and latent profile analyses with workforce-related data.

Techniques used to analyze qualitative data

Generally, when we discuss WFA, there may be an assumption that we are interested in analyzing quantitative data and where we are interested in employee attitudes and perceptions, an organization will often actively collect quantitative data (for example, with Likert scales in a survey) to represent these attitudes and perceptions (Speer et al., 2023). Of course, in the WFA space, there are often masses of qualitative data collected that can be analyzed with the right techniques (Chapter 2). Examples of qualitative data include (but are not restricted to) recorded interview transcripts, narratives in performance appraisal documentation, comments written on recruitment sites or social media, sites linked to an organization or employees (Glassdoor or LinkedIn), and, of course, text comments written in surveys.

The analyses of this data are not straightforward: analyzing it manually can take some time, and an analyst team may not always have the competency to analyze it with sophisticated techniques. However, automated analyses of qualitative data are becoming more common. More simple forms of these analysis approaches may include sentiment analyses, where a system is programmed to pick up, count, or present frequency data associated with positive or negative sentiment in the words used. However, there are many more complex techniques that can be used with qualitative data. An example is presented here by Andrew Speer and Matt Brown (Chapter 4.3), who explore using natural language processing to analyze qualitative data, focusing on qualitative comments that are collected in employee surveys.

Exploring data to see where features naturally break with decision trees

As mentioned above, a go-to form of analysis in WFA may often be to run regression analyses looking for "predictors" or "drivers" of particular outcomes (e.g., turnover, engagement, or performance). What most WFA practitioners—and many social scientists—fail to appreciate is that regression analysis, the classic "first choice" taught in statistics classes, imposes assumptions about the relationships among the variables being linear. The problem is that the actual relationships often are anything but linear: there often are curvilinear or more complex relationships, and the complexity of relationships can be compounded by interactions among the variables in the model. For example, the relationship between the proportion of females in a team and team-level engagement may not be linear, and it may also depend on whether the team leaders are male or female.

Testing for linear relationships or interactions may require the formulation of some assumptions about expected relationships and interactions before an analyst can test the complexity of the relationships. For example, an analyst may test a relationship between gender proportion in teams and team engagement if they assume that there may be a link between the two. However, other features of the environment that link or interact with this relationship might need to be examined, and prior knowledge of what features are important and how (and when) these features may become important is required.

For example, suppose that as the proportion of women in a team increases, employee engagement also increases, but this relationship may differ depending on some other features. For example, the relationship may fall away at a certain point or be different if: a) the leader of the team is male or female, b) the jobs involve customer-facing roles, and/or c) the relationship differs depending on the level of some other factor such as salary level. To test these features manually, the analyst may need to have existing knowledge about what proportion of the team is important as a possible predictor of engagement, what jobs are likely to be important, when it becomes important if there is a male or female lead, and what salary levels might be important for engagement to be activated.

Without engaging additional data sources, including talking to various stakeholders and people knowledgeable about the work setting, the analyst may not have this existing knowledge. However, the analyst can gain some insight into the potential complexity of relationships, any interactions that may be occurring, and breakpoints away from linearity in relationships by carrying out decision tree analyses. These analyses are often subsumed into more complex predictive analyses; however, decision tree analyses can be informative for the analyst who wants to understand how and where elements in the dataset may relate and/or interact. As such, the technique will be particularly useful for a workforce analytics expert. Used expertly, the analyst can also use decision tree analysis to identify patterns in the data for sense-making and validation with those who are more knowledgeable about the work setting. This is a great example of combining quantitative and qualitative data and analysis, as advocated in Chapter 3. In Chapter 4.4 below, Paul van der Laken goes through a primer on decision tree analyses.

Analyzing networks in workforce data

The use of Organizational Network Analyses (ONA) to help answer important business questions has been increasing in the field of WFA, with various advances in WFA technology. A key contributor who has helped promote using ONA for WFA is Rob Cross. He is well known for applying ONA in a number of workforce domains, including understanding optimal and/or problematic patterns of collaboration in the workplace (see the article "Collaborative Overload" in the Harvard Business Review, 2016), which may explain why Rob turned us down when we asked him to write a piece on ONA for the book!

The ability to identify how and where employees may be interacting in the workplace requires a set of analytic tools that can help track, describe, analyze, and present features of these interactions. Importantly, these can involve passive techniques or active techniques. The distinction between the two ONA techniques is important, as one requires active data collection and employee involvement (assuming employees are the network to be studied) in the data production, often with surveys; the other (passive ONA) may build network models using existing digital data that the organization may collect and store automatically as a feature of everyday work activities (or from the "digital exhaust" produced in electronic activities at work; see also the discussion in Chapter 3).

An example of data that might be used in passive ONA is email or calendar (meeting) details where an organization might track and map out interactive networks within an organization on the basis of whom employees are emailing, electronically chatting with, calling, and/or meeting with (either from calendars or meeting detail information). Using passive approaches raises ethical challenges (see Chapter 6) linked to monitoring, surveillance, and data privacy, and as such it is good ethical practice for organizations to ask meaningful permission from employees before conducting passive ONA.

ONA can be an extremely powerful technique if an organization wants to understand network and interaction patterns in the workplace. For example, being able to understand who is collaborating with whom in a large organization, and when and how they are collaborating, could be incredibly useful for those responsible for communication and information dissemination or who may have particularly wide communication networks. The myriad examples of how ONA has been applied in work contexts go way beyond this: Whiteman et al.'s case study in Chapter 4.5 is a particularly interesting example of the use of both active and passive ONA techniques.

Machine learning techniques and workforce analytics

With the increasing migration of data scientists into the field of WFA comes the increasing use of machine learning techniques. Often, when workforce analysts are conducting various analytic projects (e.g., attrition modeling), they will often (now) be using machine learning as it helps identify the best predictive model available. Machine learning can also be used to integrate and improve the predictive models when new data becomes available.

Historically, machine learning has not been used regularly within the social sciences because it is highly exploratory in its approach to analyses and can seem to be similar to the challenges with data mining discussed in Chapter 3. However, machine learning approaches can be more sophisticated than traditional data mining and can be used to help identify the best predictive model, a common approach in the field of data science.

It is important to acknowledge that machine learning is not restricted to a single analytic technique: it applies a particular set of techniques, and it may use different statistical techniques (e.g., OLS multiple regression, logistic regression, decision trees, random forests, etc.) depending on what technique is the most appropriate for the analyses. Importantly, the machine learning aspect means that the analytical technique is applied by an analytic program (e.g., Python or R) to test various possible analytic model features in order to try and identify the strongest predictive model.

In Chapter 4.6, Charlwood et al. present an example of the use of machine learning in a healthcare setting, in this case, predicting important outcomes such as the likelihood of staff making errors (in medication) and whether the patients become injured (falls), using key workforce data (e.g., staffing levels and patterns). This is an interesting example of how WFA could be used in a healthcare setting to provide important insights for the management of healthcare.

The multilevel nature of workforce data

As mentioned previously, the go-to analytic technique in WFA is likely to involve exploring relationships and identifying predictors with regression techniques. However, a key challenge for WFA is the fact that basic default multiple regression analyses will not immediately take into account the fact that data in most large organizations involve employee data structured or grouped into units (either teams, departments, locations, functions, or some other grouping). Importantly, these grouping structures may mean that different forms of multiple regression may be applied inappropriately if these structures are not taken into account. Importantly, multiple regression includes an assumption that the data objects (e.g., employees) in the data set are not related (or grouped, sharing similar experiences) in a way that is not taken into account in the analysis variables (or if these groups are not incorporated into the data modeling).

There are, however, a number of reasons why an analyst should take the multi-level nature of organizational data into account. One reason is that not including the grouped or multilevel structure of the data may violate the assumptions of the test used (Hox, 2010; Tabachnick & Fidell, 2007). Another reason is that without incorporating the grouped and multilevel nature of the data, the analysis is less likely to pick up the important role that the grouping plays in influencing the data. In WFA, a good example is engagement data within an organization that has multi-ple teams, particularly, for example, where each team has a recognized team leader who has some autonomy in how they manage (and evaluate) their team members. If, in a dataset of 2000 employees that includes engagement data and performance ratings for each individual employee, there are 100 teams with team leads who rate the employees' performance with their own approach to appraisal and who have different managerial styles, the importance of these team structures (and related team leads within each team) will be key if one wants to understand the substantive meaning of any relationship between engagement and performance in the organiza-tion. Excluding information on the team-level structure and process will ignore the key role that the team lead may play in both individual performance appraisals and (potentially) collective engagement within the team. Any analyses of this data will want to include and explicate the potential cross-level influence on variance in the data. For example, the higher-level (level 2) features (e.g., "team lead" features) may have a cross-level impact on the individual-level (level 1) features (e.g., individual engagement levels).

Some social science disciplines take the multilevel nature of data into account in cases where such a structure is clearly important. For example, data analysts in educational science are likely to be very aware that the relationship between teacher capability, competency, and performance with student attainment is likely to be highly dependent on or limited by certain characteristics of the classroom environ-ment (e.g., content subject; math versus languages, etc.), the educational resources available to the school, and particular characteristics of the student population (e.g., socio-economic status) that may be a feature of geographical location. Thus, the potential multilevel structures that would need to be considered in analyses of this kind of data may include the geographical region, the schools, the classes, the teachers, and finally, the individual students. Therefore, multilevel analysis is a common form of analysis undertaken in the field of educational psychology.

Importantly, with large organizations, many grouping structures can exist that might play a role in influencing any variation in a particular outcome of interest in a WFA project. In Chapter 4.7, van Veldhoven and Batistic discuss crossing levels linking engagement survey data with higher-level performance data. This serves as a good example of how one might consider utilizing multilevel regression analyses in WFA.

References

Cross, R., Rebele, R., & Grant, A. (2016). Collaborative overload. *Harvard Business Review, 94*, 74–79.

Edwards, M. R., & Edwards, K. (2019). *Predictive HR analytics: Mastering the HR metric*. Kogan Page.

Garvin, D. A. (2013, December). How google sold its engineers on management. *HBR*.

Hernán, M. A., Hsu, J., & Healy, B. (2019). A second chance to get causal inference right: A classification of data science tasks. *CHANCE, 32*(1), 42–49.

Hox, J. J. (2010). *Multilevel analysis: Techniques and applications* (2nd ed.). Routledge and Taylor & Francis Group.

Pearl, J. (1995). Causal diagrams for empirical research. *Biometrika, 82*(4), 669–688.

Speer, A. B., Perrotta, J., Tenbrink, A. P., Wegmeyer, L. J., Delacruz, A. Y., & Bowker, J. (2023). Turning words into numbers: Assessing work attitudes using natural language processing. *Journal of Applied Psychology, 108*(6), 1027–1045.

Tabachnick, B. G., & Fidell, L. S. (2007). *Using multivariate statistics* (5th ed.). Allyn & Bacon and Pearson Education.

Zyphur, M. J. (2009). When mindsets collide: Switching analytical mindsets to advance organization science. *The Academy of Management Review, 34*(4), 677–688.

Causal inference in HR analytics with Directed Acyclic Graphs

Nigel Guenole and Andy Charlwood

The importance of causality in HR analytics

People analytics is a nascent field that has yet to embrace the topic of causal inference. Yet understanding causality is often critically important in human resources. In some areas of management, accurate training predictions from a machine learning model might be enough to justify a decision, such as about a website design to maximize sales. As long as sales increase, it doesn't really matter what causes customers to buy more on one website compared to the next. In contrast, with people analytics problems, causes do matter. Practitioners often look to change behavior with interventions, which requires an understanding of causality. Consider the results of an engagement survey, where engagement is found to be correlated with employee turnover. Is low engagement the cause of higher turnover, or is it merely associated with it, with other unobserved variables—like poor line management—perhaps causing both low engagement and high turnover? The answer determines the right action to reduce turnover.

Furthermore, organizations have legal and ethical responsibilities to those they employ, and employees often want or are entitled to explanations for decisions that, in HR, can often be contentious. If a decision is made to offer a retention bonus to one employee but not another, an explanation saying, "It's because our analysis suggests you are not likely to leave, but your colleague is," will be inadequate. An understanding of causality can ensure a more transparent basis for such interventions. Unless causal understanding is built into people analytics projects, the outcomes reached are likely to be suboptimal. In this chapter, we explain how Directed Acyclic Graphs—a method for drawing causal inferences that can be applied with observational data and pioneered by Judea Pearl (e.g., Pearl, 1995)—can be used to examine causal effects in people analytics.[1]

DOI: 10.4324/9781003190097-7

What are Directed Acyclic Graphs (DAG)?

Directed Acyclic Graphs (DAGs) are diagrams that depict assumptions about relationships between sets of random variables. In DAGs, the variables are called vertices or nodes. DAGs describe data-generating processes that happen in the real world. For example, the weekly sales of a supermarket will be the result of a data-generating process that includes nodes like demand from customers, procurement and distribution of products, pricing compared to competitors, and the efficiency with which staff restocks shelves. The process of deciding which variables are causally related to one another is a qualitative process and requires the domain expertise of those familiar with the process under study. Presenting all of the causal assumptions about a system of variables in pictorial form is a powerful contribution DAGs make to causal inference. Once a plausible DAG has been established, it can provide a basis for estimating the magnitude of causal relationships using statistical or machine learning methods.

An example of a DAG depicting the hypothetical determinants of turnover is presented in Figure 4.1a. Assuming a DAG accurately represents the intended data-generating process, it has several important applications. First, it provides an easily understandable representation of the real-world process, which can be debated and challenged by subject matter experts. Assuming once again that the DAG is correct, we can ascertain which variables we expect to be independent, conditionally independent, spuriously associated, and causally associated. Once we have actual data on the variables in a DAG, we can check the empirical associations and independencies to confirm that the patterns of associations conform to the expectations of the DAG. Importantly, we can use the information encoded in the DAG to identify which variables we need to control for in order to purge observed relationships of non-causal effects, leaving only causal associations between variables.

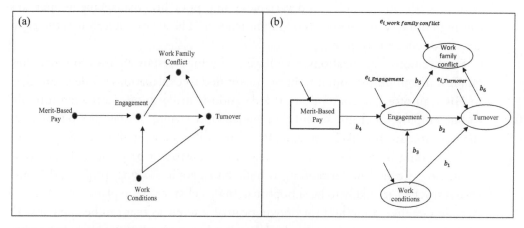

FIGURE 4.1 (a) Directed acyclic graph and (b) structural equation model.

There are a number of rules a DAG must conform to. Nodes of a DAG may be observed or unobserved, depending on whether we have data to measure the variable a node represents. Nodes may be connected to one another using directed arrows, called *edges* or *paths*. DAGs cannot contain undirected edges. Edges represent possible causal effects. A path may connect two adjacent nodes or a sequence of adjacent nodes. Common causes of two or more variables in a DAG must be represented in the DAG. A path between nodes can move along edges, going with or against the direction of the edges. Where nodes are not connected by edges, the variables are not related. A path cannot revisit itself, i.e., there can be no directed cycles (or feedback loops). Cycles are instead represented as paths that return to a different state of the same variable at a different time point. Error terms that represent parts of variables that we cannot explain are called *structural error terms*. Where structural errors affect one variable, they are idiosyncratic and are omitted from the DAG. If they affect more than one variable, the errors are correlated and must be drawn.

To illustrate these ideas, we return to Figure 4.1a, examining the determinants of turnover. The edges connecting merit-based pay, engagement, and turnover comprise a path where the travel is consistent with the direction of the arrows. The edges connecting engagement, work conditions, and turnover also comprise a path, despite the edge from engagement to work conditions going against the direction of the arrows. The edges that go from engagement to turnover to work-family conflict and back to engagement do not comprise a path, because engagement would be revisited. As stated, directed cycles are not permissible. It is not possible to revisit engagement at the *same* time point. Rather, a state of engagement at a different time would be drawn if it were consistent with theory.

In some respects, these graphical representations of data-generating processes resemble structural equation models (SEMs) in the tradition of Wright (1934). DAGs are indeed a form of SEM. The SEM representation of the DAG in Figure 4.1a is presented in Figure 4.1b. One obvious difference is the ellipses around variables in Figure 4.1b, which highlight that SEMs can easily handle latent variables. A second key difference, however, is that DAGs make no assumptions about the distributions of nodes or the functional form of the relationships between nodes. In other words, in contrast to linear SEMs, DAGs are entirely non-parametric SEMs, i.e., they do not assume variable distributions or linear relationships. This is highlighted by the equations for the two forms of models. First, we present the linear SEM equations with their parametric node distributions and assumed additive linear relationships between variables that are homogeneous for all people:

$$Turnover_i = b_1 Work\,Conditions + b_2 Engagement + e_{i\_Turnover}$$

$$Engagement_i = b_3 Work\,Conditions + b_4 Merit\,Based\,Pay + e_{i_{Engagement}}$$

Merit Based Pay $y_i = v_{i_{Merit\ based\ pay}}$

Work conditions$_i = v_{i_{Work\ conditions}}$

Work family conflict $_i = b_5\ engagement + b_6\ turnover + e_{i_{Work\ family\ conflict}}$

Different from the linear SEM representation, the non-parametric SEMs represented by DAG equations simply say that some unspecified function f transforms the variables with arrows leading into each variable to produce the variables they explain:

$$Turnover_i = f_{iT}\left(Work\ Conditions, Engagement, e_{i_{Turnover}}\right)$$

$$Engagement_i = f_{iE}\left(Work\ Conditions, Merit\ Based\ Pay, e_{i_{Engagement}}\right)$$

$$Merit\ Based\ Pay = f_{iM}\left(v_{i_{Merit\ based\ pay}}\right)$$

$$Work\ conditions_i = f_{iWC}\left(v_{i_{Work\ conditions}}\right)$$

$$Work\ family\ conflict_i = f_{iWFC}\left(Engagement, Turnover, e_{i_{Work\ family\ conflict}}\right)$$

Another key difference, in practice, is that the focal parameters of interest across the two methodologies differ. In SEMs, the parameters of the entire system of paths represented in Figure 4.1b are usually estimated. With DAGs, the focus is more commonly on identifying a sufficient set of variables that, if controlled for, will allow for the causal identification of a specific treatment on an outcome.

Relationships that produce associations between variables

A key task DAGs allow us to perform is to determine which measured (i.e., observed) relationships between variables can be considered causal relationships. DAGs further allow us to determine which variables we need to control for, or not control for, in order to allow a causal interpretation of a measured association. Consider our example in Figure 4.1a. A question in line with the first task is whether the observed correlation between engagement and turnover can be causally interpreted. The answer is no. Some of the association between engagement and turnover is going to be the result of work conditions, which is their common cause.

However, if we were to hold work conditions constant (e.g., by controlling for work conditions in a regression model, or only looking at the association within a given level of work conditions), we could give a causal interpretation to the association between engagement and turnover. More broadly, if we understand which variable associations are the result of causal relationships and which are spurious relationships, we can answer complex questions about causality from observational data. This is possible because all marginal associations (i.e., relationships where we do not control for any variables) and conditional associations (i.e., where we do control for other variables) between variables stem from three relationship forms: *chains, forks,* and *colliders* (inverted forks).

Figure 4.2a shows a *chain*. In this situation, two variables can be associated because one causes the other, either directly or indirectly. In other words, X and Z are associated, as X indirectly causes Z via Y. In the absence of other variables, the measured association between the variables can be considered a causal association. The association between X and Z could also be *blocked* (i.e., X and Z can be rendered independent) if we were to control for Y, but we would not do that if we were interested in studying mediation, a situation where the effect of X on Z is carried by an intermediary variable Y. In the example in Figure 4.1a, the relationship between merit-based pay, engagement, and turnover is a chain. If it were not for other variables in the DAG that we will soon discuss, it could be interpreted as a causal relationship.

Next, Figure 4.2b illustrates a *fork*. While there is no causal relationship between Y and Z, the variables are going to be associated because they have a common cause, X. The association between Y and Z in this instance is non-causal and is referred to as confounding. In the applied example in Figure 4.1a, the paths from work conditions to engagement and turnover comprise a fork. The presence of particular work conditions (as a simple example, job demands or task overload) can be a common cause of engagement and turnover. This prevents a causal interpretation of the relationship between engagement and turnover because some of the association between engagement and turnover will be due to work conditions, which is their common cause. However, if work conditions were controlled, the engagement-to-turnover relationship could be given a causal interpretation. This is an example of *confounding bias*, which is solved by conditioning on the common cause.

Figure 4.2c depicts a *collider* variable, Y, that appears on a path from X to Z. The relationship is called a collider path because the arrowheads collide at this variable. In this situation, no information can be transmitted between X and Z, or vice versa, because the path is blocked by Y. Whether a variable is a collider is path-specific;

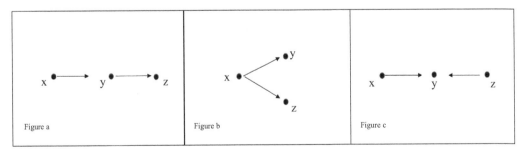

FIGURE 4.2 Relationships that explain causal associations between variables.

variables can be a collider on one path and not on another. Importantly, a non-causal association may be created between two non-causally related variables if we were to condition on (i.e., control) the common outcome of the variables, Y (i.e., if we condition on the collider). In our example in Figure 4.1, work-family conflict is a collider on a path from engagement to turnover. To give the measured relationship between engagement and turnover a causal interpretation, we need to control for work conditions (*common cause*), but we must *not* control for work-family conflict (*common effect*). Controlling for the common effect would introduce a non-causal association between engagement and turnover. This is an example of selection bias, the solution to which is not to control for the common effect.

Directional separation

Once a DAG is developed, knowing about the different variable relationships that produce or prevent non-causal associations allows us to identify sets of variables that can be controlled, or not controlled, to be confident that observed relationships between variables are causal relationships. Pearl (1995) has developed the concept of d-separation, where "d" means "directional." D-separation describes conditions that evaluate whether a set of variables exists that, if held constant or controlled, would create independence between two variables on an arbitrarily long path.[2] Selecting variables to hold constant according to these conditions allows us to control information flow and, therefore, associations between variables. This, in turn, allows us to purge variable relationships of non-causal associations.

Identifying sufficient adjustment sets

The next question we need to answer is how to identify a sufficient set of variables that will control for any confounding between a treatment and an outcome. There are several approaches that can be used; here, we discuss the backdoor criterion. First, note that a backdoor path begins with an arrow going into the treatment and is not causally related to the effect of the treatment on the outcome. By contrast, a front door path represents an effect of treatment and begins with an arrow coming out of the treatment toward the outcome. The backdoor criterion says that a set of variables is sufficient to control for confounding if it blocks all backdoor paths from the treatment to the outcome and does not block any front door paths. In our example in Figure 4.1, there is one front door path from engagement to turnover that does not require control, and there is a backdoor path from engagement to work conditions to turnover that does require control. If we were to estimate the association between engagement and turnover within the same level of work conditions, we could causally interpret the observed association.

Do-calculus

Despite the backdoor criterion and other useful rules for identifying adjustment sets, it is not uncommon to be unable to find sets of variables sufficient to control for confounding. More advanced methods are available to deal with these situations in Pearl's *do-calculus*, which can determine whether any sufficient adjustment sets exist. Programs also exist that can algorithmically check for sufficient adjustment sets (e.g., DAGgitty; Textor et al., 2011). At this point, what Gelman (2019) has described as a "division of labour" occurs between the conceptual and qualitative approaches represented by DAGs and discussed in this chapter, and the quantitative side of analytics that involves estimating the magnitudes of the causal effects with statistical modeling and machine learning techniques that control for the appropriate adjustment sets.

Conclusion

Methods for causal inference are common in economics, computer science, and epidemiology. Yet, we have seen little use of causal inference methods in people analytics. Part of the challenge is that many well-established methods require randomization of participants into intervention and control groups, but practitioners rarely have the luxury of randomization in human resources. Practitioners need to draw inferences from observational data. DAGs allow practitioners to do just that. They involve sophisticated representations of hypothesized relations between variables. A simple examination of correlations, without a conceptual model like DAGs provide, is unlikely to be sufficient for informing decisions in people analytics.

Developing credible people analytics DAGs requires close collaboration between analysts who understand DAGs and HR experts who understand the data-generating process a DAG aims to represent. Conceptual models drawn within an SEM framework often conveniently do not include confounding variables and collider variables. However, such models are likely underdeveloped. We invite readers developing such models to think very carefully about common causes and common effects of all variables that they include in their causal models. Once developed, a DAG will tell us whether the data would permit causal inferences before it is even collected. Importantly, the reliability and validity of the measures used to operationalize the DAG are critical, just as they are in every other analytical setting.

This chapter was written in 2021 when the first author participated in Statistical and Applied Mathematical Sciences Institute (SAMSI) discussion groups, where many of these ideas were discussed. If you want to know more about the ideas we have started to explain in this chapter, you can look at several resources on DAGs that we recommend to readers as being comprehensive overviews or as being highly accessible introductions. The first is *The Book of Why* by Pearl and MacKenzie

(2018). A video lecture by Elwert (2021) for SAMSI and a chapter he wrote (Elwert, 2013) also offer clear and concise introductions. We found the Coursera course by Roy (2020), "A crash course in causality: Inferring causal effects from observational data," particularly useful. Finally, we recommend that people read Huntington-Klein (2022), which clearly explains DAGs from the perspective of an economist.

Notes

1 Readers interested in how DAGs compare to the potential outcomes approach (Rubin, 1974) to causal inference can read Imbens (2020).
2 Two variables are d-separated on a path by a collection of variables, Z, if the path connecting them contains a chain and the mediator (or collection of mediators) is in Z, or if the path includes a fork and the mediator variable (or collection of mediators) is in Z, or if the path contains a collider and neither it nor its descendants are in Z. Two variables are d-separated if a set of nodes, Z, blocks every path between them.

References

Elwert, F. (2013). Graphical causal models. In S. L. Morgan (Ed.), *Handbook of causal analysis for social research* (pp. 245–273). Springer Netherlands.

Elwert, F. (2021). *Introduction to Directed Acyclic Graphs (DAGs) for causal inference.* SAMSI program on Data Science in Social and Behavioural Sciences.

Gelman, A. (2019). *The book of why by Pearl and Mackenzie.* Statistical Modeling, Causal Inference, and Social Science. https://statmodeling.stat.columbia.edu/2019/01/08/book-pearl-mackenzie/Elwert

Huntington-Klein, N. (2022). Pearl before economists: The book of why and empirical economics. *Journal of Economic Methodology, 29*(4), 326–334.

Imbens, G. W. (2020). Potential outcome and directed acyclic graph approaches to causality: Relevance for empirical practice in economics. *Journal of Economic Literature, 58*(4), 1129–1179.

Pearl, J. (1995). Causal diagrams for empirical research. *Biometrika, 82*(4), 669–688.

Pearl, J. & Mackenzie, D. (2018). *The book of why: The new science of cause and effect.* Hachette UK.

Roy, J. (2020). *A crash course in causality: Inferring causal effects from observational data.* Coursera. https://www.coursera.org/learn/crash-course-in-causality

Rubin, D. B. (1974). Estimating causal effects of treatments in randomized and nonrandomized studies. *Journal of Educational Psychology, 66*(5), 688–701.

Textor, J., Hardt, J., & Knüppel, S. (2011). DAGitty: A graphical tool for analyzing causal diagrams. *Epidemiology, 22*(5), 745.

Wright, S. (1934). The method of path coefficients. *Annals of Mathematical Statistics, 5*(3), 161–215.

4.2

Latent Class and Latent Profile Analysis

Joeri Hofmans

The goal of Latent Class Analysis (LCA) and Latent Profile Analysis (LPA) is to identify latent subpopulations of people, characterized by distinct configurations— or different profiles—of scores on a set of variables (Hofmans et al., 2020). Because of its ability to identify subpopulations of employees who score similarly on a set of variables, LCA/LPA can be a useful tool in the HR analytics toolbox. For example, HR professionals can use LCA/LPA for talent management purposes (Edwards & Edwards, 2019), identifying high potentials based on their configuration of scores on a wide range of employee performance indicators (e.g., performance ratings, employee potential ratings, competency scores, indices of culture fit, learning agility, etc.). As another example, engagement surveys often collect data on employees' satisfaction with several aspects of work. LCA/LPA can then be used to identify subpopulations of employees characterized by their unique profile of scores on indicators such as satisfaction with salary, colleagues, supervisor, job content, etc., after which those subpopulations can be targeted differently to increase their engagement.

By looking for subpopulations of employees that show similar profiles of scores on a set of variables, the goal of LCA and LPA aligns with that of cluster analysis. Unlike cluster analysis, however, LCA and LPA are based on a latent variable model that models profile membership using a *latent* categorical variable. In addition, LCA and LPA are prototypical, which means that they do not classify employees into a limited number of *mutually exclusive* subpopulations but allow for the fact that each employee has a specific probability of belonging to each subpopulation (see Morin et al., 2020).

Although the terms LCA and LPA are often used interchangeably, the difference is that the indicators in LCA are categorical in nature (e.g., employee demographic attributes), while LPA works with continuous indicators (e.g., satisfaction scores). For applied researchers, this difference has become less relevant in recent years because most software packages used for LPA can now easily accommodate

DOI: 10.4324/9781003190097-8

continuous, categorical, or count data, or any combination of those (Spurk et al., 2020). Rather than diving into the technicalities of LPA, we will highlight some best practices for readers wishing to apply LPA. Those best practices pertain to (1) data-related issues, (2) global versus local solutions, (3) deciding on the number of profiles, and (4) interpretation (Spurk et al., 2020).

1) Data-related issues. In terms of sample size, LPA requires moderate to large datasets. While avoiding rules of thumb, Nylund et al. (2007), in their simulation study, showed that a sample size of 500 would generally suffice. Apart from the sample size, one should also critically reflect on the variables to be included in the analysis. Generally speaking, those variables should be meaningfully related yet distinct (Spurk et al., 2020). For example, whereas it might be interesting to look for job satisfaction profiles (indexed by satisfaction with several aspects of the job), adding gender or age as additional profile indicators would likely make the analysis less meaningful. This does not mean that exploring the associations of gender and age with the different job satisfaction profiles is not meaningful, but rather that gender and age should be modeled as covariates and not as indicators of the job satisfaction profiles.

2) Global versus local solutions. LCA and LPA models are estimated in an iterative fashion, where the algorithm starts with an initial solution (i.e., the starting values) and iteratively updates it until further iterations offer no further improvements. A thorny issue with LPA is the potential existence of local solutions. To avoid ending up with a local rather than a global solution (imagine climbing a mountain and instead of arriving at the highest peak—being the global solution—you end up at one of the many other peaks of the mountain—a local solution), one should repeatedly run the analysis with different starting values (or the initial set of values from which the iterative procedure starts). If one repeatedly (typically at least twice) arrives at the same solution, regardless of the starting values, one can be confident that the obtained solution is the global solution and not a local one. In other words, one needs to perform the analysis more than once with different starting values to ensure that the profile solution is robust. Fortunately, most computer programs automatically do this.

3) Deciding on the number of profiles. LCA and LPA will identify as many profiles as the researcher requests. However, not all profile solutions offer an accurate description of the different subpopulations that exist in the population explored. Selecting the optimal solution (or the optimal number of profiles) should therefore be done based on both statistical and substantive grounds. Following Ram and Grimm (2009), the following steps can be taken: (1) check the solutions for error messages and statistical (e.g., no negative variances) and theoretical plausibility, (2) compare the remaining plausible models using information criteria such as Bayesian information criterion (BIC), (3) evaluate the confidence with

which people are assigned to profiles (i.e., entropy), and (4) use likelihood ratio tests to compare the selected model to models with one fewer profile. Apart from these criteria, it makes sense to add additional profiles only if doing so provides meaningful new insights into the problem and if the additional profiles are sufficiently large (according to Lubke & Neale, 2006, profiles covering <1% of the sample or profiles smaller than 25 cases should not be retained).

4) Interpretation and validation. Apart from interpreting the profiles based on the specific configuration of scores across the profile indicators and the associated labeling of the profiles, one might want to validate the solution by relating profile membership to theoretically meaningful covariates and outcomes.

LPA example

To demonstrate the usefulness of LPA, we apply it to data on characteristics people seek in a job. In the fifth round of the European Social Survey (ESS round 5, 2010), such data are available for over 43,000 individuals. In this wave of the ESS, participants were, among other things, asked to rate the importance of the following characteristics when choosing a job: a job that enables you to use your own initiative, a secure job, high income, a job that allows you to combine work and family, and a job that offers good training opportunities, using a rating scale ranging from 1 (not important) to 5 (very important). Applying LPA to these data allows us to gain a better understanding of the nature and prevalence of different profiles of the job seekers' requirements, which in turn might help companies consider the best types of employment experience to offer to new recruits.

We performed LPA in Mplus (version 8.4), using the default Mplus settings (e.g., homogeneity of variances across profiles). Performing LPA for an increasing number of latent profiles revealed that solutions for five and six latent profiles yielded error messages. Upon inspection of the other (admissible) solutions, the BIC and AIC of the four-profile solution appeared to be the lowest, suggesting that the four-profile solution provided the best balance between model fit and model parsimony. Moreover, this solution showed high entropy (i.e., .95), implying that it yielded well-separated profiles (i.e., the assignment probabilities with which people are assigned to profiles allow for a clear assignment). Finally, the profiles were meaningful and sufficiently large.

The resulting profiles are shown in Figure 4.3, revealing the existence of a profile (representing only 4% of the respondents) who, apart from scoring all characteristics relatively low, assigned very little importance to job security (i.e., the overall low, very low on job security profile). A second profile, representing about 7% of the respondents, indicated that primarily the extrinsic characteristics (security and income) were very important, while the intrinsic characteristics (initiative and training) were deemed less important (i.e., the overall low, yet high on security and

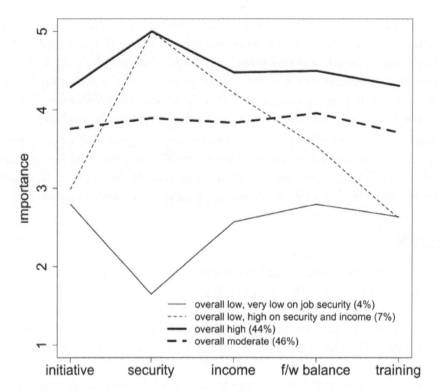

FIGURE 4.3 Overview of the average scores on the importance of initiative, security, income, family/work balance, and training opportunities for each of the four profiles.

income profile). The other two profiles differed in level, with one profile scoring all characteristics high (i.e., the overall high profile, about 44% of the respondents) and the other one scoring all characteristics moderate (i.e., the overall moderate profile, about 46% of the respondents).

Our findings clearly show that the large majority of people (about 90%) pay attention to extrinsic as well as intrinsic features of the job. Only for a minority are there important differences between those job features (either by assigning high importance to primarily security and pay or by considering job security as relatively unimportant). Hence, as an HR professional, this analysis suggests that one should pay sufficient attention to all aspects of the job to make it sufficiently attractive to most future candidates.

In conclusion, LCA/LPA is a useful tool for HR professionals because of its ability to (1) focus on patterns of scores across a range of measures rather than on individual scores, thereby shifting attention from a focus on variables to a focus on individuals, or how people score across a range of measures (Woo et al. 2024), and (2) reduce the immense complexity represented by individual patterns and possibly complex interactions between measures through a categorization of those patterns into a small number of latent profiles. Because of this balance between integration (i.e., looking at several variables simultaneously) and complexity reduction (i.e., classification into types), the method might be highly appealing to HR professionals. Moreover, the general gist of the method aligns well with the way managers may think of employees, categorizing them into types.

References

Edwards, M. R., & Edwards, K. (2019). *Predictive HR analytics: Mastering the HR metric* (2nd ed.). Kogan Page Ltd.

ESS Round 5: European Social Survey Round 5 Data. (2010). *Data file edition 3.4.* NSD - Norwegian Centre for Research Data, Norway – Data Archive and distributor of ESS data for ESS ERIC. https://doi.org/10.21338/NSD-ESS5-2010

Hofmans, J., Wille, B., & Schreurs, B. (2020). Person-centered methods in vocational research. *Journal of Vocational Behavior, 118*, 103398.

Lubke, G., & Neale, M. C. (2006). Distinguishing between latent classes and continuous factors: Resolution by maximum likelihood? *Multivariate Behavioral Research, 41,* 499–532.

Morin, A. J. S., McLarnon, M. J. W., & Litalien, D. (2020). Mixture modeling for organizational behavior research. In Y. Griep & S. D. Hansen (Eds.), *Handbook of dynamic organizational behavior* (pp. 351–379). Edward Elgar.

Nylund, K. L., Asparouhov, T., & Muthén, B. (2007). Deciding on the number of classes in latent class analysis and growth mixture modeling: A Monte Carlo simulation study. *Structural Equation Modeling, 14,* 535–569.

Ram, N., & Grimm, K. J. (2009). Growth mixture modeling: A method for identifying differences in longitudinal change among unobserved groups. *International Journal of Behavioral Development, 33,* 565–576.

Spurk, D., Hirschi, A., Wang, M., Valero, D., & Kauffeld, S. (2020). Latent profile analysis: A review and "how to" guide of its application within vocational behavior research. *Journal of Vocational Behavior, 120,* 103445.

Woo, S. E., Hofmans, J., Wille, B., & Tay, L. (2024). Person-centered modeling: Techniques for studying associations between people rather than variables. *Annual Review of Organizational Psychology and Organizational Behavior, 11*(1), 453–480.

Efficient ways to leverage untapped data sources
Using natural language processing to assess work attitudes and perceptions

Andrew B. Speer and Matt I. Brown

Organizations and researchers often engage in considerable efforts to understand employee attitudes and perceptions, such as pay satisfaction or reactions to diversity initiatives. Such perceptions are frequently assessed via surveys, which often include a mix of Likert numerical ratings as well as narrative comment boxes. There are well-established procedures for analyzing responses to Likert questions. On the other hand, text-based media such as survey comments, blogs, chat responses, and texts and emails are much more challenging to analyze. Despite providing rich and contextualized information about employees, open-ended text data are time-consuming for humans to review. This limits the interpretation of employee comments, particularly in large employee samples. As such, analytical methods such as natural language processing (NLP) are well-suited for automatically scoring employee text. In this chapter, we'll review how NLP can be applied to assess employee attitudes and perceptions.

Natural language processing of employee comments

Many organizations possess large amounts of unstructured employee data. Such qualitative organizational data are rich and contextualized data sources, and these are often leveraged by people analytics teams. For example, people analytics teams might review written exit interview responses to understand what work features are causing employees to leave. They might mine open-ended survey responses (that provide more flexibility for employee responses) for information regarding employee concerns, likely occurring in tandem with the analysis of traditional Likert responses. People analytics teams might also wish to summarize the topics of concern from data sources such as Glassdoor. Or, for teams building predictive

DOI: 10.4324/9781003190097-9

models based on organizational data (e.g., to predict turnover), people analytics teams might leverage comments from intranet blogs as an additional data source to predict worker behavior and, by leveraging more data sources, achieve a more reliable measurement of employee attitudes, perceptions, or characteristics.

Sophisticated people analytics teams can use NLP on such data sources, thus achieving efficiency when analyzing unstructured qualitative data. NLP uses computers to make sense of text data. A wide variety of NLP methods exist, and there are many software programs to conduct them (e.g., R, Python, and Linguistic Inquiry and Word Count), though a review of these topics is beyond the scope of this chapter. Instead, we'll focus on two methods that we've used to analyze employee comments to infer work attitudes and the procedures we used to develop them. These procedures were implemented using a mix of R and Python. It should be noted that this chapter was written before the introduction of large language models (e.g., ChaptGPT), which have recently made advanced NLP capabilities widely accessible across a range of tasks, including text evaluation and classification (see Demszky et al., 2023; Speer et al., 2024 for background). We will briefly return to this at the end of the chapter.

The first method applies a dictionary-based scoring procedure to classify whether a given document (i.e., set of text) discusses a particular topic referred to as theme scores (Speer, 2020). Theme scores indicate what a document is about. For example, the sentence "There is simply no option for growth in my current company" discusses the theme of satisfaction with promotion, and its theme score for this topic would therefore be higher. If a people analytics team were to develop a dictionary scoring method from scratch to derive theme scores, one approach would be to identify sets of word phrases related to topics (e.g., phrases about personal growth in relation to the topic of career development) and then count how often those word phrases occur in a document, after controlling for the total length of the text. For example, word phrases aligned with the construct of workload can be found in Table 4.3.1. This is similar to the most well-known dictionary-based NLP application—Linguistic Inquiry and Word Count (LIWC, Tausczik & Pennebaker, 2010), which uses off-the-shelf dictionaries to produce theme scores from text according to a wide range of topics. LIWC is attractive because the dictionaries are already developed and therefore can be quickly applied to open-ended data. Unfortunately, though, LIWC is not work-contextualized, and until recently, there were no comprehensive dictionaries that assess the majority of work attitudes and perceptions that organizations care about. This was a problem for people analytics teams and other researchers, as it would then require them to create theme word dictionaries from scratch if they wished to measure work-related constructs from open-ended text.

The second method we focus on is called valence scores (Speer, 2020), often referred to as sentiment scores in other contexts. Although theme scores tell us what a document is about, they do not provide information about whether a given topic is discussed favorably. Valence scores overcome this by reflecting how positively or negatively a given topic is discussed. For example, a valence score would tell an organization how satisfied their employees are with their pay based on narrative responses.

TABLE 4.3.1 Cleaned and lemmatized theme words for workload

amount	free time	tax
arduous	frenzied	timeline
assign	hard	tire
assignment	heavy	toil
backbreaking	hectic	too many
burdensome	hour	too much
burnout	light	tough
busy	load	unrealistic
chaotic	lot to	unreasonable
chill	manageable	unrelenting
deadline	nonstop	volume
delegate	of time	wearisome
demand	of work	weary
drain	my plate	workload
duty	onerous	
easy	overload	
energy	overwhelm	
exact	pace	
excessive	pile	
exhaust	pressure	
expect	quantity	
fast	rigorous	
fatigue	slow	

Note: Shown are theme-word phrases for an example construct. These phrases have been cleaned (e.g., contractions replaced, abbreviations removed) and lemmatized; thus, some word phrases may appear odd.

Traditionally, in the organizational sciences, valence scores have been created using supervised learning under the bag of words (BOW) framework. A BOW framework ignores the order of words and only considers whether a word or phrase occurs in the text. Word phrases are then treated as predictor vectors in a large data frame, which is formed after cleaning and standardizing the text (e.g., lowercasing, removing stop words, lemmatizing; Hickman et al., 2022). Software programs such as R and Python easily perform these tasks (see Hickman et al.) and automatically convert written text into such data frames, which are commonly organized so that each row represents a document (i.e., a person's narrative response) and each column is a count (or other operationalization) of which words occurred in the documents. These column vectors are then used to predict target variables such as engagement scores. For example, if engagement was measured using a traditional Likert survey, one could train an algorithm to reproduce the target engagement composite scores. The resulting algorithms are then capable of scoring text to estimate target scores and can be applied in new contexts even if only qualitative data exist. The algorithm is supervised because it tries to recreate a target variable during model training, and once trained, the algorithms can then be applied in new contexts; the target variable is only used to train the model, and once trained, the algorithms can be applied without target variable scores.

Within the context of employee attitude, the target variable is most commonly a composite of Likert items that assess a construct, such as engagement. Any machine learning algorithm could be used for this purpose, with the choice often being penalized regression (e.g., Zou & Hastie, 2005), some tree-based model (Breiman, 2001), or neural networks (Goodfellow et al., 2016). Readers are referred to James et al. (2017) for a nice introduction to machine learning.

Although BOW scoring often performs adequately in the organizational sciences, contemporary NLP leverages deep neural networks built specifically to derive meaning from text (i.e., the context and sequence of language) and, as a result, should produce more accurate valence scores. In the example case we discuss below, we leveraged transformer neural networks, which produce state-of-the-art performance on NLP tasks. More specifically, we used the bidirectional encoder representations for transformers (BERT, Devlin et al., 2018) architecture, which is composed of dense, multi-layered neural networks capable of capturing the meaning of language. At the lower layers of the neural networks are embedding vectors and layers that represent the meaning of text. At the top layer of the neural network is a prediction layer that is explicitly trained to predict the target variable (i.e., attitude or perception score).

Neural networks are powerful and flexible machine learning algorithms. However, they can require extremely large sample sizes.[1] Although this can be prohibitive, recent advancements in transfer learning allow for the application of "pretrained" neural networks built on massive datasets to then be applied to new settings (e.g., Wolf et al., 2019). In the new context, which does not require extremely large datasets, the model parameters can be gradually tweaked to be more applicable to the particular NLP task. For example, existing BERT models are freely available and trained on massive internet datasets. Such models can then be fine-tuned on employee comments to be more applicable to the purpose of attitude and perception measurement.

Text-based attitude and perception scoring (TAPS) dictionaries

Recently, Speer et al. (2022)[2] developed algorithms that create theme and valence scores for 25 commonly measured constructs from the organizational sciences. These are called the text-based attitude and perception scoring (TAPS) dictionaries, and TAPS could be useful for people analytics teams who wish to undertake NLP to process text data that might be included in employee surveys. The TAPS constructs range from satisfaction with pay and supervision to perceptions of diversity climate and stress. Using a sample of 1,506 employed respondents who responded to various narrative prompts, a total of 14,282 comments were analyzed to create the algorithms. Theme score dictionaries were formed for each of the 25 constructs using an inductive-deductive approach to identifying word phrases linked to each construct. Once again, these theme scores are used to classify what a given text is about. Likewise, valence scores were created for each of the 25 constructs. These were trained to predict Likert composites representing each construct—for example, the target score for engagement was the composite score of the Likert items "At my work, I feel bursting with energy," "I am enthusiastic about my job," and "I am immersed in my work" from the Schaufeli et al. (2017) engagement measure. The BERT transformer architecture was applied using HuggingFace (e.g., Wolf et al., 2019) in Python,[3] with 25 separate algorithms built. The pre-trained BERT models were fine-tuned on the text from the employee comments.

A k-fold cross-validation design (e.g., James et al., 2017) was used to avoid overfitting, and the reliability and validity of the developed theme and valence scores from the TAPS dictionaries were examined. The results were favorable and are summarized in Table 4.3.2. First, theme scores were substantially higher for comments coming from narrative prompts that were more relevant to the targeted construct ($\bar{d} = 2.70$). To aid interpretation, the d statistic represents Cohen's d, or the standardized mean difference. Well-established norms of 0.2, 0.5, 0.8, and 1.0 reflect small, moderate, large, and very large effects, respectively. Thus, the observed effect was very large, meaning the theme scores were highly effective at differentiating responses of construct-relevant prompts from construct-irrelevant prompts.

Second, the median split-half reliability for valence scores was 0.86, and the median test-retest reliability was 0.67. Third, the median convergent correlation between valence scores and Likert composite scores was 0.63 when the text was taken from construct-relevant narrative prompts. Additionally, when using the theme scores to filter text based on relevance, the median convergent correlation was 0.60. Lastly, valence scores were predictive of organizational citizenship behaviors measured at a later point in time (which were measured using a self-report Likert scale), explaining unique variance over and above Likert scores of the same constructs ($\Delta R = 0.04$). This speaks to the benefits of scoring employee narrative data. All told, the developed algorithms exhibited strong validity evidence, resulting in a set of algorithms that can be applied to new samples of qualitative data

TABLE 4.3.2 Final text-based attitude and perception scoring (TAPS) constructs and summary statistics

	Theme d high-how activation	Split half reliability	Test-retest reliability	Convergent r very high theme scores	Convergent r high activation
Autonomy	2.93	0.83	0.56	0.64	0.69
Organizational Commitment —Affective	2.37	0.89	0.73	0.60	0.69
Organizational Commitment- Normative	2.37	0.88	0.72	0.49	0.54
Diversity climate	5.46	0.88	0.66	0.70	0.67
Engagement	1.81	0.89	0.76	0.76	0.66
Feedback	3.23	0.84	0.66	0.58	0.56
Satisfaction with coworker	2.77	0.86	0.67	0.48	0.54
Satisfaction with pay	4.06	0.87	0.75	0.75	0.76
Satisfaction with promotion	3.48	0.86	0.69	0.73	0.73
Satisfaction with supervisor	1.87	0.87	0.60	0.58	0.74
Satisfaction with work	0.85	0.88	0.70	0.80	0.67
Complexity	2.95	0.85	0.62	0.69	0.69
Distributive justice	2.39	0.87	0.74	0.41	0.55
Informational justice	2.39	0.88	0.71	0.32	0.50
Interactional justice	2.39	0.88	0.67	0.49	0.53
Procedural justice	2.39	0.88	0.72	0.47	0.55
Ambiguity	1.82	0.81	0.64	0.64	0.62
Role conflict	2.60	0.77	0.61	0.55	0.39
Task significance	1.63	0.87	0.73	0.67	0.59
Turnover intentions	1.60	0.86	0.69	0.82	0.64
Physical demands	3.37	0.73	0.59	0.59	0.58
Work conditions	3.37	0.77	0.63	0.74	0.65
Work-family conflict	–	0.79	0.65	0.26	–
Stress	3.44	0.76	0.60	0.71	0.67
Workload	3.31	0.70	0.43	0.47	0.50
Average	**2.70**	**0.84**	**0.66**	**0.60**	**0.61**

Note: Theme *d* represents standardized mean differences between theme scores for narratives from prompts with low construct activation and prompts with high construct activation. Values of 0.2, 0.5, 0.8, and 1.0 reflect small, moderate, large, and very large effects, respectively. Split-half reliability was calculated by grouping each person's comment responses into two vectors (odd prompt responses, even prompt responses), scoring that text, and then estimating reliability for the two vectors. Test-retest reliability was calculated using two survey administrations approximately one to two weeks apart. Convergent correlations were calculated between valence scores and Likert composite scores of the same construct. Convergent correlations for "very high theme scores" were calculated within responses where the construct was likely to have been discussed (i.e., high theme score). Correlations for "high activation" were taken from narrative prompts that had a high likelihood of eliciting responses relevant to the construct of interest.

to understand employee attitudes and perceptions from text. This allows people analytics teams to automatically derive insights from qualitative comments without expensive and time-consuming manual human coding and, therefore, to more efficiently analyze existing or newly collected qualitative text.

Case study to understand gender inclusivity in a healthcare sample

As a case study applying TAPS for people analytics purposes, we scored employee comments from a sample of female healthcare providers working in an integrated healthcare system. The organization was interested in understanding perceptions of gender inclusion. Several hundred employees completed a survey that included open-ended comment responses and Likert questions to assess gender climate, defined as shared perceptions of ways in which an organization promotes gender fairness across leadership levels and measured using 12 Likert questions (Brown & Collins, 2021; Dwertmann et al., 2016). The goal of the survey was to examine perceptions of fairness and inclusion across different levels of leadership and in different roles within the organization. Rather than relying on human coding of narratives, which would be prohibitive across several hundred respondents, we automatically scored all comments using the TAPS dictionaries.

Given the nature of the survey, we focused on scoring relevant TAPS constructs. The average theme scores for diversity climate were very high, with scores at the 96th percentile. This means that the diversity climate theme scores for this sample were higher than 96% of comments provided in organizational contexts on average, or at least higher than 96% of the comments provided in the original collection of employee comments as described above. This was expected given the nature of the survey, which was diversity-focused. Other topics that respondents discussed in their responses included satisfaction with promotional opportunities (78th percentile), organizational justice (82nd percentile), role conflict (79th percentile), work-family conflict (90th percentile), satisfaction with supervisor (96th percentile), and feedback (72nd percentile). These themes were heavily discussed in the comments.

Valence scores represent the favorability of work attitudes and perceptions and, as previously described, were built using supervised transformer algorithms. These serve as a barometer of employee concerns. The healthcare providers indicated moderately low favorability for diversity climate (38th percentile), pay (39th percentile), satisfaction with promotions (40th percentile), and feedback (31st percentile). They also reported low satisfaction with supervision (28th percentile). Given these findings, the sample expressed modest concerns over diversity and factors such as pay and feedback, with more concern expressed regarding supervision. It should be noted, however, that the diversity climate valence scores deal with diversity broadly (i.e., across race concerns, gender concerns, etc.) and not explicitly with gender perceptions.

Recall that the organization was focused on perceptions of gender inclusion, and this variable was measured using a traditional Likert composite. In line with this focus, we sought to identify factors likely to drive gender climate perceptions, and the TAPS proved a useful tool for this purpose. As expected, diversity climate ($r = 0.36$), distributive justice ($r = 0.38$), and procedural justice ($r = 0.40$) exhibited moderate to strong correlations with Likert-reported gender climate perceptions. However, looking at variables that are more explanatory in nature, we found that several factors were meaningfully related to gender climate perceptions, particularly for those in advanced practitioner roles (as opposed to physicians): autonomy ($r = 0.37$), satisfaction with promotions ($r = 0.40$), satisfaction with pay ($r = 0.42$), role conflict ($r = -0.33$), work-family conflict ($r = -0.30$), and work stress ($r = -0.34$) were all meaningfully related to gender climate perceptions. Thus, these factors are ones that the organization might monitor and develop interventions for to impact gender climate perceptions for practitioners within the organization.

Conclusion

Unstructured text is a rich data source that many organizations would benefit from analyzing. Although NLP is not perfect, we believe there is utility in leveraging it to better understand employee attitudes and work perceptions. The TAPS is a tool that can facilitate such analyses and lead to useful organizational insights, and it is a method that is particularly well-suited for people analytics teams. With such algorithms built, people analytics teams can uncover themes and valence information from text data, either as a standalone form of analysis (if text is the only source of data) or as a supplement to more traditional Likert measures (if both text and traditional survey questions are used). We also want to highlight that this chapter was written before the widespread usage of large language models (e.g., GPT). Such tools provide alternatives to supervised machine learning (see Speer et al., 2024 for an example and discussion) and further enhance NLP capabilities in organizational settings.

Notes

1 The exact sample size necessary differs by problem and complexity of the data. As we'll demonstrate, by using transfer learning, neural networks can be applied with approximately a thousand cases, though we've also seen them perform adequately with several hundred respondents.
2 This work was partially funded by the 2021 SIOP Small Grant titled "Turning words into numbers: Development and validation of work attitude and perception algorithms".
3 A Python library that streamlines transformer applications.

References

Breiman, L. (2001). Random forests. *Machine Learning, 45*, 5–32.
Brown, M. I., & Collins, C. (2021). *Measuring gender inclusion climate among female healthcare providers.* Poster presented at the 36th Meeting for the Society for Industrial and Organizational Psychology, virtual conference.

Demszky, D., Yang, D., Yeager, D. S., Bryan, C. J., Clapper, M., Chandhok, S., ... & Pennebaker, J. W. (2023). Using large language models in psychology. *Nature Reviews Psychology*, 1–14.

Devlin, J., Chang, M. W., Lee, K., & Toutanova, K. (2018). *BERT: Pre-training of deep bidirectional transformers for language understanding* (arxiv:1810.04805), 1–13. https://doi.org/10.48550/arXiv.1810.04805

Dwertmann, D. J. G., Nishii, L. H., & van Knippenberg, D. (2016). Disentangling the fairness and discrimination and synergy perspectives on diversity climate. *Journal of Management, 42*, 1136–1168.

Goodfellow, I., Bengio, Y., & Courville, A. (2016). *Deep learning*. The MIT Press.

Hickman, L., Thapa, S., Tay, L., Cao, M., & Srinivasan, P. (2022). Text preprocessing for text mining in organizational research: Review and recommendations. *Organizational Research Methods, 25*, 114–146.

James, G., Witten, D., Hastie, T., & Tibshirani, R. (2017). *An introduction to statistical learning with applications in R* (7th ed.). Springer.

Schaufeli, W. B., Shimazu, A., Hakanen, J., Salanova, M., & De Witte, H. (2017). An ultra-short measure for work engagement. *European Journal of Psychological Assessment, 35*, 577–591.

Speer, A. B. (2020). Scoring dimension-level job performance from narrative comments: Validity and generalizability when using natural language processing. *Organizational Research Methods, 24*(3), 1–19.

Speer, A. B., Perrotta, J., & Kordsmeyer, T. L. (2024). Taking it easy: Off-the-shelf versus fine-tuned supervised modeling of performance appraisal text. *Organizational Research Methods*.

Speer, A. B., Perrotta, J., Tenbrink, A. P., Wegmeyer, L. J., Delacruz, A. Y., & Bowker, J. (2022). Turning words into numbers: Assessing work attitudes using natural language processing. *Journal of Applied Psychology, 108*(6), 1–17. Advance online publication. https://doi.org/10.1037/apl0001061

Tausczik, Y. R., & Pennebaker, J. W. (2010). The psychological meaning of words: LIWC and computerized text analysis methods. *Journal of Language and Social Psychology, 29*, 24–54.

Wolf, T., Debut, L., Sanh, V., Chaumond, J., Clement, D., Moi, A., Cistac, P., Rault, T., Louf, R., Funtowicz, M., Davidson, J., Shleifer S., von Platen, P., Ma, C., Jernite, Y., Plu, J., Xu, C., La Scao, T., Gugger, S., Drame, M., Lhoest, Q., & Rush, A. M. (2019). HuggingFace's transformers: State-of-the-art natural language processing, *arXiv:1910.03771*.

Zou, H., & Hastie, T. (2005). Regularization and variable selection via the elastic net. *Journal of the Royal Statistical Society: Series B, 67*, 301–320.

Decision trees and HR analytics
An example

Paul van der Laken

Introduction

Linear regression models have been the go-to tool for many scientists and analysts in the human resources (HR) domain, both in academia and in practice. Yet, not all HR phenomena can be accurately captured by defining a set of straight lines. Moreover, with the vast amount of information that organizations collect on their employees, candidates, and leaders these days, gathered datasets may often hide complex processes and patterns that their observers might be unaware of. Therefore, researchers have argued that alternative modeling approaches offer welcome functionalities that make a valuable addition to the HR analyst's toolkit (van der Laken et al., 2018). This chapter zooms in on decision tree models, examining how they can be applied within HR, their inner workings, and what advantages and disadvantages they offer over more traditional modeling approaches.

Main principles and terminology

A decision tree is a supervised machine learning algorithm that can produce non-parametric models for both classification and regression purposes. Supervised learning refers to the fact that the decision tree is built in situations where the values of both the independent and dependent variables are known. Non-parametric refers to the fact that the decision tree model does not make assumptions about the data distribution or the distribution of its errors.

The main idea behind the decision tree algorithm is to represent data as a tree of decision rules. As shown in Figure 4.4, a decision tree is upside down and starts at the top with a *root node*. Each node in the tree is either a *decision node*—where we split our data into subsets based on a test of some condition—or a *leaf node*—where a subset of data resides that we do not intend to split up any further. Each decision

DOI: 10.4324/9781003190097-10

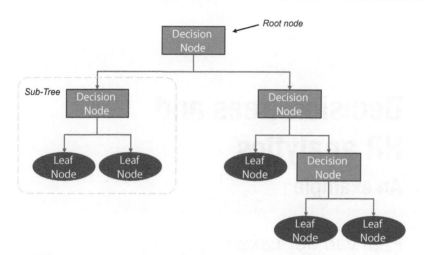

FIGURE 4.4 A conceptual depiction of a decision tree and the associated terminology.

Source: https://www.devops.ae/decision-tree-classification-algorithm/

node forms a *conditional test* that results in a (binary) yes/no decision rule, like "Is this employee a manager?", "Is this employee's engagement above 60%?", or "Does this team have more than six employees?".

Ultimately, the resulting tree can be read like a flowchart, where each internal node represents a test on an independent variable (also called a *feature*), each branch represents the outcome of the test, and each resulting leaf node represents a subset of data where the tree model estimates some class probability or mean value. The variables and cutoff values used in the tests depend on their added value for classifying or regressing the dependent variable (also called the *target*).

Dataset

In the next sections, we zoom in on an application of decision trees in HR. In this chapter, we use an implementation of CART (Breiman et al., 1984) in R (Therneau & Atkinson, 2019).

For this purpose, we generated the small artificial dataset displayed in Table 4.4.1. It contains information on 14 employees, which could be extracted from the typical HR information system. There are data on three independent variables: the commuting distance, whether the employee has a company car, and their job type. Our target is to predict the dependent variable, *turnover*, indicating whether an employee has left the organization. This is a classification problem, as we seek to predict whether employees belong to the "Yes" or "No" class regarding turnover.

The main purpose of a decision tree is to split the observations in a way that returns subgroups with the purest separation of classes. In our case, this means that

TABLE 4.4.1 Artificial dataset with employee information taken from typical HR information system

Employee name	Commuting distance	Company car	Job type	Turnover
Aziz	10	No	Manager	No
Barbara	10	No	Individual contributor	No
Constantina	10	No	Individual contributor	No
Dorus	30	No	Individual contributor	No
Eloya	30	No	Individual contributor	Yes
Felix	30	No	Manager	No
Georgina	60	Yes	Manager	No
Huy	60	No	Individual contributor	Yes
Ismael	60	No	Individual contributor	Yes
Joy	60	No	Manager	No
Karel	120	No	Manager	No
Louise	120	No	Individual contributor	Yes
Min-Ho	120	No	Individual contributor	Yes
Nyosa	120	Yes	Individual contributor	No

our leaf nodes should primarily contain employees who all score either "Yes" or "No" on the turnover variable.

Application

There are multiple decision tree algorithms, but for this example, we use CART (Breiman et al., 1984) implemented in R (Therneau & Atkinson, 2019) with specific parameter settings.[1] Moving through the different stages in the tree-building process, we demonstrate what the algorithm is doing and why.

The tree-building process starts with the full dataset of 14 employees at the root node of our tree (Figure 4.5). Here, no possible splits have been considered yet, so 100% of the total observations reside in this node. They show an average value of 0.36 on the target variable, or in other words, 36% belong to the class "Yes" and have turned over. This implies the majority of this root node belongs to class "No" (1 − 0.36 = 0.64), so this class is what our decision tree predicts for the observations in this node.

The algorithm now has to find the decision rule that best splits the two classes. For this purpose, it runs through all possible ways to divide our employees into subgroups: it examines all possible cutoff values for each of the three independent variables in our dataset.

TABLE 4.4.2 All possible splits and their Gini impurity at the root node

Independent variable	Cutoff	Gini impurity
Commuting distance	20	0.390
Commuting distance	45	0.405
Commuting distance	90	0.443
Company car	Yes	0.417
Job type	Manager	0.317

Starting with the variable commuting distance, the algorithm encounters four unique values: 10, 30, 60, and 120. This means that three binary splits are possible: between values 10 and 30, 30 and 60, and 60 and 120. For numerical variables, the algorithm uses the mean of each pair of subsequent values as a cutoff—meaning, respectively, 20, 45, and 90. The tree separates the employees who score lower than this cutoff value from those who score higher. For *commuting distance*, the algorithm thus produces three sets of possible subgroups. For categorical variables, like *company car* and *job type*, decision tree algorithms examine splits separating the categories. Our variables only have two unique values, so each produces only one possible way to split our dataset, separating employees with company cars from those without, and separating *managers* from *individual contributors*. All in all, there are a total of five ways to split the dataset (see Table 4.4.2).

In order to select the best split, the algorithm needs a way to quantify the quality of each split. There are multiple criteria metrics to determine the goodness of a binary split, and in this example, we use *Gini impurity*.

Gini impurity measures the average probability of mislabeling an observation when using a random label drawn from the current set of observations. The minimum value of the Gini impurity is 0, which implies that all randomly drawn labels are correct. This only occurs in pure nodes—like a subgroup of employees who all score "Yes" on turnover—as any randomly drawn label in such a homogeneous subgroup would be the correct one. In a subgroup that contains an equal number of employees belonging to turnover class "Yes" and "No," the Gini impurity would be 0.5, as half of the randomly drawn labels will be correct. In sum, a low Gini impurity basically reflects a more homogenous subgroup.

Our decision tree can find the best possible split by using the test that separates the subgroups and results in the lowest Gini impurity.[2] In our case, the split on job type—separating managers from non-managers—produces the lowest Gini impurity (0.317) and thus the best class separation. Hence, this decision rule is performed at the root node in Figure 4.6.

This produces two branches with associated nodes. All managers reside in the left node, representing 36% of the total dataset. None of them turned over, so this is a

FIGURE 4.5 The tree when it has only a root node, before the building has really commenced.

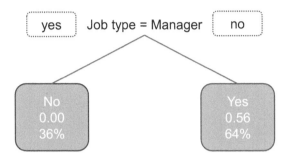

FIGURE 4.6 The decision tree with depth 1.

pure node, which explains the low Gini impurity for this split. Since the proportion of turnover in this node is 0.00, the decision tree predicts "No" for all observations. In the right-hand node, all non-managers are bundled together. This represents 64% of the dataset. The proportion of turnover here is 0.56 or 56%, so the decision tree classifies them as "Yes" for turnover.

As a pure node, the decision tree no longer needs to consider splits for the left-hand node. This left node is thus a leaf node. For the right-hand node, the algorithm again computes the Gini impurity of all possible splits (Table 4.4.3) and selects the decision rule producing the lowest Gini impurity (see Figure 4.7).

At this point, the split by commuting distance of less than 20 best separates the remaining leavers from the employees who were retained. It again produces a pure leaf node on the left-hand side (node 4), containing all non-management employ-ees with a commuting distance of less than 20. These two employees (14% of the total sample) show a 0% probability of turnover. Node 5 on the right-hand side

TABLE 4.4.3 All possible splits and their Gini impurity for node 3, containing all non-managers

Independent variable	Cutoff	Gini impurity
Commuting distance	20	0.317
Commuting distance	45	0.344
Commuting distance	90	0.481
Company car	Yes	0.417

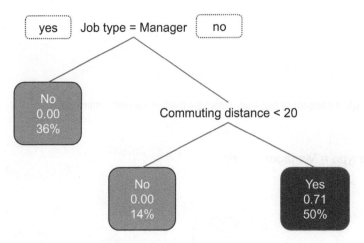

FIGURE 4.7 The decision tree with depth 2.

contains all non-managers with a commuting distance of 20 or more (50% of the total sample). They show a 71% probability of turnover.

Because node 5 is not pure yet, there are further possible splits for the decision tree to consider. We will skip the Gini details for now, but Figure 4.8 shows the next best split, based on whether these non-management employees with long commutes have a company car. If so, they end up on the left-hand side, node 6, which again is a pure node with 0% turnover.

Although the right-hand side node 7 shows a high turnover probability of 83%, it is not pure. Hence, the algorithm considers any further splits it may perform in

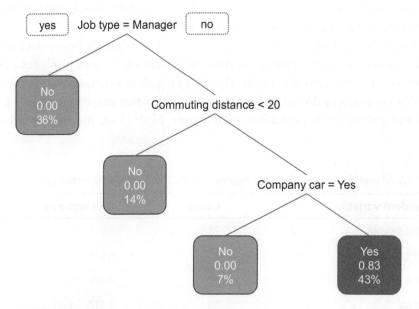

FIGURE 4.8 The decision tree at depth 3.

this node. Unfortunately, it does not find any split that can further disentangle the turnover and non-turnover cases in this impure node, so it too becomes a leaf node.

With all final nodes considered leaf nodes, our decision tree is now complete. Through three simple rules, our decision tree was able to separate almost all turnover cases from their retained colleagues. Moreover, it was able to capture two interesting non-linear patterns. First, a long commuting distance mattered only for the turnover among non-managers, and second, for non-managers with a long commuting distance, a company car further reduced turnover.

Advantages and disadvantages

This decision tree modeling approach has both clear advantages and disadvantages over more traditional generalized linear regression models.

Simple

Above all, decision trees are simple. Their output is understandable, even to non-analytical laymen, and the output decision rules are relatively easy to visualize. There are no underlying assumptions, like a requirement for normally distributed data, and as the model is just a sequence of binary tests, there are no complex parameters or formulas involved. Nevertheless, the sequential combination of simple decision rules is still able to uncover complex behaviors and processes.

This simplicity of decision trees is also evident when it comes to computation and implementation. For smaller datasets, it often takes mere seconds to build a model. Hence, decision trees can offer quick exploratory insights into your data. On top of this, decision trees are relatively easy to deploy in organizations or business processes. Just like regression formulas, you can program your decision rules in structured query language or even in an Excel worksheet. However, I would personally recommend a stable form of model deployment.

Flexible

Another main strength of decision trees lies in their flexibility. The algorithm is suitable for both classification and regression problems. Moreover, it handles both categorical and numeric features, and there is no need to standardize, normalize, scale, or otherwise prepare these independent variables. The decision tree algorithm can even handle missing values by treating them as a separate category.

This flexibility is also reflected in the "machine learning" abilities of the model. As a user, there is very little work for you to do. The decision tree algorithm can pick up any non-linearities in your data—like polynomial effects or interactions—right out of the box, without you having to explicitly specify terms or formulas. Similarly, when you are dealing with highly dimensional data (i.e., many features/

independent variables) and you are not sure what affects your dependent variable, you can simply let the decision tree find the patterns that matter. On top of this, decision tree models are relatively more robust to outliers than traditional linear regression models. All in all, there is much less work involved in finding the best predictive model when you use a decision tree algorithm.

Disadvantages

Unfortunately, all these capabilities come with some serious disadvantages.

First, building a decision tree still involves some complexity. With these algorithmic techniques, there are (hyper)parameters for you to set, tweak, and optimize.

Overfitting

This complexity is also reflected in the main problem with decision trees: they tend to overfit the data. Decision trees split your data into smaller and smaller subgroups to best fit all patterns in your training data, including those patterns that are mere (random) noise. Not only does this result in overly complex and large trees, but the modeled patterns might also no longer generalize to new data.

One way to reduce overfitting is to remove decision nodes that overcomplicate your model. This process is called pruning. An alternative is to combine the predictions of many simpler decision trees into an ensemble model, which leverages the "wisdom of the crowd."

Unstable

As a final disadvantage, decision trees are somewhat unstable. Adding a new observation to your dataset can lead to the regeneration of the whole tree, with completely different nodes, tests, and decision rules. Hence, a small change in the data can cause a major change in your model.

When to use?

Nevertheless, decision trees are still a great addition to your analysis toolbox. They allow you to explore and exploit complex non-linear effects in your dataset with relative ease and in a semi-automated way. Therefore, decision trees are a great option in situations where you have highly dimensional data, when your dependent variable is not normally distributed, when you do not know what variables have predictive potential, or when you expect many non-linearities like polynomial or interaction effects.

Conclusion

If you want to start building your own decision trees, there are some great packages in R, including *rpart* (Thernau & Atkinson, 2019), *party* (Hothorn et al., 2006), and *tree* (Ripley, 2021). This chapter's *rpart* decision tree models were visualized using the *rpart.plot* package (Stephen Milborrow, 2021). In Python, you can find decision tree algorithms included in the *sklearn* module (Pedregosa et al., 2011). A great YouTube tutorial with Python code is accessible via https://www.youtube.com/watch?v=LDRbO9a6XPU. In Julia, you can find CART implemented via the *DecisionTree* module, which is wrapped by the Machine Learning for Julia module (*MLJ*; Bloem et al., 2020).

Notes

1 Minimum number of observations for split = 1; Minimum number of observations per leaf node = 1; Minimum complexity decrease = 1e-30; and we let the maximum tree depth vary as we progress through the example application.
2 Average weighted for the size of the separated subgroups

References

Blaom, A. D., Kiraly, F., Lienart, T., Simillides, Y., Arenas, D., & Vollmer, S. J. (2020). MLJ: A Julia package for composable machine learning. arXiv preprint arXiv:2007.12285.

Breiman, L., Friedman, J., Olshen, R., & Stone, C. (1984). *Classification and regression trees.* Wadsworth International Group.

Hothorn, T., Hornik, K., & Zeileis, A. (2006). Unbiased recursive partitioning: A conditional inference framework. *Journal of Computational and Graphical Statistics, 15*(3), 651–674.

Milborrow, S. (2021). *Rpart.plot: Plot 'rpart' models: An enhanced version of 'plot.rpart'.* R package version 3.1.0. https://CRAN.R-project.org/package=rpart.plot

Pedregosa, F., Varoquaux, G., Gramfort, A., Michel, V., Thirion, B., Grisel, O., ... Duchesnay, E. (2011). Scikit-learn: Machine learning in Python. *The Journal of Machine Learning Research, 12,* 2825–2830.

Ripley, B. (2021). *Tree: Classification and regression trees.* R package version 1.0–41. https://CRAN.R-project.org/package=tree

Therneau, T., & Atkinson, B. (2019). *Rpart: Recursive partitioning and regression trees.* R package version 4.1–15. https://CRAN.R-project.org/package=rpart

van der Laken, P., Bakk, Z., Giagkoulas, V., van Leeuwen, L., & Bongenaar, E. (2018). Expanding the methodological toolbox of HRM researchers: The added value of latent bathtub models and optimal matching analysis. *Human Resource Management, 57*(3), 751–760.

4.5

Organizational network analysis (ONA) at the Broad Institute

Heather Whiteman, Andrew Pitts, and Rafael A. Sanchez

Here, we explore the use of organizational network analysis in the context of HR analytics and provide a case study of this technique in use. Organizational network analysis, often referred to simply as ONA, is a technique for studying communication, networks, and collaboration within an organizational setting. This case study is based on ONA work conducted at the Broad Institute.

The Broad Institute

The Broad Institute of MIT and Harvard is a non-profit academic research organization focused on biomedicine to improve human health. Broad was built on a foundation of collaboration across institutions and among individuals to accelerate biomedical research. Its core values include a focus on collaboration, innovation, and empowering every employee, or "Broadie," to excel. The institute's success relies on its ability to answer pressing questions about its people and a community of approximately 6,000 Broadies.

In 2020, as the COVID-19 pandemic was underway, many Broadies worked remotely, while others continued to do scientific work in labs, although with little face-to-face interaction. During this period, the People Insights team at Broad began a three-month project to address three questions about Broadie engagement, community, and collaboration:

- How do we maintain the vibrant, collaborative essence of Broad in the "new normal"?
- Who are the "go-to" Broadies that others seek out the most?

DOI: 10.4324/9781003190097-11

■ How effective are the networks of specific Broadie population sub-segments (such as early career and/or those from underrepresented populations[1])?

For a science-based research organization, it was imperative that these questions be addressed with evidence and analysis, not simply anecdotes or assumptions. So, Broad turned to ONA, a Workforce Analytics technique, to provide insights.

What is ONA?

ONA uses *network science*, which studies the relationships between different entities, to quantify and analyze the informal relationships between individuals in an organization. "A network is, in its simplest form, a collection of points joined together in pairs by lines" (Newman, 2010). The analysis can be conducted through an *active ONA* approach, which gathers information directly from individuals through their active participation, or a *passive ONA* approach, which gathers *metadata* from the "digital exhaust" that companies naturally produce, such as email, meeting, and enterprise collaboration platform data. Currently, active ONA approaches are more common since they are typically conducted using voluntary employee surveys, which many companies are more familiar with administering, and because data collection may pose fewer access challenges and employee concerns about privacy (Borgatti & Foster, 2003). Combining the two approaches may enable more unique insights than either alone. For example, active survey responses paired with passive data may identify individuals whose employee engagement may be impacted by an overload of communication.

Uses of ONA

The goal of ONA is to identify the informal networks and connections among people in an organization. It provides insights into how people communicate, collaborate, and influence one another that may not be visible through formal structures or hierarchies. ONA is one of the best tools available to illuminate the informal social structures through which work gets done. ONA can be used to assess social capital, such as the value of connections and the access to resources available to individuals, and social homogeneity, such as the common attitudes or similarity of networks and the spread or "contagion" of ideas, practices, or behaviors. The applications of ONA are as varied as the insights it can provide, as summarized in Figure 4.9.

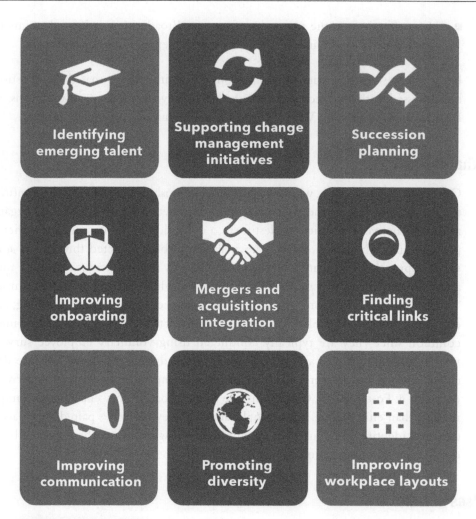

FIGURE 4.9 ONA Applications.

The Broad ONA project

As this was the first ONA project conducted at Broad, the People Insights team within the HR function began the project with a pilot across one of the organization's larger interdisciplinary disease area groups. This pilot group represented a potential respondent population of approximately 300 individuals out of the full Broad population of about 6,000. The People Insights team paid particular attention to factors that would be critical to the success of future applications of ONA, including:

■ **A true partnership between the analytics team and pilot group leadership.** People Insights started by outlining approaches to answer the questions the pilot group leadership said were top of mind for them. A deeply collaborative process then allowed People Insights to design the study in a way that would yield insights to answer those questions.

■ **Strong ethical guidelines and privacy protections.** Given that the active ONA survey would ask Broadies to name their colleagues, providing clear ethical guidelines on the use of that data and protecting the privacy of respondents was critical. People Insights had already established a people ethics charter, which allowed the analyses to proceed in ways that ensured every participant felt comfortable sharing their information and confident that the data would be used only in aggregate and in ways that would benefit Broadies.

■ **Easy-to-use tools and interfaces.** Broad worked with an external software platform, Polinode (Pitts, 2016), to design a data collection strategy that was user-friendly and easy to navigate.

■ **Broadie involvement.** High participation rates are a critical requirement for effective active ONA studies, and the People Insights team developed a detailed communications plan to ensure that Broadies in the pilot group received information about the project through multiple channels.

The Broad ONA project incorporated some relatively advanced approaches compared to ONA at a typical organization. The People Insights team chose to use both an active and a passive ONA data-gathering approach and leveraged Polinode for the collection, analysis, and visualization of network data.

In the active ONA survey, respondents were asked to nominate individuals who they felt were important to accomplishing their own work priorities, including Broadies outside of the pilot group. Respondents were then asked to provide additional network information regarding the nominated individuals, including:

■ If the respondent desired greater access to them (either in person or remotely)

■ If they were a source of expertise, energy, trust, and support to the respondent

■ How likely the respondent would be to seek input from them when a critical decision needs to be made

■ How comfortable the respondent feels initiating a conversation with them.

Next, survey respondents were asked to nominate individuals aligned with specific cultural and network relationships in three categories: reflection of Broad values, career guidance, and affinity networks. Respondents could indicate new individuals or re-nominate the same individuals identified earlier.

Finally, the survey requested participants' consent to have their email and calendar metadata analyzed. The ONA pilot group had a response rate of slightly over 70% for the active survey, and nearly all of those individuals also consented to the passive metadata analysis. With this data, the People Insights team was ready to assess work patterns, networks, collaboration, relationships, and the influence of individuals within the organization.

The analyses

Broad used several metrics to analyze and visualize the network data collected. Standard metrics included *in degree, out degree, total degree, community detection,* and *betweenness.* These metrics are based on key concepts related to the presentation and visualization of the networks, such as *node, edge,* and *layout* algorithms. In network science, a node is an entity connected to another entity via an edge (Newman, 2010). In this case, the nodes were Broad employees, and an edge existed between them if one employee (the source node) nominated another (the target node) in the active ONA survey, or if their passive data indicated communication beyond a certain threshold between them. (In Figure 4.10, each node is represented by a circle, and edges are represented by lines between the nodes.) Each node in the network could then be analyzed with respect to its out degree (relationships indicated *from* one employee to others), in degree (relationships in which others indicated a connection *to* this employee), and total degree of connections (both incoming and outgoing connections). The degree of connections for an employee provides a measure of their *centrality* within a network. Using the degree of connections between nodes and a *community detection algorithm* (called Louvain), Broad was able to identify the informal groupings or structures within the respondent population. This algorithm partitions the network into groups (i.e., *communities*) of non–overlapping nodes that have relatively denser connections with each other than with nodes in other groups across the network (see Figure 4.10).

In addition to learning about the organization as a whole, network data allow for the identification of individuals who play a critical role in connecting or "brokering" information between groups. These individuals can be identified by assessing betweenness, which measures the shortest paths between all pairs of nodes. For example, in Figure 4.11, the shortest path between node A and node E is A→B→C→D→E. Because that path (and all paths connecting nodes on the left to nodes on the right of the figure) must pass through node C, node C will have a relatively higher measure of betweenness. Even though node C has fewer direct connections than B or D, it plays a critical role in bridging two groups that would otherwise be disconnected. Because of the picture made by the placement of the nodes, this scenario has been nicknamed a "bow tie," with the employee at the center knot of the bow tie having more influence than might be visible in a formal organizational structure; this scenario may also pose an organizational risk since many players are dependent on this single employee but not on each other (Krachardt, 1993).

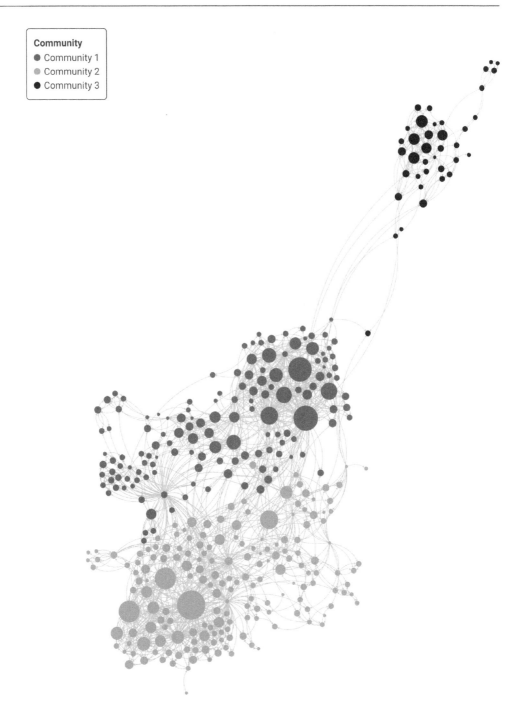

FIGURE 4.10 ONA network with 3 communities.

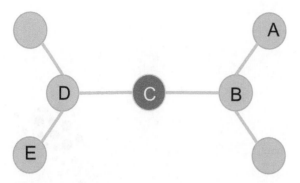

FIGURE 4.11 Node paths.

Betweenness highlights individuals whose impact on collaboration and the effective functioning of the organization may otherwise go undetected. Broad also sought to identify the individuals who were energizers, reflected Broad's values, and influenced the organization. To assess this, Broad relied on an approach developed by Polinode that accounts for three factors: total nominations, betweenness centrality, and the proportion of times individuals were identified as someone who reflects Broad's values.

Additional analyses were conducted to assess key questions regarding the effectiveness of Broadie networks at different career stage levels, to illuminate the role of affinity groups in network building, and to discover critical connectors in the organization. The passive metadata collected from consenting individuals were used to analyze the frequency and timing of communications, and to conduct comparisons of group-level work patterns both before and during the COVID-19 pandemic. As part of the project, the Broad team also calculated a range of other, more advanced metrics, which will not be discussed in depth here but include metrics such as closeness centrality, clustering coefficients, eigenvector centrality, and PageRank. With these analyses now complete, Broad had a foundation of data-driven insights on which they could base organizational strategies for engagement, community, and collaboration.

Reporting

Results were communicated through reports generated at three levels, each for a particular audience, ensuring confidentiality. First, senior leaders of the pilot group received an organizational-level report with an aggregate view of the active and passive ONA findings, including the identification of cultural influencers, energizers, and a work patterns assessment for their team. They were also provided with a summary of the findings related to the mentorship of early career individuals and diversity and inclusion. Second, leaders and individuals identified as either cultural influencers or energizers received an individual report visualizing their place in the network along with network insights they could use for personal development. Third, all Broadies who participated in the ONA project were provided with an aggregated, anonymized group-level summary.

Results and outcomes

The three-month project allowed People Insights to support the pilot group's leadership in answering their initial questions, identifying opportunities to improve the organization, and discovering areas for future exploration. The analyses confirmed some hypotheses and provided additional data to support further exploration of those topics.

The project's key findings included:

- Confirmation that collaborative activity across the pilot group had been sustained despite the many disruptions caused by the pandemic.
- Analysis of the passive ONA data indicated a marked increase in meetings. It also flagged changes to the structure of a "typical day" with extended hours on weekdays and many more weekend work hours, consistent with numerous other studies on employee working hours during the pandemic.
- These findings highlighted the need to ensure Broadies had the tools available to better manage work/life boundaries and enable sustainable work patterns in the long term.
- Other work at Broad had already highlighted a need to better support early career Broadies within the pilot group, and this study confirmed that need. It particularly highlighted the need for connectivity between more senior members of the pilot group and these early-career individuals, accelerating an initiative already in the works to build those connections.
- For some groups that had struggled to collaborate effectively in the early days of the pandemic, the analysis suggested that physically co-locating these groups and facilitating in-person interactions might help ease some of those challenges.
- However, not all groups needed such physical proximity to be effective collaborators, so this finding could not be extrapolated to all remote working and collaborative efforts.

In addition to confirming existing hypotheses, the analyses provided leadership with the opportunity to visualize the collaborative nature of the organization (even during the pandemic) and identify opportunities. The opportunities identified included:

- Promoting hybrid and in-person options around existing, remotely conducted meetings, after discovering that teams and individuals who were physically present at least two days per week had increased degrees of interconnectedness. As pandemic restrictions eased, team members were encouraged to attend social hours and in-person seminars to boost connectivity.

- Enhancing connections of underrepresented populations and early-career Broadies to more senior members across the pilot group. This analysis accelerated work on the creation of mentoring initiatives for these groups.

- Providing leaders with insights to support their own personal network development, based on the passive calendar data analysis.

- Supplying leaders with a network map and tables summarizing key external connections between members of the pilot group and the rest of Broad, to help understand where the key external connections were.

- Highlighting behaviors of teams that had maintained and even created new, boundary-spanning connections during the pandemic, so that others across the institute could emulate their level of high connectivity and collaboration.

- Identifying critical connectors who energize their colleagues and serve as culture carriers for the pilot group. The analysis suggested that investing in these individuals' continued ability to thrive at Broad was likely to garner benefits for many Broadies across the pilot group. Studying the connectivity patterns of these influential individuals also helped surface specific behaviors that others could emulate to enhance their own networks and collaborative behaviors.

The Broad team plans to leverage the outcomes of this ONA project in the future to support succession planning, encourage collaboration, and support the onboarding of new employees. ONA proved to be an ideal people analytics technique for the institute. It provided a more complete view of their organization and aligned actions with the stated values of collaboration, innovation, and empowering every employee to excel in their work.

References

Borgatti, S. P., & Foster, P. C. (2003). The network paradigm in organizational research: A review and typology. *Journal of Management, 29*(6), 991–1013. https://doi.org/10.1016/S0149 -2063(03)00087-4

Krachardt, D. (1993). Informal networks: The company behind the chart. *Harvard Business Review, 71*, 104–111.

Newman, M. (2010). *Networks: An introduction* (1st ed.). Oxford University Press., online edn, Oxford Academic, September 1, 2010. Retrieved November 30, 2022, from https://doi .org/10.1093/acprof:oso/9780199206650.001.0001

Pitts, A. (2016). *Polinode: A web application for the collection and analysis of network data.* 2016 IEEE/ACM International Conference on Advances in Social Networks Analysis and Mining (ASONAM), pp. 1422–1425. https://doi.org/10.1109/ASONAM.2016.7752435

Machine learning tools to support strategic HR decision-making

*Andy Charlwood, Danat Valizade,
Louise Winton Schreuders, and
Karen Spilsbury*

Acknowledgments

This study is funded by the National Institute for Health and Care Research (NIHR) Policy Research Programme (NIHR201429). The views expressed are those of the authors and not necessarily those of the NIHR or the Department of Health and Social Care.

Introduction

Normative theories of HR analytics stress that it should be a tool for strategy implementation, supporting evidence-based decision-making (Huselid, 2018; Levenson, 2018). However, outside of a few high-profile examples (e.g., Minbaeva, 2018; Bock, 2015; Rasmussen & Ulrich, 2015), evidence of how analytics can inform strategic decision-making about the workforce is limited. Research suggests that most HR analytics teams spend most of their time reporting data for predominantly operational purposes and are often frustrated in their attempts to utilize more advanced analytics practices to influence strategy (Levenson & Fink, 2017; Jörden, Sage & Trusson, 2021). Published examples of machine learning (ML) applications in an HR context have focused on predicting which employees will quit (Avrahami et al., 2022; Choudhury, Allen & Endres, 2021). While these ML applications provide interesting insights that go beyond traditional statistical and econometric methods, they do not help us understand how and why ML might support broader strategic decision-making. This chapter aims to provide examples of how and why specific ML methods might be desirable for this purpose. We present analyses conducted

DOI: 10.4324/9781003190097-12

as part of a collaborative research project aimed at developing the evidence base for workforce policy in long-term care environments, specifically care homes with nursing for older people in the UK. We begin by explaining the context and strategic challenges facing the UK nursing home sector.

Context: The UK nursing home sector

Care homes are an important part of societal provision for an increasing number of dependent older people. The acuity and complexity of resident care needs have risen significantly in recent decades (Clemens et al., 2021). Care homes provide a range of services, including care for older people, individuals with learning disabilities, poor mental health, and other long-term conditions, such as acquired brain injury. This range of services and people is reflected in the current care home sector. Care home services can be broadly categorized based on residents' needs, levels of dependency, and complexity caused by multiple morbidities, some of which require nursing input. Residential care homes do not employ registered nurses; residents' health care needs are addressed by local primary and community care nursing teams. In contrast, nursing homes provide both social and health care and employ registered nurses to meet residents' health care and nursing needs.

At the beginning of this study, around 95% of English care homes were run by for-profit providers. The vast majority of these providers were SMEs, with 5,500 providers operating around 11,300 homes, of which 5,200 provided nursing care, housing around 400,000 residents (CMA, 2017). The COVID-19 pandemic placed unprecedented demands on the sector, leading to rising costs, falling occupancy rates, and worsening staff shortages (CQC, 2021).

Even before the pandemic, care home providers had to navigate particularly challenging product and labor market conditions. With around two-thirds of care home beds purchased by the state (CMA, 2017), providers have to operate within resource constraints imposed by what the government is willing to pay for nursing and personal care. At the same time, homes have to deliver quality care and are held accountable by local authorities, the Care Quality Commission, and the wider public interest. Quality is central to competitive strategy. Failure to deliver appropriate quality care threatens the viability of providers' businesses, as they may struggle to attract new residents in a context where high occupancy levels are necessary to cover costs.

How can care home providers achieve and sustain quality? There is a widespread consensus that staffing is the most important determinant of care quality (Clemens et al., 2021). However, staffing is also the most costly element of providing care. Care homes that provide nursing care also face national and global shortages of registered nurses (Skills for Care, 2021; Whitney, 2021). Funding constraints mean that raising wages to encourage recruitment and retention is not an option most care home operators can afford. While care homes operate on low margins, and operators often have value-driven motives beyond profit maximization, private providers still need to achieve profitability to remain viable. This means the key strategic challenge facing home providers is how to provide quality care with severely constrained resources in order to maintain occupancy rates that ensure viability. Two specific operational workforce challenges emerge from this broader strategic challenge. First, how do we determine the amount of (scarce and expensive) nursing care needed to ensure quality provision? Second, where should the use of limited nursing resources be targeted and prioritized? In the following section, we outline how machine learning might address the first of these challenges.

Addressing strategic challenges 1: Random forest analysis to inform decisions about the sufficiency of nurse staffing

What proportion of care should be provided by registered nurses (as opposed to care workers) to ensure care quality (referred to as skill mix)? To address this question, we examine the extent to which variations in skill mix contribute to hospitalizations, and if they do, why might this be. A secondary question explores whether hospitalization risk increases with agency nurse use. Answers to these questions can help providers understand how to optimize nursing input for resident care without increasing the risk of adverse events and whether resources used to engage agency nurses are effective and necessary.

Existing research evidence on these questions is not encouraging for care home providers seeking to manage scarce nursing resources without compromising care quality. A large body of academic work has examined relationships between staffing levels, skills, and nurse-sensitive indicators of care quality. Studies tend to suggest that higher proportions of care provided by registered nurses lead to better care quality-related outcomes for residents (Spilsbury et al., 2011; Backhaus et al., 2014; Clemens et al., 2021). However, a methodological issue with existing studies is that the linear regression methods they employ typically rely on strict assumptions about the distribution of data in a population that is often unobserved and unknown (Brieman, 2001). Hence, the generalizability of such statistical models beyond observational data is often low. ML is free from such assumptions and therefore has greater potential to produce actionable insights (Leavitt et al., 2021). Furthermore, canonical regression analysis methods only identify linear relationships or pronounced quadratic effects, but relationships between skill mix and quality are more likely to be non-linear and non-monotonous. This is because a minimum threshold level of nurse staffing is likely necessary to achieve and sustain quality care, but there is also likely to be a point at which additional nurse staffing resources do not contribute meaningfully to increased quality (Spilsbury et al., 2011; Donabedian, 2003). ML methods can be particularly effective for identifying non-linear relationships that are not identifiable through regression analysis (Brieman, 2001).

Data

Staffing and quality data were shared by a large care home provider operating 186 care homes in England; their homes provide personal care, nursing care, or a mix of both. The study covers a 182-week period from September 2016 to February 2020. The unit of analysis is the care home week, resulting in 33,852 observations in the dataset (182 weeks multiplied by 186 care homes). The key outcome measure in this study is the rate of resident hospitalizations. This is a nurse-sensitive indicator of care quality because nursing care is not the primary driver of whether a resident needs to go to the hospital for treatment, but good nursing care can reduce the risk of hospitalization (for example, through prevention, early diagnosis, and treatment of chest and urinary tract infections). The provider also collected data on other nurse-sensitive indicators of care quality (e.g., falls, pressure ulcers developed in care, urinary tract infections), but we focus here on hospitalizations because it is the least likely to be biased by measurement error (accuracy of resident hospitalization records is important for billing purposes). The weekly hospitalization rate per occupied bed is around 1 in 1,000.

To make sense of the subsequent analysis, we need to consider the factors that cause the skill mix to change. Target registered nurse staffing is a relatively fixed property of each home, based on a fixed number of nursing beds per nursing post (typically, one nurse working per 30 beds, although 20 homes changed their nursing establishment over the course of the study; these changes did not impact the main results reported below). Therefore, variations in nurse staffing are primarily driven by shortages caused by sickness and absence. The provider attempts to cover nurse absences and vacancies with temporary nursing staff provided by employment agencies, but this is not always possible. By contrast, planned carer hours are determined by regular assessments of residents' care needs using an acuity assessment tool, so carer hours increase when a home has more residents and/or when residents' care needs are greater.

We include in our analysis variables that might account for changes in skill mix (nurse staffing shortages, home occupancy rates, planned carer hours) and other variables that might impact the structures and processes of care delivery (home size, the proportion of beds for residents with nursing needs, admission rates, whether there is a manager in post, and if the home has an embargo on it preventing it from taking new residents). Descriptive statistics for measures used in the analysis are reported in Table 4.6.1.

Methods

We first estimated a growth mixture model, a form of regression analysis that accounts for time-invariant home characteristics (fixed effects) and different trajectories of hospitalization among care homes over time. We then undertook a random

TABLE 4.6.1 Descriptive statistics for measures used in the study

Variable	Measurement	Mean	SD	Median	IQR
Hospital admissions per occupied bed	0.013	0.019	0.00	0.022	–
Total care hours (carer + registered nurse)	Ratio (total care hours/occupied beds)	27.8	5.46	27.37	5.77
Skills mix: Proportion of total care hours provided by registered nurses	Ratio (nursing hours/total care hours)	0.202	0.057	0.201	0.079
Proportion of planned nursing hours actually worked	Ratio (weekly worked nursing hours/weekly planned hours)	1.06	0.26	1.008	0.228
Share of agency nurses	Ratio (agency/weekly nursing hours)	0.225	0.204	0.187	0.31
Share of agency carers	Ratio (agency/weekly care hours)	0.0730	0.102	0.026	0.1139
Manager in post	Weekly records (0—no manager in post, 1—manager in post)	0.918	0.271	1	–
Planned care hours per occupied bed	Ratio (planned care hours/occupied beds)	26.141	5.344	25.65	5.943
Occupancy rate	Ratio (occupied beds/available beds)	0.88	0.2	0.891	0.172
Share of total number of beds that are for residents with nursing needs	Ratio (nursing/all beds)	0.397	0.192	0.39	0.261
Total number of beds in a care home	Number	63.31	32.723	52.0	33
Average admissions	Average daily admissions (number of residents) per week	0.131	0.19	0.143	0.156
Homes under embargo	Percentage of homes under embargo for at least one week during the observation period	0.155	0.255	0	–

Sample: 33,852 weekly care home observations across 186 care homes with nursing

forest (RF) analysis, a form of supervised machine learning. Data were split into training and test datasets. The model from the training data (75% of the data) was used to predict the outcomes in the test dataset (25% of the data), a process known as cross-validation. The RF algorithm uses bootstrapped samples from the training data to fit a series of decision tree models. It systematically compares model results, selecting those with the lowest mean squared errors (MSE) before averaging results from the best-fitting models. The training dataset model is then applied to the test dataset to check predictive accuracy. The results tell us the importance of nurse staffing and other variables in predicting hospitalizations (often described as "feature importance") and can be used to generate an accumulated local effects (ALE) plot that describes the relationship between nurse staffing and hospitalizations while controlling for other variables. Additionally, we generated individual conditional expectations (ICE) to examine how relationships in individual homes diverge from or conform to the average relationship revealed by the ALE plot (although we do not report the ICE plot due to space constraints). Overviews of the machine learning methods used can be found in Molnar (2022). We selected RF over other machine learning algorithms (e.g., artificial neural networks) due to the availability of tools like ICE and ALE plots to open the "black box" of ML analysis.

Results

Figure 4.12 illustrates the marginal effects of the relationship between skill mix and hospitalizations, as derived from the growth mixture model. It shows a statistically significant but quantitatively small linear relationship between hospitalizations and skill mix. The key finding is that when less care is provided by nurses, the risk of hospitalization is greater, but the effect size is quite small. Doubling the proportion of care provided by nurses in a care home with 30 nursing beds would reduce the

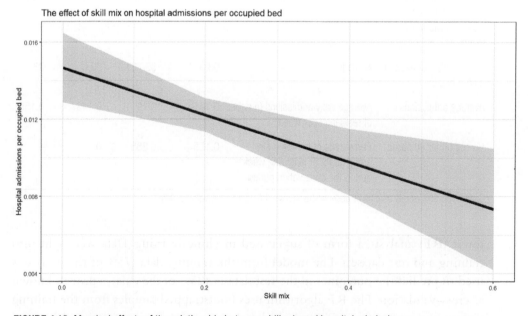

FIGURE 4.12 Marginal effects of the relationship between skill mix and hospital admissions.

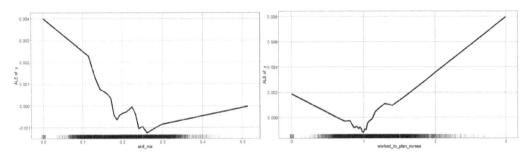

FIGURE 4.13 ALE plots showing the relationship between the weekly incidence of hospital admissions, skills mix (left panel), and the proportion of planned nursing hours actually worked (right panel).

rate of hospitalizations from around 1 in 67 per occupied bed/week to around 1 in 80, a reduction of around 3.5 hospitalizations a year.

The equivalent ALE plot from RF analysis is reported in Figure 4.13. Before examining Figure 4.13 in more detail, let's consider the feature importance scores reported in Table 4.6.2. The feature importance score for each feature (variable)

TABLE 4.6.2 Feature importance scores and model diagnostics from RF analysis

	Feature importance score (permutation error, decrease in model accuracy if a given feature is excluded from the model)	
Skills mix: Proportion of total care hours provided by registered nurses	0.011	
Proportion of planned nursing hours actually worked	0.011	
Total care hours (carer + registered nurse)	0.011	
Share of agency nurses	> 0.000	
Share of agency carers	> 0.000	
Manager in post	> 0.000	
Planned care hours per occupied bed	> 0.000	
Occupancy rate	0.011	
Number of beds in home	0.012	
Share of nursing beds	0.011	
Admissions	> 0.000	
Home under embargo	> 0.000	
Model diagnostics	**Training**	**Test**
% Variance explained	9.03	6.27
Mean of squared residuals	0.0003	0.0004

represents the absolute increase in MSE (also reported in Table 4.6.2) that would occur if a variable were removed from the analysis. The baseline MSE is 0.0004. If skill mix were to be removed from the model, the feature importance score of 0.011 for skill mix suggests that MSE for the model would increase to 0.0114. Although both of these numbers represent a relatively low MSE (i.e., the predictive accuracy of both models would be relatively high), the increase in MSE in percentage terms from removing skill mix would be very large. Table 4.6.2 shows that skill mix, total care hours, and the proportion of planned nursing hours actually worked all have a relatively large impact on the predictive accuracy of the RF models. By contrast, whether or not there was a manager in post, the proportion of nursing and carer hours worked by agency nurses and carers has no impact on the predictive accuracy of the models.

Turning now to the ALE plots in Figure 4.13, we observe that in contrast to the linear relationship in Figure 4.12, these suggest a broadly V-shaped relationship, with hospitalization risk lowest when around a quarter of care is provided by nurses. As mean skill mix for the sample is 0.201, this suggests the home provider would reduce hospitalization risk if they employed a fifth more nurses. However, the lower panel suggests that hospitalization rates are lowest when homes have the amount of nurse staffing that they planned to have and are higher when homes are both short-staffed and over-staffed. In other words, increasing nurse employment beyond what is already planned would not necessarily reduce hospitalization risk.

Combining these results with our domain knowledge of the home provider and its operations, we infer that the professional judgments of senior nurses and managers who plan nurse staffing levels have been effective in optimizing care given available resources. If the homes had less nursing care, care quality would likely suffer. However, increasing staffing beyond the planned level probably does not improve quality because the systems, processes, and behaviors for organizing and delivering care are not configured to make efficient use of the additional resources. If different (greater) levels of resources were routinely available, it might be possible to reconfigure care delivery so that quality improved, but these results suggest that increasing skill mix beyond currently planned levels within the existing system and organization of care is unlikely to result in a reduced rate of hospital admissions.

We found no relationships between agency nurse use and hospitalization risk. Combining this insight with the above results suggests that resources devoted to agency nurse use are well-targeted because risks to residents are lowest when homes have their planned amount of nurses, whether these nurses are permanent employees or provided by an agency.

Challenge 2: SHAP analysis to inform strategic decisions about resourcing priorities

So far, our analysis has identified average relationships between staffing factors and hospitalization risk. However, given nursing shortages, managers need to decide where to prioritize the allocation of scarce nursing resources. Therefore, we wanted to see if we could use ML to inform resource prioritization. We employed SHAP (Shapley additive explanations) analysis, a type of local explanatory ML analysis that can identify patterns in selected care homes relative to average predictions from ALE plots. Specifically, we used a variant of SHAP analysis called TreeSHAP, adjusted for ensemble methods such as RF and gradient boosting (Lundberg et al., 2020). We asked the care home provider to suggest a group of homes that were similar to each other but unusual in the context of the provider's wider portfolio. They suggested a group of four homes. Key differences between this group of four and the average characteristics of all homes are summarized in columns five, six, and seven of Table 4.6.3. The four homes have a lower skill mix, are much more likely to experience nursing shortages, have higher occupancy rates, have a higher share of beds where residents have nursing care needs, and are smaller. The provider also told us that these homes cater predominantly to residents with dementia and, in contrast to the wider portfolio, almost all residents are self-funding.

We attempted SHAP analysis on five nurse-sensitive indicators of care quality, although statistically valid results returned were obtained only for the falls and medication errors. Here, we focus on falls. The average number of falls per occupied bed per week for all homes is around 0.03. By contrast, the rate in the subgroup of four homes is double this at around 0.06, which equates to around 59 additional falls per year per home. Interestingly, senior staff from the care home provider (and other providers we shared the results with) all expected to see higher rates of falls in homes caring for older people with dementia. Further, they suggested that low rates of falls in this type of home could actually be undesirable because the only way to prevent falls would be to restrict the freedom and autonomy of residents to move around the home in ways that they considered incompatible with a person-centered philosophy of care.

The SHAP analysis results, reported in column two of Table 4.6.3, challenge this professional judgment, as they suggest that a lower skill mix, nurse shortages, and high occupancy rates all accounted for considerable proportions of the higher fall rate. These results imply that more nurses in these four homes would likely result in fewer falls. The broad point here is that SHAP analysis identifies staffing-related quality risks that are not visible to care home experts charged with overseeing care quality. While the results of SHAP analysis should not be used mechanistically

TABLE 4.6.3 SHAP analysis results for falls and medication errors

	1. PHI (SHAP value, falls)	2. % of difference explained, falls	3. PHI (SHAP value, medication errors)	4. % of difference explained, medication errors	5. Local value	6. Average value	7. Local average
Skill mix	0.00007	36.64%	0.00002	36.40%	0.194	0.2022	−0.008
Worked to plan nurses	0.00002	10.89%	0.00001	20.63%	0.763	1.0598	−0.297
Agency carers	0.00002	10.60%	0.00002	37.58%	0.049	0.0730	−0.024
Number of beds	−0.00001	−4.62%	−0.000004	−7.29%	46	63.310	−17.31
Occupancy	0.00004	21.69%	−0.00001	−16.18%	1.0	0.8796	0.120
Nursing beds, share	0.00004	19.38%	> 0.00000	5.16%	0.565	0.3968	0.168
Total hours per bed	0.00001	5.41%	0.00001	23.71%	26.805	27.80	−0.995

Note: Columns 1 and 3 report SHAPley values derived by the payout of the given predictor in a game theory specification of the SHAP analysis. There is no straightforward interpretation of these numbers, but we include them as an output of the analysis for information.

because the relationships we identify are not necessarily causal, they suggest lines of inquiry (i.e., what are the root causes of falls in the four-home group?), which might allow care quality to be more proactively managed, facilitating more effective targeting of managerial attention and limited nursing resources to identify and address issues of quality and optimize use of available resources.

Conclusions

While a traditional regression modeling approach suggests that the risk of hospitalization will be lower with greater nursing input into care, RF analysis points to a V-shaped relationship between nursing shortages and hospitalization risk. The implication of the first finding is that it would be desirable for care homes to employ more nurses (which is neither affordable nor realistic given nursing shortages), while the latter suggests that nurses and managers are doing an effective job of optimizing their available resources. The difference arises because the data does not fit the linear regression model particularly well, and regression methods are unable to detect the underlying non-linear relationship. Different methods lead us to quite different conclusions about the effectiveness of workforce planning and the staffing levels needed to ensure quality. The chapter has also highlighted how SHAP analysis could be used to manage risk and help organizations focus resources and managerial attention on areas where interventions might make the most difference by highlighting issues that might be missed otherwise.

In summary, we have demonstrated the potential of machine learning as a tool for testing relationships between workforce factors and aspects of quality and performance to inform strategy implementation. Based on our results, we believe that in situations where the aim of the researcher is to operationalize a plausible structural model of a data-generating process, machine learning is preferable to traditional regression methods. However, these methods are not without limitations. Causal inference methods (experimental or quasi-experimental research designs) would be needed to draw stronger causal inferences about how staffing levels and planned changes to workforce configuration cause quality and performance.

References

Avrahami, D., Pessach, D., Singer, G., & Chalutz Ben-Gal, H. (2022). A human resources analytics and machine-learning examination of turnover: Implications for theory and practice. International Journal of Manpower, 43(6), 1405–1424.

Backhaus, R., Verbeek, H., van Rossum, E., Capezuti, E., & Hamers, J. P. H. (2014). Nurse staffing impact on quality of care in nursing homes: A systematic review of longitudinal studies. *Journal of the American Medical Directors Association*, 15(6), 383–393.

Bock, L. (2015). *Work rules*. John Murray.

Brieman, L. (2001). Statistical modelling: The two cultures. *Statistical Science*, 16(3), 199–231.

Choudhury, P., Allen, R. T., & Endres, M. G. (2021). Machine learning for pattern discovery in management research. *Strategic Management Journal, 42*, 30–57.

Clemens, S., Wodchis, W., McGilton, K., McGrail, K., & McMahon, M, (2021). The relationship between quality and staffing in long-term care: A systematic review of the literature 2008–2020. *International Journal of Nursing Studies, 122*(3), 104036. https://doi.org/10.1016 /j.ijnurstu.2021.104036

CMA. (2017). *Care homes market study.* https://www.gov.uk/cma-cases/care-homes-market-study

CQC. (2021). *The state of adult health and social care 2020/21.* Care Quality Commission. Retrieved May 27, 2022, from https://www.cqc.org.uk/sites/default/files/20211021 _stateofcare2021_print.pdf

Donabedian, A. (2003). *An introduction to quality assurance in Health Care.* Oxford University Press.

Huselid, M. A. (2018). The science and practice of workforce analytics: Introduction to the HRM special issue. *Human Resource Management, 57*(3), 679–684.

Jörden, N. M., Sage, D., & Trusson, C. (2021). 'It's so fake': Identity performances and cynicism within a people analytics team. *Human Resource Management Journal, 32*(2), 1–16. https:// doi.org/10.1111/1748-8583.12412

Leavitt, K., Schabram, K., Hariharan, P., & Barnes, C. M. (2021). 'Ghost in the machine: On organizational theory in the age of machine learning'. *Academy of Management Review, 46*(4), 750–777.

Levenson, A. (2018). Using workforce analytics to improve strategy execution. *Human Resource Management, 57*(3), 685–700.

Levenson, A., & Fink, A. (2017). Human capital analytics: Too much data and analysis, not enough models and business insights. *Journal of Organizational Effectiveness People and Performance, 4*(2), 159–170.

Lundberg, S. M., Erion, G., Chen, H., DeGrave, A., Prutkin, J. M., Nair, B., Katz, R., Himmelfarb, J., Bansal, N., & Lee, S. I. (2020). From local explanations to global understanding with explainable AI for trees. *Nature Machine Intelligence, 2*(1), 56–67.

Minbaeva, D. B. (2018). Building credible human capital analytics for organizational competitive advantage. *Human Resource Management, 57*(3), 701–713.

Molnar, C. (2022). Interpretable machine learning: A guide for making black box models explainable (2nd ed.). Independently published.

Rasmussen, T., & Ulrich, D. (2015). Learning from practice: How HR analytics avoids being a management fad. *Organizational Dynamics, 44*(3), 236–242.

Skills for Care. (2021). *The state of the adult social care sector and workforce in England 2021.* Skills for Care. Retrieved March 7, 2022, from https://www.skillsforcare.org.uk/adult-social-care -workforce-data-old/Workforce-intelligence/documents/State-of-the-adult-social-care -sector/The-State-of-the-Adult-Social-Care-Sector-and-Workforce-2021.pdf

Spilsbury, K., Hewitt, C., Stirk, L., & Bowman, C. (2011). The relationship between nurse staffing and quality of care in nursing homes: A systematic review. International Journal of Nursing Studies, 48(6), 732–750.

Whitney, P. (2021). Care home industry sector report. *Hallidays.* Retrieved March 7, 2022, from https://www.hallidays.co.uk/views-and-insight/sector-report/care-home-industry

Connecting employee survey data to organizational performance indicators using micro-macro multilevel regression

Marc van Veldhoven and Sasa Batistic

Introduction to context/HR business question

Many organizations employ yearly employee surveys to monitor employee attitudes and engagement. Indeed, a specialized line of HR consultancy exists to assist organizations with employee survey design, data collection, processing, results feedback, discussion, and action follow-up (Knapp & Mujtaba, 2010; Huebner & Zacher, 2021). Several rationales underpin such employee survey-based processes of results feedback, discussion, and action follow-up. For example, how employees think and feel about their work and employment conditions, their team, their supervisor, and the organization as a whole is expected to influence their work engagement and work behaviors, thus impacting the effort invested in and the level and quality of their individual performance, and ultimately contributing to organizational performance (Cascio & Boudreau, 2010; Fulmer et al., 2003). This reasoning also underlies the HR process model (Nishii & Wright, 2008). Another rationale, more geared toward service organizations, is rooted in the service-profit chain (Heskett et al., 1994). It suggests that employees' experiences of the organizational service climate affect their attitudes and behaviors toward customers, thereby influencing positive financial returns for the organization through customer loyalty.

A common step in employee survey reporting involves aggregating survey results to the organizational level (used here as an equivalent for any relevant organizational grouping, such as teams, business units, or locations) and subsequently determining how such data might serve as indicators for "key drivers" or predictors of relevant

DOI: 10.4324/9781003190097-13

outcomes. When no actual organizational-level indicators are available for such "key driver analysis," researchers use employee survey-based aggregate scores of work engagement and/or work behaviors (Scherbaum et al., 2010; Macey et al., 2011). However, the literature commonly mentions that more "objective" organizational outcome indicators would be ideal (Schneider et al., 1998; Harter et al., 2002). These analyses connecting employee survey data to organizational-level performance indicators align nicely with the balanced scorecard/HR scorecard approaches proposed by Kaplan and Norton (1992) and Becker et al. (2001). In these approaches, indicators from various very different management domains within an organization (e.g., HR management, financial management, customer relations management) are brought together to optimize management vis-à-vis the multiple goals necessary for the organization to be successful and survive. Probably the most basic question in this context is whether employee survey information can indeed be used to predict and improve financial and/or customer-related outcomes (Schneider et al., 2003; van de Voorde et al., 2010).

Over the past decades, researchers have developed a useful set of analytical techniques for this purpose: multilevel regression. This approach connects independent variables (IVs) and dependent variables (DVs) across multiple levels of measurement. The analysis that we just mentioned—predicting financial and customer-related outcome indicators of organizations (DV) based on individual employee survey responses of the members of these organizations (IV)—is specifically referred to as micro-macro multilevel analysis. The terminology reflects the use of micro-level antecedents (e.g., individual employee survey responses) to predict macro-level outcomes (e.g., organization-level performance indicators) (Croon & van Veldhoven, 2007; Preacher et al., 2010).

In the following section, we present a brief illustration of micro-macro multilevel regression using data from a large financial services institution in the Netherlands.

Data/method

Data and context description

A type of industry that is particularly focused on financial returns and customer relations is the financial services sector. Therefore, several attempts at connecting employee survey data to organization-level performance indicators have emerged over time based on data from this specific type of industry (Mirvis & Lawler, 1977; Gelade & Young, 2005; Van de Voorde et al., 2010).

Our study focuses on a financial services institution that gradually developed its adaptation of a balanced scorecard system from the 1990s onward. This project required a lot of coordination between various management departments within the organization and involved numerous external experts (for example, university staff, data processing service providers, etc.), with each management department reaching out to their connected experts. For more background on our data context, see van Veldhoven (2005). The institution designed its balanced scorecard system to deliver optimal information at the level of individual locations, or "local branches." These branches perform similar business activities but operate in different regions of the Netherlands.

For our analysis, we connect data from "HR management" to "financial management" and "marketing" areas. The finances and control department coordinated business indicators (including financial performance), while the marketing department managed customer relations indicators. From all the indicators available, we choose to work with yearly financial productivity as our financial indicator of choice and customer loyalty as our customer relations indicator of choice.

We calculate financial productivity as the sum of all revenues deriving from banking in a local branch divided by the sum of all costs involved in banking (operations and depreciation). Customer loyalty is derived from annual customer interviews conducted for each branch, representing a weighted score based on customers' likelihood to recommend the bank to others, intention to stay with the bank, and perception of the bank's prices as acceptable. The HR department coordinates the employee survey, which has evolved to cover a wide range of topics through collaborations with academic groups in the Netherlands (co-creation). For illustration purposes, we selected a range of scales from the survey covering job satisfaction and possible predictors related to job characteristics and social organization: learning opportunities on the job, work pressure, people-oriented leadership, vision, and strategy. All of the employee survey scales were derived from the Questionnaire on the Experience and Evaluation of Work (van Veldhoven & Meijman, 1994; van Veldhoven et al., 2015).

What are the challenges of these data and how can methods help?

The indicators for financial productivity and customer loyalty are measured at the level of the local branches. This is a common situation in cross-level research where such organizational outcomes are available only at level 2, e.g., the organizational unit studied (Combs et al., 2006; Van De Voorde et al., 2010). Here, level 2 concerns local branches, but in other contexts, it may be teams, employee groups, jobs, professional groups, etc. Data about employees' attitudes and behaviors, which serve as predictors here, are usually measured at the individual level, level 1 (Edwards & Edwards, 2019).

This creates a complicated scenario where there is a mismatch in the measurement unit, which can result in the application of biased analysis and in theoretical problems. For example, when a theory proposed at the individual level (level 1) is applied at an aggregate level (level 2) without consideration (Hox, 2010; Klein & Kozlowski, 2000). Two common solutions are used in practice to solve the problem of how to analyze data measured at different levels. Both have flaws. This is elaborated and illustrated extensively in Croon and van Veldhoven (2007). We briefly repeat this here.

The first solution is to assign every case at level 1 (here, individual employees) a score for the level 2 variable. All individuals in an organizational unit (here: local branches) then receive the same value for the level 2 variable. This boosts the number of cases available for analysis while simultaneously manipulating the variance in the level 2 variable such that it is substantially smaller than it would have been if the level 2 variable had indeed been measured at level 1 (rather than assigning all individuals in a unit the same score). This solution is called *disaggregation*, and it is best avoided altogether as it is manipulative.

The other solution takes the reverse approach: All observations within an organizational unit are aggregated, usually using a mean score across all the level 1 observations within a level 2 unit. Here, we would compute mean scores for all employees in a local branch on job satisfaction, work pressure, etc., and then analyze these mean scores regarding the local branch-level outcome indicators. This solution is called *aggregation*, and it is less problematic than the disaggregation approach, but not without risk. Croon and van Veldhoven (2007) show that under certain conditions, an aggregation approach can lead to false conclusions, especially when the number of observations at level 1 or level 2 is small and when the survey scale under investigation has low levels of shared variance from one unit to the next.

Based on the limitations mentioned here, an alternative was developed and is now commonly available in multilevel analysis software (Preacher et al., 2010). This alternative is called micro-macro multilevel analysis. While this is not the place to discuss its technical details, it is best thought of as an improved variant of the "aggregation method" mentioned above. Rather than using the mean as the indicator for the level 1 variable, a "latent variable" is estimated that takes into account both the mean and the variance of the individual responses within an organizational unit.

Specific analytical method used

The data set we analyze here as an example consists of two hierarchically nested levels: 14,625 employees (level 1) nested within 175 local branches (level 2). This means there are about 112 (responding) employees in each local branch (on average), where the standard deviation is 70. The finance and control/marketing departments proposed using several control variables in our analysis. Bigger branches can be expected to generate higher financial productivity based on efficiency that is unrelated to productivity itself but more related to the scale of operations. Also, bigger branches offer more differentiated services that can be expected to generate more customer loyalty. We, therefore, use a dummy variable for "branch size" (small = 0, big = 1) as a control variable in the analysis. Similarly, it can be argued that customer loyalty can be expected to be higher when the local branch is in a rural rather than an urban area. Hence, we also employ a dummy variable for "branch location" (urban = 0, rural = 1).

The data are nested, and such data violate the assumption of data independence that underlies normal regression. Respondents within one organizational unit share similar circumstances, which are expected to be reflected in their attitudes and experiences. From one respondent to the next, the observations are therefore not independent but related systematically. The recommended approach is to use hierarchical linear modeling or multilevel regression to test for cross-level relationships. When individual (level 1) data predict outcomes at a higher level (level 2), this is referred to as micro-macro multilevel regression (Croon & van Veldhoven, 2007) or 1–2 models (Preacher et al., 2010). The basic idea of such an approach is to partition the variance of a variable in nested data into two latent components, the *between (organizations)* and the *within (organizations)* components. Basically, this means that variables assessed at level 2 have only between-component variance, and variables assessed at level 1 typically have both between and within components (Croon & van Veldhoven, 2007; Preacher et al., 2010). The assumption behind this rationale is that the between-organization component of a level 1 variable can substantially and reliably reflect the shared attitudes/behaviors/engagement of employees in local branches. If the above approach is used with structural equation multilevel modeling on raw data, explicit centering of observed predictor variables (e.g., group mean centering) is not required (Preacher et al., 2010). Lastly, it is worth noting that not all statistical packages allow for the prediction of outcomes on a higher level (e.g., branch absenteeism) (see MPlus or R for some exceptions).

Results of the data example

The results of the micro-macro multilevel modeling are shown in Table 4.7.1, and a simplified version is presented graphically in Figure 4.14, where the strength of the association between variables is represented by the line thickness.

Regarding customer loyalty, both control variables appear to matter, with customer loyalty at higher levels when the local branch is big and rural. Of the survey measures, only job satisfaction is significantly and positively related to customer loyalty. For financial productivity, the picture is different. Neither of the two control variables is significantly related to it. However, three out of four survey measures are associated. Work pressure is positively and significantly related to financial productivity, as is vision and strategy. On the other hand, people-oriented leadership is negatively and significantly related to financial productivity.

TABLE 4.7.1 Micro-macro multilevel results for financial productivity and customer loyalty

Variable	Outcome: financial productivity			Outcome: customer loyalty		
	Estimate	Standard error	p-value	Estimate	Standard error	p-value
Predictors						
Learning opportunities	0.005	0.005	0.290	−0.009	0.022	0.680
Work pressure	0.012	0.003	**0.000**	0.001	0.011	0.957
People-oriented leadership	−0.008	0.003	**0.004**	0.004	0.011	0.688
Vision and strategy	0.009	0.002	**0.000**	0.009	0.006	0.127
Job satisfaction	−0.006	0.007	0.364	0.059	0.029	**0.044**
Control variables						
Small/big local branch	0.030	0.019	0.114	−0.678	0.067	**0.000**
Urban/rural local branch	0.011	0.017	0.518	0.232	0.069	**0.001**

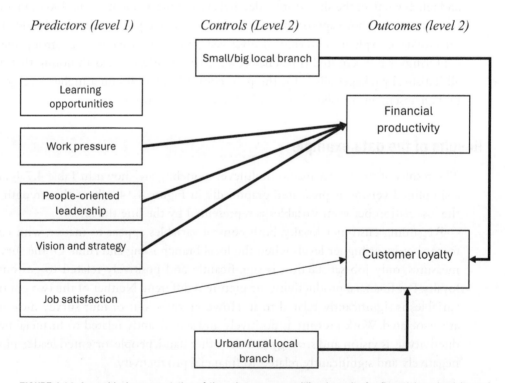

FIGURE 4.14 A graphical representation of the micro-macro multilevel results for financial productivity and customer loyalty. *Note:* The strength of the association between variables is represented by the line thickness. Thick lines represent associations that are significant at p<0.001. Thin lines represent associations that are significant at p<0.05.

Interpretation/implications

For the control variables, findings were as expected for customer loyalty but not for financial performance. There is no evidence in these data that larger branches are operating more efficiently and hence demonstrating a more positive ratio between revenues and costs (e.g., productivity). The finding that job satisfaction is associated with customer loyalty is completely consistent with the argument in the service–profit chain (Heskett et al., 1994). The results for financial productivity as positively associated with pressure are interpretable as evidence that work intensification contributes to positive organizational outcomes (Van de Voorde et al., 2012). In the literature on organizational climate, employee survey scores that evaluate the organization's vision and strategy positively can be interpreted as indicative of shared ideas about goals and means towards success of the business, so the finding that this correlates in our case with financial productivity aligns with expectations as based on Kopelman et al. (1990).

So far, all findings aligned with expectations both in the literature and among the professionals involved in our practical case. The one finding that did not immediately make sense was the significance of people-oriented leadership, but negatively. How can bad leadership be associated with good financial productivity? On closer inspection, however, it turned out that this is not how the results should be interpreted. For the people-oriented leadership scale, an average score in a local branch would have to be (far) below the midpoint of the scale to be interpreted as bad in an absolute sense. On a scale from 0 to 100, the score would need to be 50 or (considerably) lower. All the local branches in our cases scored an average between 56 and 87, with the overall mean across branches at 75. Compared to other organizations (external benchmarking; van Veldhoven et al., 2015), this is very good. There is not a single branch with bad people-oriented leadership. Then, what does the correlation with financial productivity mean? An easy way of saying it would be that compared to branches where employees deem leadership to be their very best friend, branches where employees rate their leadership as just friendly perform better financially. This was when everyone in the room started nodding that the results were actually very understandable.

We need to be careful not to attribute any causality to the findings and interpretations just mentioned. It is probably best to see the survey items that appear to be associated with business performance as potential areas for further attention, either because these are indicative of factors that contribute to (sustained) good performance or because these are areas for potential investment/improvement for the organization with an eye toward increasing performance.

Brief concluding summary/telling story

While employee surveys are often considered to be "soft data," in comparison to "hard data" like sales, costs, or profits, such "soft data" are to some extent systematically connected to business performance indicators and are hence highly relevant for HR management because they include pointers on how the human factor in the organization connects to the business.

In our data example, we found that when the proper multilevel regression method is used, findings mostly align with general theory in the area of the service-profit chain, the balanced-scorecard approach, and the HR process model. If one runs into an exception (like we did for people-oriented leadership), it is important to move from general models to local theory (Karasek & Theorell, 1990) and build one's own interpretation of how a human factor (like people-oriented leadership) aligns with the business. In this specific company, management needed to become aware of the possibility of non-linear effects, e.g., too much of a good thing, where people-oriented leadership is concerned.

References

Becker, B. E., Huselid, M. A., Huselid, M. A., & Ulrich, D. (2001). *The HR scorecard: Linking people, strategy, and performance.* Harvard Business Press.

Cascio, W., & Boudreau, J. (2010). *Investing in people: Financial impact of human resource initiatives.* Ft Press.

Combs, J., Liu, Y., Hall, A., & Ketchen, D. (2006). How much do high-performance work practices matter? A meta-analysis of their effects on organizational performance. *Personnel Psychology, 59*(3), 501–528.

Croon, M. A., & van Veldhoven, M. J. (2007). Predicting group-level outcome variables from variables measured at the individual level: A latent variable multilevel model. *Psychological Methods, 12*(1), 45.

Edwards, M. R., & Edwards, K. (2019). *Predictive HR analytics: Mastering the HR metric.* Kogan Page Publishers.

Fulmer, I. S., Gerhart, B., & Scott, K. S. (2003). Are the 100 best better? An empirical investigation of the relationship between being a "great place to work" and firm performance. *Personnel Psychology, 56*(4), 965–993.

Gelade, G. A., & Young, S. (2005). Test of a service profit chain model in the retail banking sector. *Journal of Occupational and Organizational Psychology, 78*(1), 1–22.

Harter, J. K., Schmidt, F. L., & Hayes, T. L. (2002). Business-unit-level relationship between employee satisfaction, employee engagement, and business outcomes: A meta-analysis. *Journal of Applied Psychology, 87*(2), 268.

Hox, J. J. (2010). *Multilevel analysis. Techniques and applications* (2nd ed.). Routledge.

Huebner, L. A., & Zacher, H. (2021). Effects of action planning after employee surveys. *Journal of Personnel Psychology, 21*(1), 23–36.

James, L., Jones, T. O., Loveman, G. W., Earl Sasser, Jr. W., & Schlesinger, L. A. (1994, March–April). Putting the service profit chain to work. *Harvard Business Review, 72*(2), 164–174.

Karasek, R., & Theorell, T. (1990). *Healthy work.* New York: Basic Books.

Kaplan, R. S., & Norton, D. P. (1992). The balanced scorecard: Measures that drive performance. *Harvard Business Review, 83*(7), 172.

Klein, K. J., & Kozlowski, S. W. J. (2000). From micro to meso: Critical steps in conceptualizing and conducting multilevel research. *Organizational Research Methods, 3*(3), 211–236.

Knapp, P., & Mujtaba, B. (2010). Designing, administering, and utilizing an employee attitude survey. *Journal of Behavioral Studies in Business, 2*(1), 1–14.

Kopelman, R. E., Brief, A. P., & Guzzo, R. A. (1990). The role of climate and culture in productivity. In B. Schneider (Ed.), *Organizational climate and culture* (pp. 282–318). Jossey-Bass.

Macey, W. H., Schneider, B., Barbera, K. M., & Young, S. A. (2011). *Employee engagement: Tools for analysis, practice, and competitive advantage.* John Wiley & Sons.

Mirvis, P. H., & Lawler, E. E. (1977). Measuring the financial impact of employee attitudes. *Journal of Applied Psychology, 62*(1), 1.

Nishii, L. H., & Wright, P. (2008). Variability at multiple levels of analysis: Implications for strategic human resource management. In D. B. Smith (Ed.), *The people make the place* (pp. 225–248). Erlbaum.

Preacher, K. J., Zyphur, M. J., & Zhang, Z. (2010). A general multilevel SEM framework for assessing multilevel mediation. *Psychological Methods, 15*(3), 209–233.

Scheider, B., White, S. S., & Paul, M. C. (1998). Linking service climate and customer perceptions of service quality: Test of a causal model. *Journal of Applied Psychology, 83*(2), 150–163.

Scherbaum, C. A., Putka, D. J., Naidoo, L. J., & Youssefnia, D. (2010). Key driver analyses: Current trends, problems, and alternative approaches. In S. Albrecht (Ed.), *Handbook of employee engagement.* Chapter 15, pp 182–196. Edward Elgar Publishing.

Schneider, B., Hanges, P. J., Smith, D. B., & Salvaggio, A. N. (2003). Which comes first: Employee attitudes or organizational financial and market performance? *Journal of Applied Psychology, 88*(5), 836.

Van De Voorde, K., Paauwe, J., & Van Veldhoven, M. (2010). Predicting business unit performance using employee surveys: Monitoring HRM-related changes. *Human Resource Management Journal, 20*(1), 44–63.

Van De Voorde, K., Paauwe, J., & Van Veldhoven, M. (2012). Employee well-being and the HRM–organizational performance relationship: A review of quantitative studies. *International Journal of Management Reviews, 14*(4), 391–407.

van Veldhoven, M. (2005). Financial performance and the long-term link with HR practices, work climate and job stress. *Human Resource Management Journal, 15*(4), 30–53.

Van Veldhoven, M., & Meijman, M. (1994). The measurement of psychosocial job demands. NIA.

Van Veldhoven, M., Prins, J., Van der Laken, P., & Dijkstra, L. (2015). QEEW2.0: 42 short scales for survey research on work, well-being, and performance. SKB.

4.8

Key takeaways

Martin R. Edwards

ACAI and conducting the right analyses

As discussed in the introduction of this chapter, the potential range of approaches an analyst could utilize when analyzing workforce data is considerable, with some simpler than others and some more complex. In the examples discussed above, when considering what approach to take, we are directed to a degree by the nature of the data and the analytic question we are trying to answer. If we are interested in identifying the existence of different sub-populations in our workforce population, we might use latent profiling (Chapter 4.2). If we are interested in connectivity patterns between employees, we may want to conduct ONA (Chapter 4.5). An analyst will use their judgment, of course, and they will be steered by their experience and expertise. An analyst with a data science background may take a different approach from a social scientist, for example. Consider the person-centered analysis approach: while a data scientist may prefer cluster analysis to explore sub-groups in a dataset, a social scientist may opt for latent profiling, which provides a greater array of outputs and statistics useful for testing "hypotheses."

It is not always the case that one approach is more "right" than another. However, there are some exceptions to this that might be determined by the assumptions inherent in particular statistical procedures and whether the analyses can actually do what the analyst intends when trying to answer a particular question. For example, running OLS multiple regression combining engagement survey data "predicting" performance appraisal ratings across an organization of 5,000 employees might seem straightforward and can easily be carried out with any statistical program. However, if the firm organizes its workforce into 200 teams with 200 different team leads/appraisers, the data/workforce will have an inherent grouping/multilevel structure that should be taken into account in the analyses (see Chapter 4.7, which addresses these issues with greater complexity). Thus, a straightforward OLS multiple regression analysis that treats the 5,000 employees as independent/unrelated cases may not be the "right" analysis. Also, just running multiple regression analyses predicting

DOI: 10.4324/9781003190097-14

"engagement" scores with a range of other survey items to highlight and demonstrate "key drivers" (something survey companies generally do) may not be the "right analyses." Using regression in this way assumes that it can imply causality, when in reality, such analysis is just running correlational analyses taking into account shared variance amongst the variables included. There are other analytic techniques (see Chapter 4.1) and indeed research designs that really need to be considered if an analyst wants to make stronger inferences about causality. This is not to say that multiple regression isn't a useful and informative tool in these examples, but whether it is the "right" analytic approach always needs to be asked (see the ACAI discussion in earlier chapters).

WFA applications and future

Implementation and change management

Sarah Kieran and Dana Minbaeva

Introduction

Over a decade ago, Garvin (2013) described one of the first workforce analytics (WFA) successes at Google, which involved reorienting management practices. This success aligned with the classic frame of Lewin's "unfreeze-change-refreeze" strategic change model (1947). Specifically, Garvin stressed the importance of incorporating analytics-driven change into organizational routines: "Project Oxygen … not only convinced its sceptical audience of Googlers that managers mattered but also identified, described, and *institutionalized* their most essential behaviours" (Garvin, 2013, p. 13; emphasis added).

However, numerous industry reports still claim that even the most successful WFA projects fail to lead to sustainable strategic change outcomes (Angrave et al., 2016; Van den Heuvel & Bondarouk, 2017). Indeed, as Rasmussen and Ulrich (2015) observed, "there is rarely a straight line from data and analysis to action" (p. 239). While there is not an enormous amount of evidence, estimates suggest that only one in five analytics projects is acted upon, and only one in eight initiates sustainable, long-lasting strategic change within an organization.

Why is it that although "HR Analytics may very well cause existential changes in the Human Resource Management function, and perhaps organizations as a whole" (Heuvel & Bondarouk, 2016, p. 6), most organizations struggle to translate analytics insights into the managerial actions needed to initiate, navigate, and successfully implement strategic change? We argue that this challenge stems from many organizations treating WFA activity as a standalone project, often separate from the organizational change and development plan, thus largely mirroring the popular linear, step-by-step model of planned strategic change. Many organizations suggest that, at best, it might intersect with planned change at critical junctures: beginning, middle, and end (Belizon & Kieran, 2022).

DOI: 10.4324/9781003190097-16

We propose an alternative perspective: to initiate sustainable change, WFA must be integrated into collective sensemaking and articulated through purposeful storytelling. This approach aims to create actionable narratives about how variations in human capital impact business outcomes within specific organizational contexts. With this in mind, and by acknowledging WFA's potential to challenge individual and collective beliefs about how organizations create value, we find ourselves deeply immersed in contemporary perspectives of strategic change as *schema change*.

Sometimes schema change is triggered by a crisis, such as a new competitor entering the market. Sometimes the trigger is emergent, such as the recognition of employee dissatisfaction with the organizational style of leadership and culture. Regardless, there is always a trigger or cue, signalling that the existing schema, the old way of doing things, needs to change. To change the organizational-level schema, the individual-level schema of all members must change. This process involves the organization acting as an interpretive system, engaging individually and collectively in sensemaking.

Sensemaking is an important organizational process, popularized by Karl Weick in his book *Sensemaking in Organisations* in 1995. It is a contemporary perspective on change management, challenging much of what we have learned about the importance of having a plan or programme with key stages to manage change, as presented by Kotter (1996). Sensemaking has gained increasing attention in recent years as organizations become increasingly complex and uncertain, with change becoming a norm of organizational life.

When we consider the ACAI model, introduced in Chapter 1, we see how WFA acts as both the driver and an underpinning process of strategic change. In the "**A**sking the right questions" phase, organizations identify and better understand the need for change, which may even trigger change in some cases. As the right data is **C**ollected and **A**nalyzed, it assists change agents and other stakeholders in understanding the potential consequences of change, eventually arriving at some shared understanding and thereby **I**nfluencing the organization towards the right decisions. The sensemaking process is a crucial underlying mechanism that connects all phases of the ACAI model.

In this chapter, we explain and examine the critical linkages between WFA, sensemaking, and successful organizational change. We start with a brief overview of the strategic change literature, introduce the concept of organizational sensemaking, and outline the process and stages of sensemaking as they might interact with WFA.

Contemporary perspectives of strategic change

Strategic change is one of the most extensively researched phenomena in organizational science. Its definition as an organization "altering its alignment with its external environment" (Ven & Poole, 1995) positions strategic change as an "event," necessitated from time to time in an organization's life cycle. Consequently, traditional approaches to strategic change have employed planned programmes of transformation with a beginning, middle, and end.

There is, of course, a critical tension between the need to manage and control the strategic process and the upheaval strategic change creates within organizations. Therefore, many authors, such as Appelbaum et al. (2012) and Cummings et al. (2016), argue that tried and tested models, like those developed by Lewin (1947) and Kotter (1996), provide solid foundations for organizations to control, manage, and account for their strategic change efforts. Notably, these programmed approaches highlight the important role of using data – or, more broadly, evidence – at various points in the process to inform the vision for change, support the business case, track and monitor progress, and ultimately measure success.

However, despite a wealth of evidence on the dos and don'ts of strategic change, organizations continue to struggle to sustain successful organizational outcomes on the back of strategic change initiatives. Many organizational efforts fail, with reports indicating 30% to 70% are unsuccessful (Balogun & Hailey, 2008; Fay & Lührmann, 2004). Although deciding what to change is complex in itself, delivering on that vision is also an issue, as up to 50% of strategic decisions fail for reasons related to their implementation rather than formulation (Raes et al., 2011).

Thus, the last-century perspective that strategic change could be planned, directed, and managed through a wide range of implementation methods has been repeatedly challenged (Bartunek & Woodman, 2015). The very notion of a change plan, or that strategic change is an episodic event, is strongly criticized. Eminent authors (see Clegg, et al., 2021) call for organizations to consider fundamentally reframing and rethinking the processes used to understand, formulate, and implement strategic change initiatives.

Recently, we have begun to contemplate that certain management domains are not merely plans or programs to execute; rather, they represent dynamic organizational capabilities. For example, strategizing is increasingly viewed less as a plan and more as a practice within the organization. Instead of writing up a strategy, the focus is on engaging in ongoing strategic activities (Balogun et al., 2014).

Similarly, change is now viewed less as a staged plan and more as an interpretation, storytelling, or a series of conversations that need to occur within the organization. It involves rethinking what might be important for the organization and how it could be executed, considering factors such as who, when, and to what end. This perspective focusses on *schema change* as the foundation of strategic change (Brown et al., 2016; Maitlis & Christianson, 2014; Sandberg & Tsoukas, 2015). We elaborate on this concept below.

What is organizational sensemaking?

Sensemaking is defined as a process of cognitive interpretation and action triggered by an event for which organizational members have no existing mental model or schema (Gioia & Chittipeddi, 1991; Weick, 1995). Within organizations, sensemaking takes place at all levels and among all members. While individuals strive to comprehend ongoing changes, successful strategic change requires a collaborative effort. Sensemaking is fundamentally a collective and social activity (Bartunek et al., 2006; Cornelissen, 2012).

Sensemaking isn't a planned part of strategic change; it's non-linear and ongoing. It's an iterative, cyclical process without a clear beginning, middle, or end. In organizations, people often act quickly, sometimes without fully understanding the situation. Karl Weick suggests that action can precede full comprehension; true understanding often emerges only after action is taken. Understanding deepens as responses unfold, leading to the emergence of a new organizational framework and successful strategic change.

The sensemaking literature to date, particularly in the context of organizational strategy and strategic change, highlights the importance of achieving a *shared schema*. Organizational success hinges on members reaching a shared understanding of the present and future. This involves social sensemaking through dialogue, storytelling, and information exchange.

Through these interactions, stakeholders reflect and interpret, a process known as sensegiving (Gioia & Chittipeddi, 1991). During this process, they seek out information to help them make sense of things. This information may be both formal (reports, data, briefings) and informal (observations, events, stories). Increasingly, and of particular relevance to WFA in strategic change, we have come to understand that the sensemaking process is not about the distribution of meaning from leaders (or, in our case, the HR or WFA team) down through the organization. Instead, it facilitates the creation of shared schemata across all parts of the organization through the sensemaking processes.

Notably, entrenched schemas can impede renewal by limiting attention to familiar events. Therefore, for strategic change to occur, existing schemas must be disrupted, a process known as *sensebreaking*. Thus, sensemaking is both a response to change signals and a critical process for realizing the need for strategic change.

WFA as sensemaking

Let us start by looking at the stages of sensemaking in which the WFA team and its organizational stakeholders are expected to engage.

Envisioning (leadership sensemaking)

In organizations, strategic change typically (but not always) commences when senior leaders' sensemaking is triggered by their "noticing" the need for change. They assess relevant issues based on experience, knowledge, and their existing individual and collective schemas. Individually and collectively, they interpret and discuss, and eventually, they develop shared understandings and ultimately advance a plan for strategic change.

For envisioning to occur, however, senior leaders must be prompted in some way to change their existing schemas used for navigating organizational tasks and events (Gioia & Chittipeddi, 1991; Maitlis & Christianson, 2014). Some new cue or unequivocal event must signal the need for change. Such cues may come from scanning the external environment or discussing business development or strategy implementation. Though this scanning can occur naturally, it is also critical for senior leaders to challenge themselves to constantly scan the horizon and "uncover" new cues in their internal and external environments. It is proposed here that consistent application of and attention to WFA in organizations becomes an underpinning process in triggering the envisioning stage of sensemaking. This is relevant for the first phase of the ACAI model, where WFA teams are encouraged to ask the right questions.

WFA is best equipped to focus senior leaders' attention on various opportunities and challenges related to organizational human capital through phases two and three of the ACAI model – collecting the right data and conducting the right analysis. For example, establishing an interactive HR dashboard contributes to the scanning and review of existing organizational capabilities that could trigger the envisioning stage of sensemaking. Even the pure visualization and articulation of changes in human capital in printed reports could enable constructing and reconstructing interpretations at the top table, thereby assisting leadership sensemaking.

As automation, AI, and machine learning advance, they will assist in exposing potential "triggers" by combining and processing huge chunks of external and internal human capital data. For example, at the beginning of the COVID-19 pandemic, many organizations created a crisis management dashboard. Decision-makers needed accurate information about the workforce: who, how many, and where. Expatriates, international assignees, and mobile workers needed to be relocated quickly. Business leaders also needed detailed data about the temporary workforce or any other forms of nonstandard employment.

Some WFA teams decided to go one step further and map the workforce data against the publicly available COVID-19 datasets. In the Visier webinar "How to Use Analytics During the COVID-19 Crisis," Jeremy Shapiro explained, "You can show your leadership team where employees are and who is most at risk by embedding public data into your systems." Further, there were also examples of WFA teams creating their own risk assessment index. One of the analysts explained,

Demographic data could be a good starting point: we know age and gender matters; in some instances, we have medical records or sickness leaves; we know their location. To that we could add the nature of their work in terms of exposure to many people, the need for physical contact, the need of relocation, etc. Soon you will have enough data to calculate the actual trend in employees' infection rates based on job role, location, etc.

WFA can also provide focussed cues, zooming in managerial attention to a specific area that needs change or at least managerial attention, phase four of ACAI: Influence the right decisions. For example, at Maersk Drilling, the WFA team joined forces with health and safety experts to investigate how many injuries could be prevented by increasing various aspects of employee engagement. The team researched engagement, managerial commitment, and safety. It generated a model connecting safety climate at the organizational level, personal knowledge and motivation, safety performance, safety violations, and injuries. It found connections between estimates of training, aspects of engagement, and incidents ("near-misses"), as well as incidents with injuries and fatalities. The WFA lead of this project commented,

> We communicated the finding to different stakeholders and subsequently to the broader Maersk community through our intranet. I cannot describe the direct impact of this study [on initiating a specific change program]. ... However, showing a clear link between aspects of employee engagement, especially managerial commitment and safety performance, has surely helped drive an agenda of "employee commitment matters."

For WFA functions with low maturity, leadership sensemaking could also be a chance to push forward the analytics agenda. For example, in the mid-2010s, Novo Nordisk, a Danish-based pharmaceutical multinational, was looking at significant expansion. In the ten years leading up to 2014, Novo Nordisk had doubled in size, and in the next ten years, the company planned to add another 20,000 employees worldwide.

During this period of active growth, the focus on corporate culture and its core values was high on the agenda of Lars Sørensen, then CEO of Novo Nordisk. In this case, leadership sensemaking was triggered because Novo Nordisk encountered an event (unprecedented employee growth outside of Denmark) for which it did not have an existing schema to guide its response. Sørensen asked, "What are our core values? We have a lot of values, but which ones are the absolute fundamental and create a true bond between the company and its employees?" Knowing its core values was crucial because such knowledge could guide the company in onboarding new employees, integrating newly acquired businesses, and creating a tighter cultural alignment with the business strategy. This quest, in turn, triggered the initiation of the first big HR analytics project at Novo Nordisk, named "Future Bond," to identify the core values that bond Novo Nordisk and its employees.

Signalling (leadership sensegiving)

Once senior leaders achieve a shared understanding of the need for strategic change and agree upon an embryonic plan, the process moves into a signalling stage of sensegiving. This communication and influencing process aims to convey the shared understanding of the need for and vision of strategic change to the broader organization. Through announcements, events, signals, and symbolic actions, it communicates that existing organizational schemas are no longer appropriate and shares new, preferred schemas.

This activity introduces ambiguity that, while creating anxiety for organizational members, can also facilitate the beginnings of a positive view of change if well-managed by senior leaders. This stage of sensemaking can return us to phase one of ACAI, where new questions arise and the process of data collection and analysis recommences. This highlights the iterative nature of sensemaking as strategic change unfolds.

For WFA, the signalling stage of sensegiving involves the development and communication of relevant logical and reasonable change messages. For example, in the aforementioned "Future Bond" project, the HR data and analytics team prioritized formulating and communicating the project's mission. Through iterative dialogue with senior leaders and the broader organization, the following mission emerged: "To enable a qualified stakeholder dialogue about the Future Bond and what Novo Nordisk must do to embrace future workforce expectations while at the same time stay true to our values and who we are." The work then continued to formulate an overarching research question for the project. After several iterations with the organizational stakeholders, the final research question read as follows: "Given the continued global growth, the increase in global compliance requirements, the increased pressure for performance and changing future workforce expectations, how do we ensure the healthy growth of Novo Nordisk while protecting our strong one-company culture?"

Although there was ample space for interpretation and ambiguity, the formulated mission and research question helped the team strengthen the shared understanding and proceed with the operationalization of the analytics project, as well as specify the precise steps to be taken by both WFA and, more broadly, HR functions. In this regard, WFA becomes a key tool for senior leaders to appropriately communicate the need for change to the rest of the organization and signal "how we go about it."

Re-visioning (collective, organizational sensemaking)

Once the need for strategic change is triggered, a stage of re-visioning begins as organizational members, particularly middle managers, attempt to make sense of the proposed strategic change. Individual and collective sensemaking occur in a sequential and reciprocal fashion that encompasses increasingly broader groups. By gathering information, observing senior leadership, and sharing stories with others, organizational members develop their understanding and shared meanings and respond accordingly. This response may include resistance as old interpretive schemas prevail over the need for change.

WFA then becomes critical for gathering additional information to enable a broader organizational understanding and interpretation of an appropriate, highly contextualized response to the plan for change. Information gathering may include employees' experience, expertise, instinct, and external and internal data relevant to their role and position in the organization, reflective of evidence-based management principles. For example, the LEGO Group has historically had very high employee engagement scores – consistently around 14 points above the benchmark. In the mid-2010s, the engagement scores remained very high, but the organization experienced a decline in the Employee Net Promoter Score. This worried management and the owning family, who have always been strongly dedicated to high employee engagement and ensuring that LEGO is a great place to work. To facilitate broader organizational understanding and interpretation, LEGO introduced a pilot initiative called "HuddleUp." It consisted of a short poll on engagement every two weeks, with subsequent follow-ups and team conversations based on the results. Another initiative was the creation of an Employee Engagement Task Force[1] to dig deeper into the engagement data, discover pressing issues, and conduct interviews to determine whether these issues were real and problematic for the organization. The head of the LEGO HR analytics team at that time reflected on the importance of having a dedicated task force to guide collective sensemaking: "Remember that different people read and interpret data differently. Therefore, the right people need to be involved from the beginning by, for example, putting together a diverse taskforce that helps digest the data."

At times, WFA needs to be engaged in explicit sensebreaking, whereby old schemas are challenged and new ways of seeing the world emerge. This is described as the need for organizations to reconsider and question the schemas developed through prior sensemaking (Lawrence & Maitlis, 2014; Maitlis et al., 2013). WFA plays a powerful role in this regard. Organizational members will seek out a range of information to inform their interpretation of the change – both individually and collectively.

The aforementioned "Future Bond" project included numerous briefing sessions with people and culture leadership, HR business partners, and executive sponsors from the leadership team. During this process, stakeholders asked the analytics team to provide additional insights on specific issues while simultaneously generating more general WFA to be drawn upon as needed and appropriate, for example, to test various interpretations and move toward a common, shared understanding. Further, to understand global megatrends and workforce preferences, both inside and outside of Novo Nordisk, the analytics team engaged in a detailed review of research by leading human capital consultancy firms (Corporate Leadership Council/CEB,

Deloitte, PwC, McKinsey, etc.). It also gathered inputs from existing in-house surveys, ongoing HR projects, and all senior HR people in Novo Nordisk that could be relevant to the "Future Bond" investigation and conducted in-depth interviews with key executives.

During re-visioning, if the sensemaking process is too loose and "informal," relying on organizational stories and rumours, it can derail strategic change (Mantere, 2008). WFA is key to ensuring the sensemaking process is directed and informed appropriately for all stakeholders at different levels of the organization, leaning into phase three of ACAI but focussing on influencing the right decisions. As organizational members reach shared understandings of the best way forward, WFA can frequently be used by senior leadership to reinforce and confirm these new understandings for those who may disagree. Organizations rarely reach a unanimous consensus on strategic change initiatives. What matters is that the process is open and equitable, and those who still do not fully agree see the "sense" in the path of action chosen by the majority.

Energizing (collective, organizational sensegiving)

This final energizing stage of sensemaking involves the engagement of organizational members in the vision for strategic change while simultaneously seeking to influence the details of the senior leadership's proposed interpretive schemas with their collective understandings. This stage, while often overlapping with the previous re-visioning stage and potentially still involving resistance by some organizational members, also signals the end of the initiation phase of strategic change as the organization moves toward action.

Because the cyclical sensemaking process relies on the continuous redrafting of the event, more information is shared and understood, but an accurate interpretation may never be reached (Weick et al., 2005). Instead, organizational members seek a plausible interpretation of the event, which will allow them to act. Even though others may have different interpretations, key individuals must diagnose the nature of the event plausibly so that it can be managed, coordinated, and distributed as appropriate (Balogun & Johnson, 2004).

In the "Future Bond" project, the analytics team completed the quantitative analysis and presented the results to senior management. The WFA lead of the "Future Bond" project recalls,

> There were a lot of interesting findings. Firstly, and most importantly, we answered the CEO's quest. Knowledge of the "Future Bond" WFA is needed as Novo Nordisk WFA is facing a huge growth, among others, by acquisitions. As a global company, with the strongest growth outside of Denmark, having a strong focus on the key elements of the bond between employees and the company WFA is crucial.

At the energizing stage, the WFA team should have a strong emphasis on storytelling and communication of results in the process of (re)gaining management attention. "Turning analytical insights into concrete business actions begins with effective storytelling with data" (Minbaeva, 2018, p. 5). The WFA team working with Future Bond saw establishing and maintaining formal and informal interactions with HR business partners as crucial for developing HR analytics functions. The "Future Bond" project results were presented at the targeted workshops for HR business partners (HRBP). The workshop aimed to share the results, but most importantly, to increase the HRBPs' knowledge about what analytics could offer for their businesses and to begin a dialogue.

From this point forward, WFA becomes about embedding strategic change throughout the organization. Unfortunately, WFA teams often feel that "their job is done" once they present the results of the analytics to the problem owners or senior leadership. If the WFA team loses control of how the results are regarded and interpreted in the broader organization, their validity can be compromised. Even if the WFA team spends time "developing a story" but leaves the actual interpretation to the organization, the stakeholders can still misuse the information to drive their agenda or confirm their predictions (confirmation bias) rather than embracing the "big picture" of the results. Encouraging the internal and external exploration of information through sensemaking is known to lead to a positive and controllable interpretation of strategic change issues (Gioia & Chittipeddi, 1991; Rouleau & Balogun, 2011), making the role of the WFA team critical in this process.

Additionally, increasing strategic control through guided, collective sensemaking is associated with higher levels of strategic action and increased performance for the organization despite any risks that may present during the strategic change (Rouleau & Balogun, 2011). Therefore, although an absolute, accurate interpretation may never be reached (Weick et al., 2005), during the energizing stage, the WFA team needs to control the emergence of the new *schema*. This requires the unlearning, destruction, or breaking down of meaning as organizational members are required to reflect on, question, and reconsider the sense they have already made, review their underlying assumptions, and re-examine their course of action (Maitlis & Christianson, 2014).

The creation of a new, shared schema through unlearning and learning may be the ultimate goal of WFA. When the results of WFA projects are communicated, as organizational members reflect, share interpretations, and gather more information, sensemaking can lead to noticing new, related events that require a reinterpretation of previous understandings. For example, in Novo Nordisk, the organization used a narrative of "Future Bond" for a while, but most importantly, the project sparked attention to WFA and resulted in the initiation of multiple follow-up projects related to the "Future Bond" findings. As the WFA lead explained,

While it is a little hard to say how findings are being followed within concrete initiatives, this project at least started to form the agenda around WFA. Most importantly, it helped me to get a "license to operate" and continue building and developing our WFA function, investing in new organizational capabilities and starting to think about larger analytics projects.

Creating sustainable change

The final, but equally crucial, role of WFA in the process of strategic change is to measure its outcomes and impacts. Although organizations are improving their abilities to act on the results of their WFA projects, too few collect data focussed on the consequences of their analytics-based decisions and actions. What actions have been taken, and where? How have they been operationalized? What changes are evident in the variables? The formal analysis of follow-up data reveals the effectiveness of the decisions and actions, helps identify how actions can be modified or changed to better achieve the expected output, and highlights those actions that are harmful and should therefore be stopped.

Moreover, reviews of the processes of data gathering, analysis, and action implementation serve as a source of learning. They make it easy to assess the entire analytics-based decision-making process, exploit opportunities, and avoid risks. It is important to consider the WFA process outside the specific business problem to leverage general lessons that can be applied to future analytics-based solutions for subsequent business problems. All these benefits will be missed if the follow-up stage is forgotten.

We are reminded here that sensemaking is not like a planned programme of change. While it can be presented in stages – as we have done here – it is not linear. It is messy, dynamic, iterative, and ongoing within an organization (Cornelissen et al., 2011; Cunliffe & Coupland, 2012; Sandberg & Tsoukas, 2015). Thus, the end of one WFA project creates new triggers, cues, and events for a new cycle of sensemaking.

Evidence shows that more highly performing organizations place as much emphasis on the management of meaning as on the management of information (Sutcliffe & Weber, 2003), and the development of strong sensemaking environments within an organization can lead to a competitive advantage (Kieran et al., 2022). We can clearly see how WFA has the power to play a key role in – or be a key capability within – the strategic change process when considered an integrated part of a sensemaking process. It is not merely about providing WFA on demand but about becoming part of the process of sensemaking itself.

This requires WFA teams to "perform" sensemaking and craft meaningful, engaging, compelling, and appropriate messages around strategic change to facilitate these conversations, set the scene, and ultimately deliver successful outcomes for the organization (Rouleau & Balogun, 2011). As David Green said, "You can create the best insights in the world, but if you don't tell the story in a compelling way that resonates with your audience then it is highly likely that no action will be taken" (Rouleau & Balogun, 2011, p. 5). Therefore, it is important to ensure that the audience experiences these insights as compelling, which is why Heuvel and Bondarouk (2016) stated that competencies, such as storytelling, should reside within the analytics team.

> Also, they would need to have the capability to advise on the outcomes in a way that is appealing to management, which implies they should also be able to link the outcomes to the business strategy and challenges management is faced with.
>
> *(p. 25)*

Evidence suggests that high-reliability organizations operating in dynamic, high-risk contexts are more likely to develop strong sensemaking schemas, whereby even weak cues trigger sensemaking (Weick et al., 2005). Juxtaposed with this, other organizations operate in contexts where deviancy becomes normalized, positive asymmetry becomes institutionalized, and even the worst is interpreted as positive (Dunbar & Garud, 2009; Maitlis & Christianson, 2014). WFA can uncover such deviancy by acting as a form of sensebreaking.

It is also known that some organizations engage in what has been termed immanent sensemaking, where daily routines are interpreted in the same way to the point that organizational members engage in absorbed coping; they know the prevailing schema and respond spontaneously (Sandberg & Tsoukas, 2011, 2015). To avoid such organizational complacency, building strong WFA teams creates WFA projects that underpin and accelerate sensemaking so that an organization is guided to constantly scan its horizon and become more responsive to internal and external cues, thereby moving WFA activity toward an organizational capability.

Conclusion

WFA powers strategic change capabilities in organizations. Analytics leveraged to trigger support for individual and collective interpretation – and guide consensus building – enable sensemaking and lead to more sustainable strategic change outcomes (Kieran et al., 2022). Given the accelerated forces most organizations contend with in the contemporary business landscape, appreciating and fully leveraging the potential of WFA has never been more needed. Therefore, we argue that the WFA team's understanding of the power of sensemaking and its role within this process, particularly at different stages, is vital for increasing the legitimacy and impact of WFA in organizations.

Note

1 http://www.slideshare.net/Competitiveness/lego-presentation-the-use-and-usefulness-of
   -employee-engagement-surveys-myths-and-realities

References

Angrave, D., Charlwood, A., Kirkpatrick, I., Lawrence, M., & Stuart, M. (2016). HR and analytics: Why HR is set to fail the big data challenge. *Human Resource Management Journal, 26*(1), 1–11. https://doi.org/10.1111/1748-8583.12090

Appelbaum, S. H., Habashy, S., Malo, J. L., & Shafiq, H. (2012). Back to the future: Revisiting Kotter's 1996 change model. *Journal of Management Development, 31*(8), 764–782.

Balogun, J., Bartunek, J. M., & Do, B. (2015). Senior managers' sensemaking and responses to strategic change. *Organization Science, 26*(4), 960–979.

Balogun, J., & Hailey, V. H. (2008). *Exploring strategic change.* Pearson Education.

Balogun, J., & Johnson, G. (2004). Organizational restructuring and middle manager sensemaking. *Academy of Management Journal, 47*(4), 523–549.

Balogun, J., Jacobs, C., Jarzabkowski, P., Mantere, S., & Vaara, E. (2014). Placing strategy discourse in context: Sociomateriality, sensemaking, and power. Journal of Management Studies, 51(2), 175–201.

Bartunek, J. M., Rousseau, D. M., Rudolph, J. W., & DePalma, J. A. (2006). On the receiving end. *The Journal of Applied Behavioral Science, 42*(2), 182–206.

Bartunek, J. M., & Woodman, R. W. (2015). Beyond Lewin: Toward a temporal approximation of organization development and change. *Annual Review of Organizational Psychology and Organizational Behavior, 2*, 157–182.

Belizon, M., & Kieran, S. (2022). Human resource analytics: A legitimacy process. *Human Resource Management Journal, 32*(3), 603–630.

Brown, A., Colville, I., & Pye, A. (2016). Sensemaking processes and Weickarious learning. *Management Learning, 47*(1), 3–13.

Clegg, S., Crevani, L., Uhl-Bien, M., & By, R. T. (2021). Changing leadership in changing times. *Journal of Change Management: Reframing Leadership and Organizational Practice, 21*(1), 1–13.

Cornelissen, J. P. (2012). Sensemaking under pressure: The influence of professional roles and social accountability on the creation of sense. *Organization Science, 23*(1), 118–137.

Cornelissen, J. P., Holt, R., & Zundel, M. (2011). The role of analogy and metaphor in the framing and legitimization of strategic change. *Organization Studies, 32*(12), 1701–1716.

Cummings, S., Bridgman, T., & Brown, K. G. (2016). Unfreezing change as three steps: Rethinking Kurt Lewin's legacy for change management. *Human Relations, 69*(1), 33–60.

Cunliffe, A., & Coupland, C. (2012). From hero to villain to hero: Making experience sensible through embodied narrative sensemaking. *Human Relations, 65*(1), 63–88.

Dunbar, R. L. M., & Garud, R. (2009). Distributed knowledge and indeterminate meaning: The case of the Columbia shuttle flight. *Organization Studies, 30*(4), 397–421.

Fay, D., & Lührmann, H. (2004). Current themes in organizational change. *European Journal of Work and Organizational Psychology, 13*(2), 113–119.

Garvin, D. (2013, December). How google sold its engineers on management. *Harvard Business Review.*

Gioia, D. A., & Chittipeddi, K. (1991). Sensemaking and sensegiving in strategic change initiation. *Strategic Management Journal, 12*(6), 433–448.

Kieran, S., MacMahon, J., & MacCurtain, S. (2022). Simple rules for sensemaking praxis: How HR can contribute to strategic change by developing sensemaking capability in organisations. *Human Resource Management Journal, 32*(2), 299–320.

Kotter, J. P. (1996, March). Why transformation efforts fail. *Harvard Business Review*, 59–67.

Lewin, K. (1947). Frontiers in group dynamics: II. Channels of group life; social planning and action research. *Human Relations, 1*(2), 143–153.

Maitlis, S., & Christianson, M. (2014). Sensemaking in organizations: Taking stock and moving forward. *Academy of Management Annals, 8*(1), 57–125.

Maitlis, S., Vogus, T. J., & Lawrence, T. B. (2013). Sensemaking and emotion in organizations. *Organizational Psychology Review, 3*(3), 222–247.

Mantere, S. (2008). Role Expectations and Middle Manager Strategic Agency, *Journal of Management Studies, 45*(2), 294–316.

Minbaeva, D. (2018). Building credible human capital analytics for organizational competitive advantage. *Human Resource Management, 57*(3), 701–713.

Lawrence, T., & Maitlis, S. (2014). The disruption of accounts: Sensebreaking in organizations [Working paper]. Simon Fraser University.

Raes, A. M. L., Heijltjes, M. G., Glunk, U., & Roe, R. A. (2011). The interface of the top management team and middle managers: A process model. *The Academy of Management Review, 36*(1), 102–126.

Rasmussen, T., & Ulrich, D. (2015). How HR analytics avoids being a management fad. *Organizational Dynamics, 44*, 236–242.

Rouleau, L., & Balogun, J. (2011). Middle managers, strategic sensemaking, and discursive competence. *Journal of Management Studies, 48*(5), 953–983.

Sandberg, J. & Tsoukas, H. (2011). Grasping the logic of practice: Theorizing through practical rationality, *Academy of Management Review, 36*(2), 338–360.

Sandberg, J., & Tsoukas, H. (2015). Making sense of the sensemaking perspective: Its constituents, limitations, and opportunities for further development. *Journal of Organizational Behavior, 36*(S1), 6–32.

Sutcliffe, K. M. & Weber, K. (2003). The high cost of accurate knowledge, *Engineering Management Review, IEEE, 31*(3), 11–11.

van den Heuvel, S., & Bondarouk, T. (2016). The rise (and fall) of HR analytics: a study into the future applications, value, structure, and system support. Paper presented at 2nd HR Division International Conference, HRIC 2016, Sidney, New South Wales, Australia.

van den Heuvel, S., & Bondarouk, T. (2017). The rise (and fall?) of HR analytics. *Journal of Organizational Effectiveness: People and Performance, 4*(2), 157–178.

Van de Ven, A. H., & Poole, M. S. (1995). Explaining development and change in organizations. The Academy of Management Review, 20(3), 510–540.

Van Den Heuvel, S., & Bondarouk, T. (2016). The rise (and fall?) of HR analytics: The future application, value, structure, and system support. Academy of Management Proceedings, 2016(1). https://doi.org/10.5465/ambpp.2016.10908abstract

Weick, K. E. (1995). *Sensemaking in organizations*. Sage.

Weick, K. E., Sutcliffe, K. M., & Obstfeld, D. (2005). Organizing and the process of sensemaking. *Organization Science, 16*(4), 409–421.

Ethics and workforce analytics

Martin R. Edwards

Effective workforce analytics implementation and ethical considerations

As discussed throughout the book, the key phases considered important to follow when implementing effective workforce analytics (WFA) involve the following ACAI approach:

- Phase 1: **A**sk the right questions
- Phase 2: **C**ollect the right data
- Phase 3: Conduct the right **A**nalyses
- Phase 4: **I**nfluence the right decisions

We propose that these phases should be approached in any WFA project and present this as our ACAI model of workforce analytics. As mentioned in Chapter 2, when deciding what the "right" questions are, collecting the "right" data, conducting the "right" analyses, and ensuring the "right" decisions are influenced, the WFA team needs to incorporate ethical considerations into deciding what is the "right" thing to do. Doing the "right" thing includes acting ethically and addressing the ethical challenges associated with workforce analytics project implementation.

Some WFA questions may seem "useful" for a business, but that does not necessarily mean that the organization should conduct these analyses; they may not be the "right" questions to answer from an ethical perspective. Also, WFA projects involve data, and although it might be possible to collect lots of different data, some data collection activities can raise ethical challenges. Collecting private data, for example, or engaging in data collection activities that violate individual rights to privacy may

DOI: 10.4324/9781003190097-17

be ethically problematic. Thus, some data collection activities can be "wrong" rather than "right" because they breach ethical standards.

As an example, it is well documented that in 2020, H&M received a record fine for violating the European General Data Protection Regulation. H&M reportedly recorded an extensive range of data on employees (some very private data) to profile them for decision-making purposes within the employment relationship. In general terms, the features of this project can definitely be considered a standard workforce analytics-based project: collect data on employees, analyze and create profiles to be used for decision-making purposes. However, this was clearly not "right" as a WFA project in a number of ways.

Examples of clear breaches of ethics such as the H&M case are easy to understand, and are ones that an organization's leadership will strive to avoid. More challenging for any WFA initiative are the less egregious ethical issues prevalent in decisions made about data and analyses. The topics covered in this chapter that fit that profile include problems with data validity (determining the correct metrics to use; imperfections with performance ratings; missing data; data transparency); algorithms and bias created by AI and machine learning; technologically-enabled monitoring of employee activities; employee privacy, including the issue of consent; and global variation in regulatory frameworks. The chapter ends with a ten-step framework for ethical workforce analytics.

Ethical competency: An essential competency for WFA

While ethics may not be the first consideration for an emergent WFA team when deciding what kind of analytics project to introduce to their organization, almost every WFA project has an ethical dimension, making ethical consideration essential. HR analytics activities have multiple ethical considerations. In this section, we discuss some of these challenges.

The vast majority of WFA projects work with some aspect of employee data, whether it is analyzing characteristics of potential recruits during the selection stage, employee performance data, workforce diversity characteristics, sickness absence data, or employee turnover data. Thus, almost all WFA projects risk creating an ethical breach or violating data privacy regulations, potentially leading to ethical dilemmas. Furthermore, the impact and outcome of WFA projects may involve making recommendations for HR practice choices or directing selective investments (e.g., who to hire, reward, or promote). These projects can have profound impacts, with a high potential to inadvertently create problems of bias and (indirect) discrimination.

Historically, WFA experts did not prioritize the ethical dimension of WFA. A cursory scan through some of the earlier texts (Guenole et al., 2017; Sesil, 2014; Soundararajan & Singh, 2017) focused on WFA reveals little to no guidance on ethics and, in some places, no mention of ethics at all. This omission represents a fundamental blind spot in the earlier focus on WFA as the field developed. However, this has changed. The ethical component of WFA now takes center stage in the field. As an example, the global conference network People Analytics & Future of Work (PAFOW) recently adopted "People Data for Good" as its tagline for networking events (details below).

The increasing interest in and recognition that WFA operates in an ethical context is also gaining attention in academic literature. A number of recent reviews have highlighted a range of ethical issues (some of which we discuss below) emerging in the field. For example, Tursunbayeva et al. (2021) set out some of the main ethical challenges emerging in WFA, including: risks of analytics contributing to bias and discrimination; potential psychological and social profiling of employees (and potential employees); the dehumanization of employees and performance through reducing people or behavior to numbers; and the increasing threat to employee privacy and autonomy posed by digital (and analytic) surveillance in the workplace. In addition to these points, in their review, Gal et al. (2020) argued that WFA faces ethical challenges due to a lack of algorithmic transparency. They also noted that algorithmic nudging and the datafication of people could restrict employee creativity, virtues, and ability to flourish (Gal et al., 2020).

McCartney and Fu (2022) also highlighted that ethical and privacy concerns go hand in hand as WFA becomes more popular. They emphasized that WFA-related data collection in activities such as recruitment (e.g., facial recognition data) raises data privacy concerns, while the passive collection of employee data also presents privacy- and monitoring-related ethical challenges. This includes concerns about invasive data collection, which is often automated and algorithmically driven, and may lead to selective investment. Also, organizations run the risk of HR dehumanization, where HR decisions about employees are driven by algorithms, further distancing employees from the HR process. In a recent WFA special issue, Edwards et al. (2022) highlighted that these ethical challenges are proliferating alongside the field's growth, and that ignoring or being unwilling to recognize the ethical context of WFA risks creating a blind spot that could expose the WFA field to legal and ethical challenges.

While we do not address all the ethical challenges highlighted in recent reviews, in the following section, we discuss some of the key ethical considerations that contextualize the field of WFA.

The inevitability of facing ethical challenges

Almost all HR decisions have an ethical context, and consequently, almost all WFA activities have an ethical context. HR analytic-driven decisions are ethical decisions and activities. As Wicks (1996) argued, business decisions cannot be separated from ethics; business decisions are not devoid of ethical content. Although the primacy of business decision-making considerations has occasionally been suggested as mainly focusing on profit (Friedman, 1970), this perspective is extremely limited from an ethical standpoint. From the Friedman perspective, strategic goals and business interests are the primary concerns of decision-makers in organizations, and the main ethical concern (if there is one) should be considering shareholders. Related to this, for many decades, theorists have debated and discussed the notion that managers have a right, or prerogative, to hire and fire to help ensure businesses operate as efficiently and profitably as possible. However, this prerogative is potentially limited by what is referred to as the "managerial prerogative" (McKinlay & Zeitlin, 2006). This concept can usefully be considered with regard to ethics and HR, and indeed WFA. From a WFA perspective, the idea that the organization has every right to analyze data linked to employees to ensure it can operate under the best or optimal (or profitable) conditions falls neatly into this idea of managerial prerogative.

When running a business or organization where employees are paid, the business surely has the prerogative to exercise due process by analyzing employee activities, such as their comings and goings, to ensure the business runs efficiently and that money spent on wages is not wasted. On the surface, who could argue with that? However, such a position follows the idea that organizations can logically separate decision-making linked to economic activities from any ideas around ethics or that business decisions can be considered "ethics-free." This idea, sometimes referred to as the separation thesis (Sandberg, 2008), is generally seen as untenable (Harris & Freeman, 2008; Freeman et al., 2010).

More often than not, when business decisions are made, value is created for some agents or people, and that value may be taken from someone else (Freeman et al., 2010). Some people may benefit from business decisions, and some may be harmed. Some business decisions may enable the fulfillment or recognition of some people's rights and realize some people's values, while other people's rights and values are neither recognized nor fulfilled. This is why Wicks (1996) and others (e.g., Harris & Freeman, 2008) highlighted that business decisions inevitably involve ethics.

WFA is in no way immune from this. In fact, some HR analytic activities draw managers into realms of ethical analysis or ethical relevance in ways that other business activities do not. For example, if potential, current, and past employee data are being used in a predictive algorithm that is applied as a basis for who should or should not be short-listed for a job, this may well introduce ethical challenges linked to social justice (if there is a bias in the algorithm that means certain groups are less likely to be recommended) or informational justice (if the algorithm applied is not transparent). Different HR analytic activities are likely to invoke different ethical challenges. Importantly, ethics is a complex field, and there are many ways of considering whether a business practice, WFA project, or otherwise, can be considered ethical (or not). An ethical judgment involves a value judgment, and it is important to recognize there are no black-and-white frameworks that one can draw on when making value-based judgments.

Ethical lenses and HRM

A chapter that focuses on the ethics of any organizational or business activity should address what is meant by ethics. If we are suggesting that engaging in WFA activities may raise ethical challenges and that an awareness of this needs to be something WFA teams take seriously, we need to be able to define what we mean by ethics. A cursory consideration of this question may lead to a response along the lines of "ethics is the consideration of whether something is right or wrong." However, the issue of ethics is much more complex than this, as philosophers have debated for millennia, and we do not propose to present a solution in this chapter. Ethics and ethical judgments of whether something (such as a particular HR activity) can be considered right or wrong will inevitably involve subjective attitudes, perceptions, and value-based (moral or otherwise) judgments.

In recognition of this, in this section, we present the idea that ethical judgments are likely to be bound by, and situated in, particular ethical frameworks held by the person making a judgment of right or wrong. In taking this position, we recognize previous work carried out in the field of ethics and HRM by Winstanley and Woodall (2000). They argued that, in judging whether HR practices can be considered ethical or not, these judgments will depend on a selection of ethical frameworks or lenses. The authors set out a range of possible ethical frameworks that can be used as a basis for making ethical judgments. For the reader interested in the conceptual issues regarding how ethics is defined, please continue in this section. For those who prefer to skip to the ethical issues around specific WFA decisions, please skip to the next section.

Each of these frameworks has an entire body of literature behind them, and giving them due space for discussion here is beyond the remit of this book. However, a selection of these frameworks or lenses can be used to help us reflect on different aspects of HR activities, specifically WFA. The chief frameworks we draw on include utilitarianism, justice-based ethical frameworks, deontic- (or Kantian)-based frameworks, stakeholder theory, corporate social responsibility, and sustainability-based frameworks. For reference, we briefly set out these frameworks in Table 6.1 and Figure 6.1. We summarize these frameworks not to provide an exhaustive reference of ethical frameworks but to help the reader note some of the basic components and elements of different ethical positions.

One of the challenges in reflecting on HR analytic practices from an ethical standpoint (which this chapter does) is that an ethical judgment of context is not absolute, and each framework is a lens through which the reader can position or consider a value-based judgment of right and wrong. Reflecting on the different frameworks and considering them one by one may mean an HR practice invokes an ethical challenge to a varying degree depending on the framework considered, or that particular frameworks may be more relevant or easily applied when (potentially) considering the ethical context of the business activity, decision, or problem.

TABLE 6.1 Ethical frameworks summary

Utilitarianism. This ethical framework focuses on outcomes and ends. J.S. Mill and Jeremy Bentham are associated with the ethical principles of utilitarianism. The key idea is that actions that can help to "achieve the greatest amount of good for the greatest number of people" and benefit rather than harm people can be considered right forms of action. Thus, the outcomes and ends are positive (often favoring the majority over the minority; Norman, 1983).

Deontic or Kantian perspectives. Key arguments from a deontic or Kantian perspective center on the idea that we are duty-bound to do the right thing and that we should treat people with respect and follow rule-based ethical principles that are not justified by the outcome of actions (Norman, 1983; Winstanley & Woodall, 2000). Also, we should not act in ways or treat humanity only as a means to an end but always consider the careful treatment of people, which leads us to the idea that we should always respect human rights.

Stakeholder theory. Although each of the ethical frameworks presented here has important implications for considering the ethics of HR practices, stakeholder theory has a special place when it comes to WFA. Freeman (1984) is generally credited with presenting stakeholder theory, which has had a considerable impact on business. More recent contributions (e.g., Freeman et al., 2010) have also helped to identify the ethical scope of the theory in business. As mentioned above, Freeman et al. (2010) suggested almost all business decisions have ethical content, and taking this further, almost all WFA projects have ethical content. A key idea behind stakeholder theory is that business decisions, or decisions made by businesses, will often affect multiple stakeholders. These stakeholders may be shareholders, employees, supply-chain partners, customers, or broader groups from the (local or otherwise) community. Because business decisions may affect one or more of these groups positively (they may benefit) or negatively (they may lose out or be harmed in some way), those making decisions in business need to consider how stakeholder groups are affected. Stakeholder ethical theory is particularly relevant to WFA because often (but not always) the primary target of the analytics is the employee stakeholder (or potential employees or customers). Also, a key professed aim of WFA projects is to help organizational profitability and productivity or to help show a return on an investment (Larsson & Edwards, 2021), which will serve the interests of the shareholder or business owner as a stakeholder. However, these targets or beneficiaries are specific stakeholder groups that may have different interests, and this needs to be recognized.

Corporate social responsibility (CSR). While social responsibility can be seen as a framework separate from stakeholder theory, recent definitions tend to integrate a stakeholder perspective when defining social responsibility (Aguinis, 2011; Morgeson et al., 2013). Some of the early roots of CSR as a perspective (Davis, 1960) can be considered to be defined by what the organization *should not* purely focus on; that is, the achievement of profit and compliance with regulatory edicts. CSR was framed by Waldman et al. (2006) as business actions that focus on or promote social good that go beyond focusing on fostering bottom-line return or actions that organizations carry out because legislative rules require them to. Carroll (1979) also suggested organizations need to focus on a range of responsibilities, specifically those that are economic, legal, ethical, and discretionary, as a model of CSR. Importantly, although CSR and stakeholder frameworks are often linked, a key aspect of CSR is that organizations have a responsibility beyond shareholders in the pursuit of profits, and both can be drawn on when considering the ethical context of WFA.

Organizational sustainability. As with stakeholder theory, a sustainability ethical framework is often subsumed into a broader lens of CSR (or ESG). An organization that acts with social responsibility will generally need to consider ideas of sustainability regarding the social environment and resources (which includes employees). Organizational sustainability as a focus is linked to the idea that organizational and corporate activities need to emphasize the importance of exerting efforts to conserve (rather than consume) natural environmental resources. Organizational sustainability means to "lessen the burden of economic activity on the environment and ensure that the activity can be sustained over time"!

(Continued)

TABLE 6.1 (Continued)

(Pfeffer, 2017, p. 34) to ensure the resources required will not be exhausted. However, the resources that need protecting and sustaining are not just physical resources; they include social resources, cultures, cultural values, and communities. This social aspect of sustainability falls within the framework of CSR. However, several theorists have specifically applied the idea of sustainability to employees as a core focus. Pfeffer (2017) discussed the importance of organizations carefully managing levels of stress in the workplace and considering the impact of work on employees' immediate social environment (family), the effects of layoffs on communities, the social implications of inequality, and issues of providing health (insurance)-based safety nets to workers. Also, Ehnert (2009) and Ehnert and Harry (2012), in discussions of sustainable HRM, specifically focused on employees as the resource that needs to be developed, conserved, and invested in rather than used up or exhausted, and these authors specifically focus on sustainable HRM practices. One of the responsibilities included in a sustainable HRM perspective is the organization's need to assess and consider the negative impact of its practices on employees as a social resource; interestingly, this would most likely involve or directly require a WFA project!

Social justice. A broad ethical framework linked to social justice is connected to a range of other ethical frameworks mentioned above. However, the reference to social justice takes into account the idea that there are social inequalities in the world that may often lead to discrimination against certain groups and that it is a fundamental human right for people not to be subject to discrimination on the grounds of membership in particular (often marginalized) social groups.

Organizational justice-based frameworks. This ethical framework is linked to decades of research in the field of HR and organizational behavior that explores different (important) dimensions of organizational justice but can also be linked to some of the other frameworks raised here (e.g., social justice and deontic frameworks). The categories are distributive, procedural, interactional, and informational justice, largely based on Colquitt's (2001) framework. The idea is that, in making management decisions, employees should be treated fairly and, where possible, with equity. Distributive justice refers to the idea that resources and rewards are distributed fairly on the basis of inputs and effort expended in the workplace (or on the basis of equal value). Procedural justice is distinct from distributive justice in that organizations need to be fair and transparent in making decisions and setting out procedures. Informational justice is linked to the idea that the organization should provide information to employees about issues that affect them. Interactional justice involves the idea that employees can expect to be treated with dignity and respect by their organization (and managers).

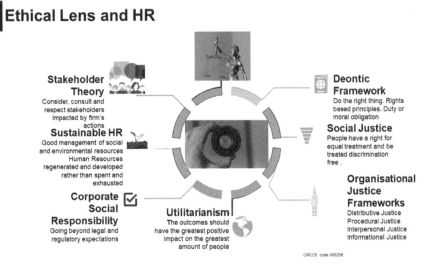

FIGURE 6.1 Ethical lenses and HR.

Ethical challenges with the validity of data used

Most HR data is bad data.

(Buckingham, 2015)

While WFA teams often face challenges linked to the quality and validity of data, the availability of that data may not immediately present an ethical challenge. However, using bad or invalid data in analyses can easily lead to a range of very challenging ethical problems. Almost all WFA teams spend much of their time addressing quality issues with data. These quality issues involve a broad scope.

When WFA teams want to collect and integrate data derived from multiple sources and systems (e.g., pay data, engagement data, talent data, performance data, sales data, recruitment data, and selection data), this information is often recorded differently and held by different teams in different parts of the organization, in different physical locations. A challenge with integrating different sources of data is that they may store and define data differently. Combining these different forms of data may lead to challenges in data interpretation and issues of quality. Also, WFA teams may need to integrate historical data into a central data source; sometimes historical data is collected in different ways by different teams and stored in different systems over time. The different systems may have stored different types of information (and fields) for the same potential construct, and definitions of particular data elements may vary over time (e.g., ratings of performance, an organization may change from a three-item rating scale to a five-item rating scale over time, thus changing the meanings of the numbers). See also the related discussion in Chapter 3.

Combining historical data from different systems and teams into a longitudinal dataset for project analyses poses a scientific validity challenge. Most HR analytic teams should deal with this issue, yet many people working in WFA roles have not been trained to recognize or manage these challenges. This raises many difficulties for the data analytics team that hopes to pull together a dataset to analyze. There may be missing data at different times, and some data fields may have different meanings. Often, the WFA team makes multiple assumptions about the data's meaning during analysis. The validity and quality of these data are crucial to their appropriate and correct use in analytics.

From an ethical lens, using invalid or poor-quality data as a foundation for analyses (whether applying algorithms or not) that may influence selective investments can invoke ethical challenges, especially if some employees benefit and some lose out as a result of analyses with validity issues. Using invalid data may invoke ethical concerns related to justice perspectives (procedural), and other social justice challenges may arise if systematic bias results from analyses driven by poor-quality data.

While Buckingham (2015) asserted that most HR data are bad data, Charlwood and Guenole (2021) suggested that this is a misconception and instead argued there are various analytic techniques that can help alleviate or manage errors in measurement. These techniques (e.g., structural equation modeling and latent variable modeling) are potentially useful for HR data linked to survey data (e.g., engagement survey data) and can, in some places, be used with other data forms. However, it's debatable whether these analytic techniques can adequately address challenges such as missing data, incorrect data, invalid integration of different data fields with differing definitions, or invalid use of measures as proxies for other constructs or measures. Although data validity may not immediately be considered an ethical issue, the challenges that invalid data and measures can bring to the HR analytic sphere can have significant ethical implications.

Validity of data and the wrong metric

A common challenge in HR analytics is the lack of accurate measures for specific constructs in a project. This is where a proxy measure may be used. However, this approach can lead to significant (potentially problematic) assumptions about employees or employee behavior based on proxy measures that may not actually represent a good, accurate, or reliable measure of the construct it is supposed to represent.

Here is a blunt example of this issue: Barclays Bank (BBC, 2020) was in the press for introducing an electronic monitoring system that tracked whether employees were active on their computers. Whether someone is active on their desktop computer could be considered a proxy for productivity. However, there could, of course, be many activities a person does in their job that do not involve them being active on their desktop computer. This could include things such as meetings with coworkers and clients, reading or consulting physical documents, or any other activity that may involve job activities that do not involve typing.

Other examples of metrics that may be used in WFA, where data are collated to produce a metric representing a particular performance evaluation construct, include data linked to employee email activity or meeting patterns as a measure of productivity. In 2020, Microsoft (MS) introduced a passive metric in its MS365 suite that produced a "productivity score" for employees linked to the degree to which people interacted over email, whether they utilized online meetings, and whether they collaborated with MS365 online files (Hern, 2020). Whether these are valid measures or proxies for performance or productivity can be questioned. Similar issues could be raised with this metric as with the Barclays productivity measure.

Many assumptions are made about whether these types of proxy scores actually represent true, accurate, and valid measures of employee productivity. If not, is it fair or just to use these scores in this way? Issues around procedural fairness and justice will be invoked if judgments are being made about employees on the basis of their scores associated with a problematic proxy measure. The ethical challenges become greater as the consequences of variation in these scores increase in importance or severity. This kind of issue can also become problematic if a score or metric is used as a proxy for performance when certain demographic groups (e.g., women) are indirectly affected negatively (e.g., whether the organization invests in different people on the basis of these measures) by the blunt use of this proxy; social justice ethical challenges may be triggered as a result.

Valid data and metrics of performance

Because a key purpose of WFA is often to help employees and organizations be more productive, the validity of performance measures and performance metrics associated with employees is a particularly important concern. A key metric often used in this regard is a performance appraisal rating. However, the use of performance appraisal scores or measures, and metrics associated with these, have substantial data quality and validity challenges.

First, performance ratings are usually given by a supervisor and typically are subjective, as they require a (potentially biased) human to interpret and judge performance. Subjective judgments often do not accurately reflect true variation in employees' performance (Longnecker & Ludwig, 1990), and there are a multitude of possible positive and negative motives a manager may have for deliberately providing an inaccurate rating of performance. Importantly, potential motives that lead to inaccuracies in performance ratings may well be driven or influenced by the rater's own systematic biases in the first place.

Other challenges affecting the validity of performance appraisal ratings arise when an organization wants to assume a particular distribution of these ratings. Often, when this happens, managers' initial ratings of employees' performance may be adjusted after a calibration meeting where active pressure is placed on initial ratings to ensure that, overall (either vertically or horizontally in the organization), a particular distribution of ratings is produced. This practice challenges the validity of the performance rating as an accurate measure of performance. (See also the discussion of problems with forced rating distributions in Chapter 3.)

While performance ratings and measures are valuable data that WFA teams would often want to have for potential analytics projects involving performance, these ratings are often prone to validity problems at their foundation. If this lack of validity and error in measurement is linked to biases in some way, the use of this data to help make suggestions for selective investment could easily invoke further ethical challenges that the analytic team may end up being responsible for.

Missing data

In almost all WFA projects where data are collated and engineered before any analyses are conducted, there will be missing data. Whether this involves missing fields for particular individuals, teams, or other categories of workers, or missing data due to missing workers (in a dataset), the challenge of what to do with this missing data raises several potential ethical issues. If there is something systematic about which data (e.g., demographic data) is missing for whom (e.g., particular minority groups or teams may have missing data), then the likelihood of bias will increase in any analyses produced from these data. Williams et al. (2018) discussed this issue in relation to missing data and algorithms. As discussed below, attempts to impute data from existing cases in a demographic category that has a greater-than-usual proportion of missing data can fundamentally exacerbate any bias that may exist in the data initially. Therefore, careful treatment of missing data and its potential adverse impact needs to be thoroughly examined to reduce the potential for ethical challenges arising. See also the discussion of data cleaning in Chapter 3.

Data transparency: An ethical obligation

One of the responsibilities that academic researchers have when they publish articles in top scientific journals is to be explicit about the nature of data used and completely transparent about what measures are used and how any measure is created. This is part of the process of being rigorous scientists: documenting publicly the methods used so they can be replicated by other researchers. One of the implications of being completely transparent in the methods and measures scientists use is that if there is a validity problem with the methods, this will be open for discussion in the scientific review process.

This approach is equally important for WFA teams. Transparency can help ensure a more ethical approach to analyses, meaning the analyst or researcher has not deceived nor made inappropriate assumptions in the process of setting up and conducting the analysis. With WFA, this transparency will help ensure any potential problems with the data and assumptions made during the analysis are recognized. This is essential for alerting any stakeholders who are affected by the results to the potential limitations of the insights generated.

As investment decisions are often made as a result of a WFA project, there is a risk that certain stakeholders (e.g., potential and current employees) could be negatively affected by an analysis built on bad data or invalid measures. This, therefore, raises ethical challenges that HR teams need to address. Thus, a key capability for WFA teams is the ability to identify weaknesses in the measures or data used and the willingness and capability to articulate these weaknesses in any WFA projects. Because of the potential ethical challenges associated with using poor-quality or invalid data in HR analytic projects, HR analytic teams need to adopt an approach of transparency in their analytics undertakings.

Algorithms, ethics, bias, and unequal outcomes

The issue of ethics linked to bias associated with HR analytic activities has become a topic gaining increasing attention. Often, bias and ethical challenges are linked to (i.e., associated with but not restricted to) the outcomes of utilizing algorithms, AI, and machine learning in HR. As mentioned above, recent reviews in the area of WFA (Tursunbayeva et al., 2021; Vigden et al., 2021; Edwards et al., 2022) that discuss ethics almost all highlight the problem that applying predictive algorithms in HR (which may be used to help organizations make investment decisions) introduces challenges associated with bias.

Several authors have specifically discussed the ethical challenges that algorithms, AI, and machine learning bring to the HR table. Recent examples include Gal et al. (2020), Meijerink et al. (2021), and Charlwood and Guenole (2021). The latter highlights the paradoxical challenges of AI and machine learning for HR and discusses issues of bias that algorithms may produce. The issue of algorithmic application potentially leading to biased outcomes has been discussed in the general data analytics and business analytics fields for some years (examples include Someh et al., 2019; Martin & Waldman, 2021; and Williams et al., 2018).

What kinds of biases can arise when applying algorithms in HR? The answer depends on what algorithm is being applied. It has been argued that AI can be used in a range of different HR applications to help HR make investment decisions. Predictive algorithms are being used for short-listing candidates for jobs; for giving recommendations on the suitability of short-listed candidates; for determining who should and could be deemed talented, trained, or promoted; or for flagging who is likely to leave.

The nature of the HR application is likely to affect the outcome of the bias. For example, if analytics and algorithms are used to assess applicants for short-listing, there is potential for bias linked to determining who is considered suitable for short-listing. For those who are short-listed, an algorithm may be applied to suggest the potential fit for the job and whether the candidate is likely to perform well and stay at the organization. If there is bias involved in this process, the outcome of the bias is significant for the individual, affecting whether they can get a job or not. With attrition-based algorithmic applications that predict who is likely to consider leaving (or not), the outcome of any bias in these algorithms will likely affect who gets special attention (or not) in an attempt to reduce the likelihood of people leaving. Thus, the nature of the application will determine the impact of any bias in any algorithm.

Sources of bias in algorithms

The potential sources of bias in an algorithm are many. One of the key sources of bias involves the idea that predictive analyses may be applied (usually with regression techniques) to look at previous records linked to employees; to sort and profile data; and to look for trends that may help explain, predict, or account for whether (and what potentially explains) employees who were found to perform well or were more likely to stay in the organization. Two of the challenges with looking at previous patterns and profiles of employees who were found to perform well are that (a) a potentially arbitrary characteristic (e.g., gender) may be linked to or associated with performance ratings and (b) people in general have (potentially discriminatory) biases toward or against a particular group or people with particular characteristics.

The bias may be systematic; that is, it may be reinforced by an organization's systems and culture that indirectly benefit certain groups. However, it may be due to a person's inherent direct or indirect discrimination against certain groups. This could include sexism, ageism, racism, and any other relevant "-ism." This issue has been well documented and revolves around the idea that if an organizational system has an inherent bias, then an algorithm that is produced as an outcome of analyses that explore trends and patterns will itself be influenced by the existing biases that are present or emerging in the data due to the inherent bias in the organization (Edwards & Edwards, 2019). Thus, an analysis that identifies a pattern from historical data that seems to indicate males are associated with higher levels of performance than women may actually be picking up previous patterns of bias in the organization and end up reinforcing this bias by suggesting male candidates will perform better; therefore, males may get a higher predictive score in a performance analysis. The idea is that the existing bias becomes "baked in" to the algorithm.

Societal biases are also a potential source of bias in organizational data. Organizational bias revolves around the idea that some form of bias in an organization may be feeding further bias in the application of an algorithm. However, some biases that exist in an organization are linked to, and potentially caused by, existing patterns of differences in society. This will produce apparent patterns of bias that are caused by, reflect, and represent external societal patterns and trends. This issue was raised by O'Neil (2017), whose book *Weapons of Math Destruction* highlights how selective recruitment algorithms may be excluding certain groups in society because not everyone is on a level playing field and not everyone has the same opportunities to thrive.

As an example, with WFA, a mining organization may have more males in engineering jobs than females because fewer women may study engineering at university than males. Therefore, a trend analysis that explores features that predict performance and promotion patterns in an organization may show that males are more likely to be promoted than females. A range of other societal-related biases or differences that exist may also be propagated within organizations, and the algorithm that drives recommendations based on these patterns identified in the analyses will again reinforce wider societal biases.

As mentioned above, there are data quality and validity challenges that lead to bias. One of the things that Williams et al. (2018) discussed is that algorithms can discriminate or be biased due to lacking or missing data in the system. For example, if a particular group of employees with certain characteristics are more prone to mistrust their employer (perhaps because of their status as a minority group or because they have been mistreated), they may also be more likely not to complete certain questionnaires that an organization circulates to try to collect information on employees. In such a situation, when an analyst looks for patterns in data to explore predictors of performance, the systematic patterns of missing data associated with certain groups may mean these groups end up being even less likely to be identified as potential predictors of higher performance. Additionally, there are various strategies for imputing missing data (which may be used by an analyst), and these may involve the analytic extrapolation of data. In this case, extrapolation is driven by a smaller number of cases in this particular group, which could further reinforce any bias that may exist against these groups.

Adverse impact

One of the key developments in the field of analytics is that WFA teams need to become adept at deciding where algorithms are being deployed to make predictions or recommendations involving selective investment decisions or adverse impact audits of algorithms. If algorithms are used in predictive analyses to develop recommendations, the degree to which these algorithms lean toward recommending particular demographic groups (which may represent an algorithmic bias) needs to be checked. This needs to be done to ensure the algorithm does not have an adverse impact on employees who hold particular characteristics (Speers, 2021; Charlwood & Guenole, 2021). As an example of adverse impact in action, if an analytics team invests money in trying to reduce turnover (maybe by providing training and development opportunities or pay raises) and the algorithm finds that white males of a certain age group (younger perhaps) are associated with a greater tendency to leave the organization, it may be the case that this algorithm is leading to an inherent bias against white males of a certain age group. This needs to be checked.

There are arguments that if an adverse impact is found with the application of a particular algorithm, then adjustments can be made to the algorithm to adjust or weight the importance of certain group characteristics so that the inherent bias is no longer propagated in recommendations (Speers, 2021). This is a potential solution for the problem of a biased algorithm. However, there is room for discussion and debate (Charlwood & Guenole, 2021) about the degree to which interventions can be applied to adjust the algorithms and steer them away from a particular leaning in recommendations. This remains a thorny issue for WFA where AI or machine learning is used to make selective investment recommendations.

Frameworks for evaluating algorithmic bias

A recent contribution to the literature on bias in AI is from Landers and Behrend (2023), who fully explore the scope of bias in AI applications and set out a framework of questions that those responsible for engaging automated algorithms and AI can use to evaluate for bias. The authors highlight that bias in the application of AI can be considered through a number of lenses. These include: (a) individual fairness attitudes as a lens linked to perceptions that the outcome of an algorithm (and its recommendations) is perceived to be unjust with regard to distributive, procedural, or informational justice; (b) considerations that the algorithms may lead to biased outcomes from the perspective of legal regulations, or moral or ethical judgments (which would include, for example, that the algorithm discriminates against particular groups); and (c) the lens of bias from a technical or statistical perspective—for example, where the model that produces biased outputs is being pushed toward these outcomes by a systematic (biased or erroneous) feature of the data or the analytic model setup. These three frameworks cover a broad range of possible meanings for bias but demonstrate that the breadth of scope of "algorithmic bias" (which is beginning to be used extensively in the field) is in itself a complex notion.

WFA teams need to stay abreast of the complexities of the notion of "algorithmic bias" or "biased AI" to avoid the potential ethical pitfalls that the unwary may stumble into. Usefully, Landers and Behrend (2023) set out a 12-component auditing framework that would be helpful for a WFA team to use to audit the bias in their own use of algorithms. This includes the following (taken from Landers & Behrend, 2023, p. 9): The audit components that a bias auditor needs to consider include the importance of assessing aspects of the analytic models themselves, including aspects linked to input data, model design, model development, model features, model process, and model outputs.

In addition to these components related to model features, Landers and Behrend (2023) also highlighted that a bias auditor should consider how the information produced by the models is received and enacted. They emphasized that how those who receive the model output interpret and respond to the results is key in determining bias. In addition, bias auditors need to consider the consequences and effects of the model outcomes on those directly affected and how regulatory agents may consider and evaluate the model's impact. Finally, they highlight the need to consider broader aspects ("meta" components) that affect the degree to which model application is likely to be biased. These include the cultural contexts of those involved in the model design and use, what cultural assumptions are being made with regard to the appropriate use of the model and outputs, respect for generally considered ethical standards associated with the use of algorithms, and the aspects of the analytic research project design (e.g., is the design robust and valid and can claims being made about the model and its results hold up to methodological scrutiny?).

This framework is but one possible framework that can be considered by those interested in assessing whether an algorithm or analytic model (be it automated or otherwise) is prone to bias and, therefore, runs the risk of involving an ethical challenge. The ability of a WFA team to understand these complexities and apply such a framework is important as the field develops.

Algorithmic transparency and explainability

Coinciding with the recent growth in the use of algorithms in the HR sphere, and the challenges being raised with the potential for bias in algorithms, is the argument being presented for algorithmic transparency and, subsequently, algorithmic explainability (Holzinger et al., 2019; Charlwood & Guenole, 2021). The push in the field of analytics to ensure algorithms are transparent and manageable is discussed by Schildt (2016) and, more recently, by Gal et al. (2020) and Meijerink et al. (2021). Arguments made for algorithmic transparency and explainability focus on the importance of being able to crack open the algorithmic black box to understand and manage the potential impact, ethical or otherwise, of these new digital applications.

One of the challenges with the introduction of AI and machine learning in the HR sphere, either to help predict particular HR outcomes or to help recommend selective investment decisions, is that these applications may considerably impact employees (and potential employees) due to the risk of bias and the need to explain these systems to the workforce. Importantly, if challenged, the HR analyst responsible for deploying an algorithm must be able to explain why, for example, a particular investment (e.g., to hire or not) is being recommended by the system. If a manager asks, "How does this algorithm work, and why is it selecting this particular candidate over others?" the deploying HR practitioner must be able to explain the workings of the recommendation. Failing to do this not only risks making the HR function appear incompetent but also demonstrates a lack of expertise in auditing the algorithm for bias.

The HR profession's capability to engage in statistics (and indeed algorithms) has been questioned (Angrave et al., 2016), and significant training may be needed before HR has the necessary levels of statistical and analytic capability (Edwards, 2019; Kryscynski et al., 2018; Huselid, 2018). However, HR's ability to interrogate and explain algorithms (when deployed) affecting current and potential employees is essential if the application of these analytic techniques can be considered ethical. HR is the interface between the organization and employees who are the individual-level stakeholders at the receiving end of the algorithmic deployment. From an ethical lens of stakeholder theory, therefore, this necessitates that HR can engage with algorithms, explain them to employees, and audit their potential adverse impact that may result from them. As Charlwood and Guenole (2021) argued: "Without HR involvement in negotiating the development of AI with those affected, the risks of unfair and biased AIs that negatively affect workers will likely increase."

Humans in the loop

An emerging ethical challenge from the growing use of AI and algorithms is the potential removal of humans (whether HR or managers) from the interface between the organization and employees (or potential employees). This raises an ethical challenge that this digital analytic technology is running the risk of dehumanizing the management of the employment relationship. As De Cremer and Kasparov (2021) argued, despite calls for AI and technology to be designed to avoid ethical challenges, there are inherent dangers in allowing technology to take a leading role in decision-making. This can result in decisions and actions that are devoid of ethical considerations. As Charlwood and Guenole (2021) suggested, major questions remain around who or what is accountable when an algorithm that has "learned" and makes recommendations or decisions leads to discriminatory outcomes. Despite proposed attempts to intervene with algorithms and conduct audits of the impact of analytics or adverse impact audits, algorithms are not ethical.

It is important, as many have argued, that HR practitioners who engage with analytics and algorithms develop the necessary competency to determine how and what the algorithm is doing. Algorithms cannot act ethically; they do not have the ability to make human judgments, and as De Cremer and Kasparov (2021) suggested, technology needs more, not less, human involvement in this regard. The recent arguments being proposed about the importance of human oversight in algorithmic applications follow this train of thought. This is something the General Data Protection Regulation (GDPR) in Europe is focusing on: algorithms should not be left to run, adapt, and make decisions without a human in the loop to assess their impact. Importantly, the more technology is used in HR to help make decisions around selective investment, the more people will be needed to consider and assess the potential nature and impact of these algorithms.

A fully-fledged WFA team needs data!

A fully-fledged WFA team has to be able to address the sophisticated application of automated algorithmic prediction systems that recommend and highlight who would be good to hire, who are potential key future leaders, who needs training, who might be a flight risk, who needs a pay raise, who is a well-being risk, etc. The team will also likely need to address systems used to nudge employees toward conduct and carry out activities that may help with their development (e.g., training programs) and well-being (e.g., taking breaks). Such a team would also need to be experts in algorithms and in addressing and understanding the potential ethical challenges of a fully operating WFA team.

For such a team to be fully functioning, with the inclusion of an array of analytic projects, significant automation of data collection and monitoring would be required to fulfill their analytic potential. This may mean an investment in new technologies or systems that collect additional data, which can help provide insights into different aspects of employee psychological states, well-being states, and different features of behavior and performance at work. From an ethical lens, this can potentially invoke some interesting challenges. It raises the question of whether WFA activities that seek to use and collect an increasing amount of data on employees may be doing so at the cost of employees' rights to privacy and their rights as legitimate stakeholders to expect that aspects of their personal selves (and movement) are respected with dignity and not mined for the purposes of the organization (and profit).

The increased capabilities and scope of organizational monitoring of employee activities

Associated with the increasing use of WFA is an increasing array of digital HR-related technology (Bersin, 2023) that acts as an interface between employees and their organizations. These increasingly sophisticated technologies enable a greater volume and wider variety of employee data, correlating with an increase in monitoring of employee activities.

The degree to which monitoring and surveillance invoke ethical challenges depends on several factors, including the ethical framework one considers. For example, if an organization engages in sophisticated data collection and monitoring with the goal of ensuring employee well-being is not being harmed, then the outcome of the activity will be key. From a utilitarian perspective, a goal of serving the "greater good" in terms of "ends" may mean it can be considered an ethical activity due to positive aggregate economic outcomes, potentially justifying any ethical challenges associated with monitoring and surveillance. In contrast, a deontic or Kantian perspective emphasizes that the ends do not determine whether something is considered ethical, and individual rights (e.g., privacy) must be considered.

Aside from the ethical challenges, there is little doubt that recent digital HR technology developments have increased the capability, likelihood, and scope of potential monitoring of employees. This increasing scope includes recent developments in the capabilities of operating and IT systems, such as MS Office and MS 365, which employees use daily. The use of software systems that either overtly or covertly monitor employee activities appeared to increase during the COVID-19 pandemic (Wood, 2020, in *ABC News*; Hern, 2020, in *The Guardian*; Banks & Fai, 2020, in *The Financial Review*), though their use was already reportedly increasing before the pandemic (Economist, 2018). As employees were working from home more, there was a reported "surge" in organizations utilizing monitoring software that tracked employees, took random screenshots of employee computer screens, recorded how much time employees were idle on their computer or spent on a website, and monitored emails and other internet activities.

Aside from specific software systems that are available to monitor employee activities, basic computer operating systems are now opening up this potential. The capability of digital meeting and calendar systems such as MS Outlook, MS Teams, Zoom, and other systems to passively record, collate, and report on employee electronic activities has increased. As mentioned, in 2020 MS Office introduced facilities that would monitor and report productivity metrics linked to their electronic movements (e.g., emails responded to and meetings scheduled) and provide reports to managers (*Hern*, 2020).

Recent reviews of research on electronic monitoring and surveillance at work (Ravid et al., 2020; Ball, 2021) present an incredibly rich body of research highlighting an extensive range of methods used to monitor employees and the potential outcomes (positive and negative) that monitoring can have on employees and factors that influence these outcomes. In particular, the report by Ball (2021) to the European Commission discussed how digital developments are widening the scope and breadth of monitoring and surveillance activities at work. This includes the potential increase of biometric monitoring technology, such as wearable devices, and the tracking of location and movement through digital camera surveillance and other location-tracking technologies.

WFA and monitored data

The availability of recorded and traced data linked to employee activities, movements, emailing, and meeting activity is increasingly used by WFA teams to answer a range of different business questions. This invokes the ethical challenges of surveillance, monitoring, and data collection of employee activities with WFA. The ethical challenges of monitoring are combined with ethical challenges that may come to the fore when organizations begin to analyze these data and potentially make selective investment decisions.

Employee privacy: A core concern for WFA teams

One of the biggest ethical challenges accompanying the growth of WFA and the increased sophistication of digital technology for data collection and analysis is the issue of privacy intrusions related to employee data. In a recent review of workplace privacy issues, Bhave et al. (2020) outlined a range of issues linked to privacy in the workplace. Not all of the issues are directly related to WFA; however, some issues are. Bhave et al. (2020) highlighted a central problem with regard to privacy: employees may have some expectations and desire for privacy, but employers may also have expectations that they can collect and analyze extensive information regarding their employees. There may be a mismatch in these two sets of expectations that can create an ethical challenge.

This issue is linked to the point made earlier about managerial prerogative. Organizations may see it as their prerogative and expect to access and analyze employee data. In particular, employers may expect access to data detailing what the employee is doing during work time, including, for example, location data. The Bhave et al. (2020) discussion points out that this mismatch of expectations highlights some of the ethical concerns about whether organizations are potentially interfering with employees' right to privacy. In most societies, employees have a legal right to privacy; almost all reviews of WFA that touch on ethical challenges highlight this as a key and increasingly important ethical issue. As mentioned, Kantian ethical perspectives can be drawn on when considering issues around the ethics of individual rights, and a violation of rights can be deemed unethical—even in societies where there is no explicitly defined legal right to privacy.

The right to privacy, especially regarding data that is collected, stored, and analyzed, is enshrined in the European GDPR (Edwards & Edwards, 2019; Charlwood & Guenole, 2021). There have already been a number of high-profile cases where employers have been found to breach these privacy regulations; for example, IKEA (fined €1m) was deemed to be monitoring employees unnecessarily, and H&M (fined €35.3m/£32.1m) was found to be analyzing and creating profiles of employees' (potentially sensitive and private) health and attendance records. The GDPR provides an important framework of ethical principles that cover both data collection and use of analyses, but importantly, privacy is key.

Regardless of the legal environment in which an organization operates within a particular country, a socially responsible perspective requires organizations to go beyond the legal minimum set of guidelines for ethical action. As such, WFA teams need to be able to justify their position on privacy from a strong ethical perspective.

Frameworks for avoiding ethical challenges with privacy: Principles of privacy

Molitorisz (2020) provides a particularly useful framework of five fundamental principles of data privacy linked to digital developments regarding data and the internet. This framework can be used to assess the privacy challenges of WFA: consent, transparency, anti-deception, anti-coercion, and balancing principles.

Molitorisz contends that, for any act or process that significantly affects a person's or group's privacy with particular regard to personal or sensitive data, certain principles should be followed: (a) consent should be sought and respected; (b) the organization must be transparent and fair in its dealings regarding a person's privacy;

(c) the organization must refrain from conduct that is misleading or deceptive in the use of data and information linked to employees; (d) organizations must not be coercive in their dealings regarding a person's privacy; and (e) the right to privacy needs to be balanced in the context of other rights (e.g., security and freedoms of information and speech; Molitorisz, 2020, pp. 262–267).

Applying this set of principles to WFA projects and the use of employee monitoring and data access should withstand a good degree of ethical scrutiny regarding privacy because it goes beyond legislative minimum requirements and could therefore be considered socially responsible. This set of principles is rights-based and also procedurally (and informationally) just. It also fully considers the individual employees as key stakeholders. In today's era of rapid information dissemination on the internet and social media, such a socially responsible approach to protecting employees' privacy will help insulate the organization's reputation in the marketplaces for both customers and employees.

Frameworks for avoiding ethical challenges with privacy and monitoring: Principles of moderation and disclosure

Another useful nonregulatory framework for guiding WFA teams in their activities is proposed by Ambrose et al. (1998) when considering the ethical status of employee monitoring systems. The two key ideas they draw on are linked to the ethics of monitoring and include the rule of moderation and the rule of disclosure. The rule of moderation stipulates that organizations should act in moderation and not monitor or track (and subsequently analyze) information or data that can be considered private or sensitive or that may be perceived as crossing a line of privacy for employees. This may well include, for example, analyses of employee emails.

The rule of moderation, as applied by Ambrose et al. (1998), also relates to acting in moderation regarding the extent to which performance is monitored in a way that places employees under undue pressure. The rule of disclosure is particularly important because it touches on the ethical lens of informational and procedural justice frameworks. The rule says that organizations need to fully inform employees about the depth and scope of what is being monitored. According to Ambrose et al. (1998), the full disclosure of what an organization is doing with employee data, why they are monitoring and using employee data in a particular way, and the extent to which employees are being monitored is key to avoiding ethical challenges, such as coercion, a breach of employee rights of privacy, and any other analytic activities that may invoke an ethical challenge.

Wright et al. (2015) present another useful framework for managers to use in detecting ethical challenges in their monitoring activities. They set out a range of questions different stakeholder groups (including service providers, policymakers, and consultancies) should ask themselves when engaging in surveillance. From an

HR analytic perspective, many key questions in this guide would help ensure that employee-based monitoring does not breach ethical standards. We do not set out these questions in detail here; instead, we refer the reader to the source document. One example question that managers need to ask with a WFA project is, "Has a privacy impact assessment been conducted?"

Consent as an ethical principle

The use of employee-related data linked to personal information or collected on their movements or behavior without their knowledge exposes the organization to breaching ethical standards and concerns across several dimensions. Both of the privacy frameworks mentioned here, which consider employee rights to privacy, discuss the importance of consent. From an ethical HR lens, we can draw on the deontic framework to consider whether the organization may be doing the right (or wrong) thing when monitoring and analyzing employee data. Asking for consent from employees before initiating analytics projects and being concerned with employee rights to privacy will help the organization avoid invoking a deontic or Kantian ethical challenge (in this regard)—which helps protect its reputation among customers, current and prospective employees, and leaders.

Beyond a deontic perspective, monitoring and analyzing employee data may also raise a stakeholder challenge that the organization is not taking the interests of employees seriously nor considering the potential impact of the policies on employees. This is especially the case if the reason for carrying out the project is to boost productivity and performance, which will ultimately benefit the organization and its shareholders as a stakeholder group, potentially at the expense of the interests of employees as a stakeholder group. This is particularly relevant if the organization is breaching, in some way, employee rights to privacy or principles of procedural and informational justice.

For WFA teams to ensure they do not breach potential ethical boundaries, transparency and the disclosure of what information and data are being used, and how and why they are being analyzed, are key elements that will help determine whether analytics projects are considered ethical. Because new projects are often introduced by analytics teams that may use data in ways the organization has not previously, this idea of disclosure and consent suggests that employees need to be consulted on any new use of their data. This would necessitate a communication program to be implemented that regularly updates staff when new projects are being introduced. This would also be important for new joiners who may not have been abreast of previous communication activities. However, organizations rarely do this, and the challenge of disclosure and consent is often covered by policies that are communicated to staff at the outset when they join, to which they are often expected to sign their consent.

The challenge lies in these disclosure and consent policies often being extremely broad to enable employers to use employee data in various forms of important business analyses. Frequently, analytics teams undertaking new analysis projects need to seek consent or, at the minimum, allow employees to have some control (or perception of control) over what their employer does with data (private or otherwise). This, of course, can create a challenge for organizations that may need employee data for a new analytic project that uses data in a new and different way that may extend or stretch their existing data use arrangements or policies.

A good example of this challenge is the recent growth in the use of organizational network analyses, particularly passive rather than active organizational network analyses. Active organizational network analyses involve distributing surveys to employees that can help demonstrate employee networks (by asking employees who is in their network, etc.) and enable the organization to build an understanding of how people are linked. Passive organizational network analyses, however, involve the organization collecting data from its electronic system of communication or scheduling (e.g., calendar system). This distinction is key in determining whether the analyses are likely to cross any ethical boundaries.

For example, organizational network analyses that use email traffic and calendar activity may well go beyond what an organization has formally communicated to staff in a policy regarding the kind of data that may be collated and analyzed. This is an example of a project where employers may need to seek additional consent. When consent is sought, the organization face the challenge of not all employees being willing to have their electronic activities analyzed. As mentioned above, there may be some mismatch between employees' sense of what is private and the organization's perspective of what is private employee data, and this is an example of where there may be a stakeholder expectation mismatch.

Global variation in data use regulatory frameworks

One of the challenges for HR analytics teams that operate in multinational organizations or organizations where employees are based in different parts of the world is the variation across the globe in terms of regulatory frameworks that may influence what activities are considered legally acceptable. For example, Europe is covered by the GDPR, which has broad sweeping powers to ensure organizations comply with a whole range of different data protection and privacy principles, along with guidelines on important issues such as the nonhuman oversight of the application of AI. Importantly, from a WFA perspective, this legislation covers employees and the use of employee data. However, other countries have less rigorous legislative frameworks covering employee data and data use (e.g., Australia has an employee data exemption to their privacy regulation, even though working for a government organization gives some coverage), which means WFA teams will have to be on top of regulatory frameworks across different countries if their organization covers multiple regions.

Ethical workforce analytics for good

This chapter has focused on the ethical challenges that WFA can introduce. There is always an ethical context to WFA activities; however, this does not necessarily mean the ethical context will always lead to a negative ethical judgment regarding the WFA team activities. Assuming various safeguards and guidelines have been implemented, there is considerable potential for WFA to do good. Some aspects of data held on employees are not necessarily private and easily fall within the range of data that is well within an organization's ethical remit to analyze. Furthermore, there are many HR analytic projects whose analyses lead to good and positive outcomes while also remaining ethical.

An example of this is when an organization conducts analytics to try to identify whether particular minority (diverse) groups are receiving equal treatment compared to the majority within the organization; this could be patterns of pay, progression, appraisal ratings, performance ratings, or turnover statistics. When these projects are undertaken with the aim of helping identify where there may be challenges to social justice (where unequal outcomes are identified), the ethical status of these projects is unlikely to be challenged. Other examples of projects "for good" may include trying to assess any potential negative impact of HR practices on employees (e.g., shift patterns on employee well-being and sickness absences). Such analytics projects would come under the purview of sustainable HRM.

Heather Whiteman, University of Washington

People Data for Good

People analytics success is often measured by the degree to which it enables an organization to meet its objectives. However, when we consider the power and impact that people analytics-informed decisions can have on the lives and livelihoods of the people involved, is this an adequate measure of success? Is it enough to measure how people data does good for the organization, or should it also do good for people? To embrace "people data for good" is to ensure that "people analytics" means "analytics for people," not just "analytics about people."

Terms like "good" or "bad" are subjective, but we can consider them on a spectrum that ranges from actions that are clearly unethical to actions that create positive outcomes for all involved. I believe people analytics' success should be measured not only in terms of its usefulness to the organization but also with regard to its place on this spectrum.

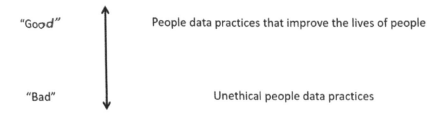

FIGURE 6.2 Good to bad people data practices.

People analytics leads to outcomes that affect real people in very real ways. As such, there will be few, if any, instances when a practice could be considered truly neutral. Let's say one wants to assess a people analytics practice. The first step is to determine if it has privacy issues, "creepiness," or legal concerns, followed by assessing if the outcomes/decisions lead to positive or negative consequences. If no ethical issues are found and no changes will be made as a result, it can be tempting to label the analysis as a "neutral" fact-finding mission. The thinking may be, "It may not do 'good,' but at least it's not doing bad, right?" Maybe. The next step is to ask if there is an undesirable status quo in the organization (e.g., selection bias, exclusivity, inequity) that the data is helping to reinforce. Could the data, if used differently, alter this status quo for the better? If so, then the ethical implications of the people analytics practice are a bit more complicated than they may seem on the surface. People data for good requires not merely avoiding new harm but also efforts to bring about change for a better future.

While complicated, the effort of using people data for good should not be overwhelming or discouraging. There are analytical techniques that identify and mitigate biases and increase inclusivity. There are platforms based on sound principles for using people data for good. There are people analytics teams in organizations creating ethical people data practice standards, such as in the Broad ONA Case Study (mentioned in Chapter 4) or Rio Tinto (as discussed in this chapter), that can serve as models and provide inspiration. Consider connecting with other people analytics professionals in the community who are committed to promoting the responsible and ethical use of people data, analytics, and artificial intelligence for the benefit of individuals, organizations, and society at large. Alternatively, create your own people data for good pledge, outlining the standards you will follow and the practices you will uphold to place people at the heart of your work while ensuring the fair, ethical, and secure use of people data.

People data for good is not an action but a movement; one that poses tricky questions and complicated answers. But it is also one that provides an opportunity for everyone (no matter how small a role each person plays in the decisions and actions that affect the lives of people at work) to unleash the power of data "for" people, not "to," "on," or "about" them.

Analytics ethics charters

One strategy a WFA team can employ to ensure ethical issues are always considered is to set out an analytics ethics charter that commits the analytics team and members to act ethically in their dealings. Rio Tinto is an example of an organization that has an ethics charter (Figure 6.3) and trains its analytics teams to work within this charter. A strong aspect of this ethics charter is that it covers privacy, security, and fairness, and it pledges to be transparent and unbiased in the work the analytics team does.

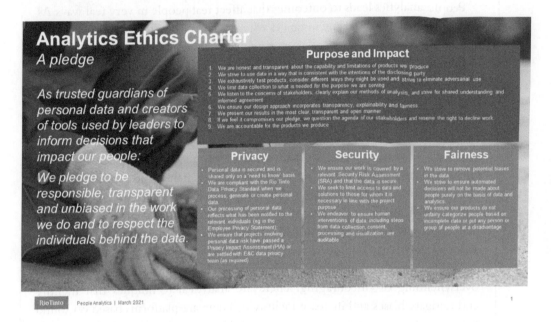

FIGURE 6.3 Rio Tinto ethics charter.

Ethical workforce analytics—a ten-step framework?

As discussed, the potential scope of ethical issues that workforce analytics considers, and the ethical issues that can be involved in WFA, are varied. This chapter addressed a number of issues that need to be considered to help employers ensure they do not fall foul of an ethical challenge. We summarize some of the most important below.

1) **Communication:** Employers need to clearly inform employees about which employee data are stored and how they use their data. This needs to be updated and communicated regularly. Where employee behavior and activities (including electronic activities) are monitored, this needs to be declared to employees with full transparency.

2) **Consent:** Where possible, employees need to be asked for consent whenever data related to an employee is collected and analyzed. While some employee

data that is collected is not likely to be considered private (and could be considered more the property of the organization), where data has the potential to encroach on privacy (e.g., vaccination status, biometric data, protected status data, video recording data), consent must be sought, and the consent needs to be genuine; employees need to be able to withdraw from its use.

3) **Restriction of monitoring and surveillance:** Because the monitoring of employees can invoke ethical challenges linked to privacy rights, organizations need to use moderation when it comes to monitoring and surveying employees. Monitoring should be deployed only when absolutely necessary, and there should be no monitoring in spaces of privacy nor where access is required to data that may be perceived as private by employees. This needs to be declared (following the principle of communication). The organization also needs to conduct a privacy impact assessment to ensure the monitoring and analytics activity does not interfere with employees' rights to privacy.

4) **Frameworks of transparency and disclosure:** Following communication, the WFA team must ensure their analytic methods' data use is transparent. Where assumptions are made about the use of proxy measures, these need to be declared and discussed. Also, where algorithms are used, these need to be transparent. The analytic team needs to be able to discuss the features of the algorithms when applied and communicate these within the principles of explainability.

5) **Bias audits:** Large-scale bias audits covering a range of possible aspects of bias should be conducted. This includes potential bias associated with model features such as the data used, model design, development, features, process, and outputs. In addition, how model outputs are interpreted and responded to, the impact and effects of the model on recipients, and how they fit with regulatory frameworks and recognized ethical frameworks where available (e.g., with the use of AI) need to be audited. The HR analytics team needs to consider the cultural contexts of those involved in the model design and use (i.e., what cultural assumptions are being made about the appropriate use of the model and outputs). The aspects of the analytic research project design also need to be questioned (i.e., whether the design is robust and whether claims about the model hold up to methodological scrutiny).

6) **Humans in the loop:** Unfettered automated algorithms are likely to lead to ethical challenges because the computers and programs involved lack the human insight required to make ethical judgments. Many ethical frameworks (including, for example, the GDPR) now require humans to be in the loop to ensure decisions that impact people (employees) are not made without some human oversight. Where automated processes are introduced that have the potential to nudge employees or be used to make selective investment decisions (e.g., who to short-list), these systems should be overseen by a human.

Also, where investment decisions could affect people's livelihoods or well-being, algorithms should be seen as advisory but require human oversight.

7) **Overreach of the managerial prerogative:** One of the key challenges with WFA that could lead an analytics team to fall foul of an ethical challenge is that many different analytic projects may end up crossing ethical lines. While there is a wide scope of analytic activities that fall under everyday managerial or operational planning and analysis activities, an analytics team cannot automatically ethically analyze any data they have access to. Thus, analytics teams need to ensure that an overreach assessment is conducted for any analytics project. Is this project necessary? Are we going beyond what can be reasonably considered ethical managerial activities and prerogatives?

8) **Stakeholder assessment:** Any WFA team about to embark on a project needs to conduct a stakeholder assessment process that considers which stakeholders are impacted by the project, what their interests or stakes are in the project, how they may be affected by it, and whether they would benefit or suffer as a result. Obviously, the key stakeholder to consider from an ethical perspective is employees, but different projects may have different stakeholders who may be affected. Therefore, each project requires stakeholder assessment.

9) **Analytic project ethical framework assessment:** In addition to a stakeholder assessment, a full consideration of potential ethical challenges in an analytic project requires an ethical framework assessment to be conducted. This involves considering the project from the ethical lenses highlighted above. What ethical implications does this project have from a social responsibility perspective? What ethical implications does this project have from a utilitarian perspective? While most WFA projects may have a reasonable ethical standing or status, there may be specific projects where particular ethical frameworks are invoked. For example, some projects may invoke stakeholder challenges, some may involve sustainability challenges, some various justice challenges, some utilitarianism challenges, and some privacy challenges.

10) **Do not forget the human in workforce analytics:** Whether an organization uses the label workforce analytics, people analytics, or something else, the main focus of analytic work in these teams will be employee-related data in many shapes and forms. With analytics, it is easy to reduce employees and their attitudes, emotions, and behaviors to numbers; the team and organization must always remember these numbers relate to humans and ensure the humanity linked to the numbers is not lost. While the notion of recognizing human sentiment is not mentioned as an ethical framework above, it is central to Hume's framework of sympathy, which involves having the capacity to be moved or affected by the happiness or suffering of others when making judgments of what is right or wrong. This may be an important place to end this chapter on

the ethics of WFA. As Edwards and Edwards (2019) raised, "Do not forget the human in Human Resource/HR Analytics."

Key take-away: ACAI and effective (and ethical) workforce analytics implementation

The discussion above highlights the complexity of the ethical landscape that workforce analytics experts must navigate. These issues must be considered and addressed for an organization to ensure that the element of "right" in the four ACAI phases of effective workforce analytics implementation can withstand potential ethical challenges. Thus, from an ethical lens, the four phases of effective implementation of workforce analytics can be considered as follows:

- Phase 1: **A**sk the right (ethical) questions
- Phase 2: **C**ollect the right data (that does not breach ethical frameworks)
- Phase 3: Conduct the right **A**nalyses (in an ethical way)
- Phase 4: **I**nfluence the right decisions (that do not transgress ethical considerations)

At every phase of the WA implementation, the analyst needs to ask, "Is this 'right' from an ethical perspective?" and also holistically consider how the phases combine. For example, it might be 'right' or reasonable to consider evidence and data linked to employee activities and performance to help inform decision-making; however, if the evidence and data collected on employees are highly private and personal, building profiles with this data will render other parts of the process "wrong" from an ethical perspective. Furthermore, if the analyses conducted reinforce bias in data collected or produce biased results or outcomes, this will raise challenges in making the "right" decisions based on the interpretation of output from the analyses.

References

Aguinis, H. (2011). Organizational responsibility: Doing good and doing well. In S. Zedeck (Ed.), *APA handbook of industrial and organizational psychology. Maintaining, expanding, and contracting the organization* (Vol. 3, pp. 855–879). American Psychological Association.

Ambrose, M. L., Alder, G. S., & Noel, T. W. (1998). Electronic performance monitoring: A consideration of rights. In M. Schminke (Ed.), *Managerial ethics: Moral management of people and processes*. Chapter 4, 61–80. Lawrence Erlbaum & Associates.

Angrave, D., Charlwood, A., Kirkpatrick, I., Lawrence, M., & Stuart, M. (2016). HR and analytics: Why HR is set to fail the big data challenge. *Human Resource Management Journal, 26*(1), 1–11.

Ball, K. (2021). *Electronic monitoring and surveillance in the workplace: Literature review and policy recommendations*. Publications Office of the European Union.

Banks, D., & Fai, M. (2020, July 16). The new challenge for bosses: Spy or trust? *Australian Financial Review.* https://www.afr.com/work-and-careers/workplace/the-new-challenge -for-bosses-spy-or-trust-20200713-p55bo3

BBC. (2020, February 20). What are the rules on workplace surveillance? *BBC News.* https:// www.bbc.com/news/explainers-51571684

Bersin. (2023). https://joshbersin.com/2023/06/the-next-generation-of-hr-software-has -arrived-finally/

Bhave, D. P., Teo, L. H., & Dalal, R. S. (2020). Privacy at work: A review and a research agenda for a contested terrain. *Journal of Management, 46*(1), 127–164.

Buckingham, M. (2015, February 9). Most HR data is bad data. *Harvard Business Review.* https:// hbr.org/2015/02/most-hr-data-is-bad-data

Carroll, A. B. (1979). A three-dimensional conceptual model of corporate social performance. *Academy of Management Review, 4*(4), 497–505.

Charlwood, A., & Guenole, N. (2021). Can HR adapt to the paradoxes of artificial intelligence? *Human Resource Management Journal, 32*(1), 729–738.

Colquitt, J. A. (2001). On the dimensionality of organizational justice: A construct validation of a measure. Journal of Applied Psychology, 86(3), 386–400.

Davis, K. (1960). Can business afford to ignore social responsibilities? *California Management Review, 2*(3), 70–76.

De Cremer, D., & Kasparov, G. (2021). The ethical AI—paradox: Why better technology needs more and not less human responsibility. *AI and Ethics, 2*(1), 1–4.

Economist. (2018, March 28). There will be little privacy in the workplace of the future: AI will make workplaces more efficient, safer—and much creepier. *The Economist.* https:// www.economist.com/special-report/2018/03/28/there-will-be-little-privacy-in-the -workplace-of-the-future

Edwards, M. R. (2019). HR metrics and analytics. In M. Thite (Ed.), *e-HRM: Digital approaches, directions & applications.* Chapter 6, 89–105, Routledge.

Edwards, M. R., Charlwood, A., Guenole, N., & Marler, J. (2022). HR analytics: An emerging field finding its place in the world. *Human Resource Management Journal, 34*(2), 326–336. https://doi.org/10.1111/1748-8583.12435

Edwards, M. R., & Edwards, K. (2019). *Predictive HR analytics: Mastering the HR metric* (2nd ed.). Kogan Page.

Ehnert, I. (2009). *Sustainable human resource management: A conceptual and exploratory analysis from a paradox perspective.* Physica Heidelberg.

Ehnert, I., & Harry, W. (2012). Recent developments and future prospects and sustainable human resource management: Introduction to the special issue. *Management Review, 23*(3), 221–238.

Freeman, R. E. (1984). *Strategic management: A stakeholder approach.* Pitman.

Freeman, R. R., Harrison, J., Wicks, A., Parmar, B., & de Colle, S. (2010). *Stakeholder theory: The state of the art.* Cambridge University Press.

Friedman, M. (1970, September 13). The social responsibility of business is to increase its profits. *New York Times Magazine,* 122–126.

Gal, U., Jensen, T. B., & Stein, M. K. (2020). Breaking the vicious cycle of algorithmic management: A virtue ethics approach to people analytics. *Information and Organization, 30*(2), 100301.

Guenole, N., Ferrar, J., & Feinzig, S. (2017). *The power of people: Learn how successful organizations use workforce analytics to improve business performance.* Pearson FT Press.

Harris, J. D., & Freeman, R. E. (2008). The impossibility of the separation thesis: A response to Joakim Sandberg. *Business Ethics Quarterly, 18*(4), 541–548.

Hern, A. (2020, December 3). Microsoft apologises for feature criticised as workplace surveillance. *The Guardian.* https://www.theguardian.com/technology/2020/dec/02/ microsoft-apologises-productivity-score-critics-derided-workplace-surveillance

Holzinger, A., Langs, G., Denk, H., Zatloukal, K., & Müller, H. (2019). Causability and explainability of artificial intelligence in medicine. Wiley Interdisciplinary Reviews: Data Mining and Knowledge Discovery, 9(4), e1312.

Huselid, M. A. (2018). The science and practice of workforce analytics: Introduction to the HRM special issue. Human Resource Management, 57(3), 679–684.

Kryscynski, D., Reeves, C., Stice-Lusvardi, R., Ulrich, M., & Russell, G. (2018). Analytical abilities and the performance of HR professionals. *Human Resource Management, 57*(3), 715–738.

Landers, R. N., & Behrend, T. S. (2023). Auditing the AI auditors: A framework for evaluating fairness and bias in high stakes AI predictive models. *American Psychologist, 78*(1), 36–39.

Larsson, A.-S., & Edwards M. R. (2021). Insider econometrics meets people analytics and strategic human resource management. *International Journal of Human Resource Management, 33*(2), 1–47.

Longnecker, C., & Ludwig, D. (1990). Ethical dilemma in performance appraisal revisited. *Journal of Business Ethics, 9*(12), 961–969.

Martin, K., & Waldman, A. E. (2021). Are algorithmic decisions legitimate? The effect of process and outcomes on perceptions of legitimacy of ai decisions. *Journal of Business Ethics, 183*(1), 653–670.

McCartney, S., & Fu, N. (2022). Promise versus reality: A systematic review of the ongoing debates in people analytics. Journal of Organizational Effectiveness: People and Performance, 9(2), 281–311.

McKinlay, A., & Zeitlin, J. (2006). The meanings of managerial prerogative: Industrial relations and the organisation of work in British engineering, 1880–1939. *Business History, 31*(2), 32–47.

Meijerink, J., Boons, M., Keegan, A., & Marler, J. (2021). Algorithmic human resource management: Synthesizing developments and cross-disciplinary insights on digital HRM. *The International Journal of Human Resource Management, 32*(12), 2545–2562.

Molitorisz, S. (2020). *Net privacy: How we can be free in an age of surveillance.* McGill-Queen's University Press.

Morgeson, F. P., Aguinis, H., Waldman, D. A., & Siegel, D. S. (2013). Extending corporate social responsibility research to the human resource management and organizational behavior domains: A look to the future. *Personnel Psychology, 66*(4), 805–824. https://doi.org/10.1111/peps.12055

Norman, R. (1983). *The moral philosophers: An introduction to ethics.* Oxford University Press.

O'Neil, C. (2017). *Weapons of math destruction: How big data increases inequality and threatens democracy.* Crown.

Pfeffer, J. (2017). Building sustainable organizations: The human factor. *Academy of Management Perspectives, 24*(1), 2–21.

Ravid, D. M., Tomczak, D. L., White, J. C., & Behrend, T. S. (2020). EPM 20/20: A review, framework, and research agenda for electronic performance monitoring. *Journal of Management, 46*(1), 100–126. https://doi.org/10.1177/0149206319869435

Sandberg, J. (2008). Understanding the separation thesis. *Business Ethics Quarterly, 18*(2), 213–232.

Schildt, H. (2016). Big data and organizational design—The brave new world of algorithmic management and computer augmented transparency. *Innovation: Organization & Management, 19*(1), 1–8.

Sesil, J. C. (2014). *Applying advanced analytics to HR management decisions: Methods for selection, developing incentives, and improving collaboration.* Pearson Education.

Someh, I., Davern, M., Breidbach, C. F., & Shanks, G. (2019). Ethical issues in big data analytics: A stakeholder perspective. *Communications of the Association for Information Systems, 44*(34), 718–747. https://doi.org/10.17705/1CAIS.04434

Soundararajan, R., & Singh, K. (2017). *Winning on HR analytics: Leveraging data for competitive advantage.* SAGE Publications.

Speer, A. B. (2021). Empirical attrition modelling and discrimination: Balancing validity and group differences. *Human Resource Management Journal, 34*(1), 1–19. Advance online publication. https://doi.org/10.1111/1748-8583.12355

Tursunbayeva, A., Pagliari, C., Di Lauro, S., & Gilda, A. (2021). The ethics of people analytics: Risks, opportunities and recommendations. *Personnel Review, 51*(3), 900 921. Advance online publication. https://doi.org/10.1108/PR-12-2019-0680

Vigden, R., & Hindle, R. (2021). Exploring the ethical implications of business analytics with a business ethics canvas. *European Journal of Operational Research, 281*(3), 491–501.

Waldman, D. A., Siegel, D. S., & Javidan, M. (2006). Components of CEO transformational leadership and corporate social responsibility. *Journal of Management Studies, 43*(8), 1703–1725.

Wicks, A. C. (1996). Overcoming the separation thesis. *Business & Society, 35*(1), 89–118.

Williams, B., Brooks, C., & Shmargad, Y. (2018). How algorithms discriminate based on data they lack: Challenges, solutions, and policy implications. *Journal of Information Policy, 8*, 78–115. https://doi.org/10.5325/jinfopoli.8.2018.0078

Winstanley, D., & Woodall, J. (2000). The ethical dimension of human resource management. *Human Resource Management Journal, 10*(2), 5–20.

Wood, P. (2020, May 21). Employee monitoring software surges as companies send staff home. *ABC News*. https://www.abc.net.au/news/2020-05-22/working-from-home-employee-monitoring-software-boom-coronavirus/12258198

Wright, D. Rodrigues, R., Raab, C., Jones, R., Szekely, I., Ball, K., Bellanova, R., & Bergersen, S. (2015). Questioning surveillance. *Computer Law & Security Review, 31*(2), 280–292.

Building the workforce analytics function

Steven McCartney and Dana Minbaeva

Introduction

Over the past several years, workforce analytics (WFA) has seen significant growth in popularity, with organizations worldwide leveraging workforce data to aid in making strategic decisions (Angrave et al., 2016; Marler & Boudreau, 2017). Accordingly, we have seen numerous examples of organizations effectively implementing the ACAI model (introduced in Chapter 1) to demonstrate the impact of WFA and how organizations can effectively utilize workforce data to make critical decisions in areas such as diversity and inclusion, recruitment and selection, and training and development (Buttner & Tullar, 2018; Falletta & Combs, 2020; Minbaeva, 2018; Peeters et al., 2020; van der Togt & Rasmussen, 2017). However, despite its popularity among practitioners and advances made in the field, what remains nascent are studies illustrating the dualistic nature of WFA maturity, how this shapes the development of WFA functions, and their evolution among different organization types. Furthermore, a holistic view of the various elements required to achieve the desired level of WFA maturity and to build an effective WFA function in contemporary organizations is needed.

In this chapter, we address these gaps by proposing a new WFA maturity matrix, offering a much-needed shift in thinking toward WFA maturity. In addition, we propose a framework for building effective WFA functions, including team composition, and the relative advantages and disadvantages of different choices available when building a WFA function.

In the following sections, we set the stage by first outlining various perspectives concerning WFA maturity and the need for a more expansive view thereof. In doing so, we challenge the established view of WFA maturity as a linear process that evolves in a predictable manner from low-level operational reporting to highly sophisticated advanced analytics. Instead, we argue that the equilibrium between

DOI: 10.4324/9781003190097-18

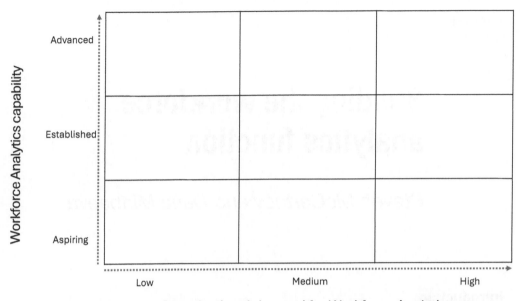

FIGURE 7.1 Workforce analytics maturity matrix.

"push" and "pull" factors (Cascio & Boudreau, 2017) defines the desired level of WFA maturity. "Pull" factors represent the level of demand from the broader organizational context for knowledge that the WFA projects generate, while "push" factors capture the WFA team's capabilities to generate such knowledge (see Figure 7.1).

Next, drawing on the ACAI model, we outline each of the "push" and "pull" factors that help shape the development of the WFA function, emphasizing those "push" factors that are under the control of WFA functions. Building on the logic of supply ("push") and demand ("pull"), we apply these concepts to improving the effectiveness of the WFA function. We propose that an effective structure depends on the needs of the organization and is best situated at a point of equilibrium between supply and demand. We conclude the chapter by addressing various options for setting up the WFA function based on the desired level of capability and their relative advantages and disadvantages.

Unique to this chapter, we leverage insights into the development of WFA functions and maturity derived from interviews conducted with expert WFA professionals. These interviews and quotes support and strengthen the arguments we make throughout the chapter.

Setting the stage: WFA maturity

From the early days of WFA' popularity, the key question has been, "What does good WFA look like?" Companies have been curious to see the best-in-class standards and best practices to gain inspiration and better understand where to go and what to aim for. Meanwhile, practitioners and scholars have also contentiously debated the concept of WFA maturity. For instance, according to various consulting firms and professional associations, WFA should be considered a continuum, with the function's maturity determining the extent of analytics that may be performed (Chartered Institute of Personnel and Development (CIPD), 2019; Deloitte, 2019).

For example, Deloitte (2019) claimed that WFA can be classified into four distinct levels: operational reporting, advanced reporting, advanced analytics, and predictive analytics. Likewise, the CIPD (2019) built upon this premise, suggesting that WFA operates on five levels: operational, descriptive, diagnostic, predictive, and prescriptive. This perspective has spread to the academic literature on WFA, where scholars such as Margherita (2022), Sivathanu and Pillai (2020), and Marler and Martin (2021) address the various levels of WFA. For example, according to Margherita (2022), WFA follows a linear three-stage maturity model. At its lowest level, "descriptive," WFA focuses on using data to answer questions concerning what has happened. Next, the "predictive" stage focuses on what might happen in the future and why. Finally, the "prescriptive" stage determines the actions to take in response to the analysis.

More recently, McCartney and Fu (2022b) expressed their belief that WFA maturity plays an important role in conceptualizing and developing value-added WFA programs:

> [Workforce Analytics] should be seen as situational, falling along a spectrum where organizations at the low end of maturity report on descriptive statistics. In contrast, organizations at the highest and most mature level of workforce analytics can utilize descriptive statistics and more advanced forms of technology (i.e., artificial intelligence, machine learning and organizational network analysis tools) to analyze workforce data to perform predictive and prescriptive analytics.
>
> *(p. 8)*

As can be seen, many scholars have categorized WFA maturity based solely on the principles of Phase 3 of the ACAI model, which relates to the degree of analytical and statistical capabilities of the individual or WFA team. Although this is an essential component of analytics maturity, we argue that to fully realize business value from WFA, it is equally important that organizations have the demand for new knowledge that WFA projects create and the willingness to implement actionable solutions derived from them. For example, if a WFA team has the required analytical competencies to deliver sophisticated predictive analyses, but there is no appetite for actions from the organizational side (Phase 4), the business value of WFA would be negligible. Therefore, progressing WFA for business value creation necessitates working with two axes (along two dimensions simultaneously).

This sentiment aligns well with current thinking among influential WFA leaders. For instance, Heather Whiteman, former VP, Global Head of People Strategy,

Analytics, Digital Learning, and HR Operations and current Associate Teaching Professor at the University of Washington School of Information, asserts:

> There is a difference between analytics maturity, meaning what you're capable of doing with analytics, versus the organization's maturity to use analytics. I have seen instances where the data approach itself is very advanced, where they are using some machine learning, very technical stuff. However, I would still consider the organization to not be very mature from an analytics standpoint. … Plenty of organizations have a really high demand for workforce analytics, but they don't know how to use it.

Accordingly, we argue that WFA maturity evolves through the interaction between two dimensions: (a) the WFA team's capabilities and (b) the organizational demand for actionable insights that WFA projects create (see Figure 7.1). In Tables 7.1 and 7.2, we suggest that each of the two dimensions comprises three levels, and we offer examples to illustrate their differences.

For organizations and human resources (HR) departments to begin building capabilities in WFA, it is crucial to be aware of the equilibrium required between "pull" (i.e., organizational demand for WFA) and "push" (i.e., the supply of WFA capabilities). This is particularly important in the context of the ACAI model because the manner in which data can be collected (Phase 2), analyzed (Phase 3), and presented (Phase 4) is predicated on the position of the organization or department within the WFA maturity matrix at that moment (Margherita, 2022; Marler & Martin, 2021). Likewise, the organizational demand for data and insights from

TABLE 7.1 Levels of WFA capabilities

	Aspiring	Established	Advanced
Analytical competencies	Uses reporting tools via HCM interface, basic visualization skills. Excel superuser.	Enables trusted diagnostic reporting and delivers insights via dynamic BI tools.	Conducts bespoke predictive analytics using SPSS, Stata, R, Python, or similar software; open to experimentation with AI and ML.
Data quality and processes	Uses clean and reliable data, typically from a single source (e.g., HCM system).	Uses data from multiple sources, organized and transformed within a single environment, e.g., DW/SQL.	Uses structured and unstructured data from across business functions, with high-volume data processing tools.
Business partnering ability	Delivers basic HR reporting, leading to increased understanding. Limited decision-making impact.	Offers advanced insights to leaders and HRBPs that may guide operational and tactical decision-making.	Influences business planning and HR strategy. Offers tactical sparring and hypothesizes about foreseen HR management issues.

TABLE 7.2 Organizational demand for WFA

	Low	Medium	High
Analytical requests derived from the digitalization of business processes	How many and who? What happened and when? Reporting figures (e.g., headcount trends, hires, promotions, and exits), internal comparisons. Teams or functions review HR data.	Why did it happen? Is it good or bad? Linking HCM KPIs to organizational priorities (e.g., time to hire). Linking HCM practices to costs using external benchmarks, insights into employee experiences. Functions or BUs apply insights.	What might happen next? What should be done? Knowledge about internal collaboration patterns and networks. Linking the root causes of HCM issues to business outcomes. Forecasting to avoid over- and understaffing, simulating HCM impacts of business scenarios. BUs or enterprise adapt significant changes.
Analytical and data-driven culture	Limited implementation of data and analytics for decision-making. Decisions based on personal experience rather than evidence. Reactive decision-making processes.	Functional or BU decisions are based on data and analytics. Analytics focus on answering functional or unit challenges. Analytical and data-driven culture enacted by functional or BU leader.	Strategic business decisions encompass data from all facets of the organization. AI and ML outputs highly influence strategic decision-making and change management activities. Focus on answering business questions with data. Data embedded into the values of the organization.

stakeholders and the ability to implement actionable solutions directly relate to the required level of a WFA team's capabilities.

In the following sections, we outline and provide in-depth insight into the "push" and "pull" factors that impact WFA functions and play a pivotal role in their paths within the WFA maturity matrix.

What are the push factors?

Once organizations and HR departments have determined their level of analytics maturity, it is then critical to begin building upon the "push factors" that enable building and strengthening WFA capabilities. We define "push factors" as circumstances or criteria that must be met for WFA to be available within the HR department. These factors provide the "supply" for building effective and sustainable WFA capabilities.

We identify three overarching push factors critical to establishing effective WFA. To build organizational capabilities in WFA and provide actionable insights through workforce data, the following conditions must be met: (a) the workforce analyst or members of the WFA team must have the proper knowledge, skills, abilities, and other characteristics (KSAOs); (b) the department must have data quality procedures and processes in place; and (c) the workforce analyst or members of the WFA team must have the ability to partner with the business. We discuss each push factor in detail in the subsequent sections.

Skills and competencies required for building workforce analytics capabilities

Given the expanding number of HR functions embracing WFA to make more informed and data-driven decisions, many HR departments are now employing workforce analysts (McCartney et al., 2020; Huevel & Bondarouk, 2017). This newly emerging role has become a unique addition to the HR function that focuses on collecting, analyzing, and implementing workforce data to generate actionable solutions to various HR and organizational challenges. Moreover, this role differs from traditional HR roles, such as HR business partners or HR generalists, given the technical nature of the tasks involved (McIver et al., 2018; Huevel & Bondarouk, 2017).

As discussed earlier, the maturity level of the WFA capability impacts the sophistication of analytics that can be generated. At the aspiring level of WFA maturity, a single analyst may oversee all aspects of the ACAI process. Therefore, this role requires a broad set of KSAOs to manage the entire ACAI process (Andersen, 2017; McIver et al., 2018).

Several scholars and professional associations worldwide have made suggestions regarding the KSAOs that workforce analysts require to generate value-added WFA. Many scholars emphasize the need for robust data management skills (Andersen, 2017), storytelling and visualization (Andersen, 2017; McCartney et al., 2020; McIver et al., 2018), strong business acumen (Andersen, 2017; Ellmer & Reichel, 2021; McCartney et al., 2020; van der Togt & Rasmussen, 2017), and proficiency with technology including human capital management (HCM) systems such as Workday, SAP SuccessFactors, and Vizier, as well as open-source statistical platforms like R and Python (Ellmer & Reichel, 2021; Falletta & Combs, 2020; McCartney et al., 2020; McIver et al., 2018; Pessach et al., 2020). Similarly, HR professional associations share comparable views on the KSAOs required for analysts to generate insights through workforce data. The Society for Human Resource Management (SHRM), for instance, asserts that workforce analysts require proficiency in using data to predict and suggest improvements to workforce challenges through analytical skills and statistical knowledge (SHRM, 2016).

Although a wide range of KSAOs is theorized among scholars and practitioner associations, it is also important to consider the perspective of WFA leaders tasked with recruitment and the overall strategic direction of the WFA program. Thomas Rasmussen, former Senior Vice President, Digital and Automation, People and Culture at Vestas, stated the following:

You need a deep understanding of scientific methods, right? 'Cause you know workforce analytics is an applied science. You need to know how to do a regression. You typically need to code, so knowing how to code is important. You also need to know about and research design all of that stuff, right? And then in addition to that, having a deep statistical skill set, and you need to be really, really, really good at telling the story on the results, so translating it from something that you would put in a journal to something that you can present in front of executives.

Another WFA leader, Pete Jaworski, Head of People Data and Analytics at A.P. Moller-Maersk, stated the following:

> The core capability in essence of the workforce analysts is being able to understand what the problem is defined, what the potential solution is, and then feedback a recommendation based on insights so that that's the consulting capability that's really core to the role.

The views expressed across three perspectives (i.e., scholars, practitioner associations, leaders) are similar, and WFA leaders' views align well with current assumptions that scholars and professional associations make regarding the KSAOs WFA professionals require to enact the ACAI model and offer insight through workforce data. Recently, in an attempt to consolidate the three perspectives concerning the desired KSAOs for workforce analysts, McCartney et al. (2020) developed a comprehensive competency model through an extensive literature review and interviews with WFA professionals. Their review uncovered six competency buckets that HR analysts require to perform value-adding WFA: storytelling and communication, consulting, research and discovery, technical knowledge, HR and business acumen, and data fluency and data analysis. Accordingly, workforce analysts operating in functions at the aspiring level of WFA maturity require a blend of these six competencies to offer insights through workforce data.

Data quality and processes

The second "push" factor critical to the successful development of WFA capabilities relates to Phase 2 of the ACAI model, which emphasizes high-quality data that are error-free and easily accessible. According to McCartney and Fu (2022b), "If teams cannot trust HR data given the likelihood of missing values and wrong entries, having the analytical understanding and capabilities will only aid in running inaccurate analysis, thus generating little to no value" (p. 28). Furthermore, making decisions based on inaccurate data may result in implementing solutions that fail to address the underlying or root problem, potentially causing more harm than good (McCartney & Fu, 2022a).

Despite HR departments' heavy investments in data infrastructure and efforts to centralize workforce data over the past years, several issues persist regarding data quality and effective data processes (Boudreau & Cascio, 2017; Minbaeva, 2018). For instance, Boudreau and Cascio (2017) note that although advances have been made in technology, systems often remain unable to "talk" to each other and are designed with legacy WFA structures in place. Likewise, Minbaeva (2018) argued that most organizations still remain unsure of the types of data available to them, where they are stored, and how multiple datasets can be integrated. Equally important is the emerging concept of data governance, which further enhances the policies and procedures implemented to ensure the accuracy and completeness of organizational data (Green, 2017; Peeters et al., 2020; Shet et al., 2021).

Building capabilities to ensure data quality and establishing processes to ensure data are complete and accurate are critical steps in the ACAI model and building WFA capabilities overall. Accordingly, in this section, we detail how to build organizational capabilities in WFA by illustrating how organizations leverage HR technology platforms to aid in collecting and storing workforce data. In addition, we review the types of data collected to help make strategic workforce decisions. Finally, we present evidence on how HR is implementing data governance policies to ensure the accuracy and completeness of data.

Business partnering ability

The third "push" factor in building sustainable WFA, closely aligned with Phases 3 and 4 of the ACAI model, is the capacity for the workforce analyst or WFA team to partner with various business units (BUs) across the organization. This partnership allows the analyst or team to provide insights through analytical capabilities that inform strategic decision-making and influence change management activities (see the discussion in Chapter 5). As with the two previously mentioned "push" factors, this factor is also impacted by the level of analytics maturity: organizations operating in different quadrants of the WFA maturity matrix possess different capabilities. These capabilities determine the insights workforce analysts and teams can generate, as well as their influence and impact on decision-making.

At the aspiring level of WFA maturity, analysts or functions can deliver basic reporting capabilities, including descriptive statistics on demographic information, turnover, and headcount. Although important, these types of descriptive statistics, often referred to as HR metrics (Huevel & Bondarouk, 2017), exert limited influence on decision-making and change management. As Boudreau and Cascio (2017) assert:

> At best these kinds of data represent operational or advanced reporting, and not strategic or predictive analytics that incorporate analyses segmented by employee population and that are tightly integrated with strategic planning.

While these data can be informative, they can also lead to a focus on the operations of the HR function, rather than on the effects of human capital decisions and investments on organizational outcomes. (p. 122)

WFA professional Pete Jaworski notes:

> HR metrics have been a starting point [at my organization]. I've had to make the rounds and do a bit of work with the different functional heads asking which metrics do you want to use? And once we know that, then we can plan for what's going to get into a dashboard or plan. … [HR metrics] is all about connecting the dots for HR partners.

At the established level of WFA capability maturity, WFA teams have more breadth and depth in the insights they can provide. This is partly because of their access to technology, including HCM systems coupled with business intelligence (BI) tools. For instance, according to McCartney and Fu (2022b), BI tools are being integrated with modern HCM systems to allow for greater functionality. The end result is an increased ability to generate more advanced insights that can help shape and guide operational and tactical decision-making by business and HR leaders. Discussing how COVID-19 has positively impacted the impact of WFA, Thomas Rasmussen states:

> COVID has led us to look at a lot of different things that we probably normally wouldn't look at. So, for example, there is a lot of focus on the employee. In particular, well-being more so than usual where it's looking at how are our employees coping? … We've also done some research, for instance, around hybrid work in terms of our diversity agenda and how this may affect different demographic groups in the organization.

As can be seen, organizations operating at the established level of WFA wield significantly more influence with the insights they can provide. They can transcend operational reporting and simple descriptive statistics to offer recommendations to drive evidence-based decision-making.

At the advanced level of WFA capability maturity, as illustrated in Chapter 3, HR departments can leverage existing technology platforms coupled with automation to influence workforce planning and HR strategy. For example, HR departments may implement artificial intelligence (AI) and machine learning (ML) algorithms to apply predictive and prescriptive analytics to future HR or business challenges. Heather Whiteman offers this example:

> We implemented a full talent management system built on capabilities and skills data connections where individuals could rate their own skills, and capabilities

get feedback from their managers and from peers. We could then validate those skills through an objective criterion. It allowed us to offer employees an assessment of what skills they most need to work on and directly linked them to those learning assets in our learning catalog. It would prompt employees based on how they rated themselves. For example, it would say, hey, you know you indicated that you're only a three on this skill, but did you know people in your role are typically a four? Here are a couple of courses aimed specifically at getting someone from level three to four. ... We also built in some predictive algorithms and other machine learning to say, did you know you're actually an 85% fit for this other role in a different department? And oh, by the way, there's a job posting.

Similarly, Alexis Fink offers the following example of how automation and ML can help generate prescriptive analytics:

Automation can be a great analytical tool if you are looking for areas of risk. If I am going out and doing analysis manually, I can probably do interactions between two or three variables, and I will probably be doing them in large chunks. But a machine can go out and do many, many, many more permutations. ... So, for example, companies right now are transitioning to remote work. Using automation, we can start to figure out which teams are vulnerable or struggling, and what indicators are most important for flagging teams at risk. The ability of a machine to go out and find whatever those indicators may be – things like manager feedback, or attrition, or missed objectives, or whatever else – and then take that data and quickly identify the ten most risky combinations. From there, organizations can engage the managers to address the issues with those teams. This can be done at a much finer level of granularity, and with much more speed if we use a machine.

Altogether, workforce analysts or members of WFA teams partner with organizational stakeholders to enable strategic decision-making and "influence the right decisions." As we have shown, this influence manifests at levels of sophistication. At the aspiring level, stakeholders receive analytics in the form of descriptive statistics that highlight the current state of several key performance indicators (KPIs) and HR metrics. However, these offer little decision-making power. In contrast, BUs more frequently consult HR departments operating at higher levels of maturity on specific challenges rather than general HR metrics, thus providing additional insights that enable more strategic decision-making.

HR technology and data management

Over the past 60 years, HR technology, such as human resource information systems (HRISs) or HCM systems, has significantly influenced how employee data are collected, stored, and managed (Kim et al., 2021). As defined by Kavanagh et al. (2015), an HRIS is "a system used to acquire, store, manipulate, analyze, retrieve, and distribute information regarding an organization's human resources" (p. 17). Likewise, HR technology has enabled organizations to effectively enhance the delivery of HR services and support decision-making through various types of data (Kim et al., 2021). As such, HRISs and HCM systems are a key element of the ACAI model: they form the foundation for *"Collecting the right data"* and building sustainable WFA (see Chapter 3). These systems enable the storage of data required for conducting analysis and generating actionable insights. To illustrate, Tim Haynes, VP of Organizational Development and People Analytics at Jazz Pharmaceuticals, stressed the importance of HR technology:

> [HR technology] is very, very important by definition, whether it is Workday or any of the other global HCMs. I think the principle is having a single system that has your core workforce data, especially if you are a global multinational company. … Having a single HCM makes life a lot easier from an analytics perspective.

Technological advances in cloud software platforms have made HRIS platforms more affordable and commonplace within organizations (Johnson et al., 2016; Plessis & Fourie, 2015). Johnson et al. (2016) note that increased technology capabilities at lower costs have allowed smaller organizations that previously could not afford HRISs to invest in more cost-effective cloud-based technologies. However, despite this advancement, organizations operating at the aspiring level of WFA maturity may lack the resources or managerial buy-in to invest in these platforms.

A paradox exists where "the team responsible for HCA [human capital analytics] needs data to prove its point, but top management needs proof before it will invest" (Minbaeva, 2018, p. 703). As a result, data collection may be rudimentary, relying on basic technology. Moreover, workforce data at this level are commonly fragmented and collected across several different systems. Organizations at the aspiring level of WFA often collect data from forms and manually transfer it into Excel documents or databases. As mentioned earlier, this practice causes several issues, including a lack of understanding or awareness of where specific data are stored, how to access them, or if they are even available. Several WFA professionals address this. Tim Haynes states:

> A lot of organizations still do not have a single HCM [system]. They then need to connect lots of different data from different systems, and when you are facing that situation, there is always a risk of data not getting connected in the right way, and it is just complex and creates a lot of work.

Likewise, Maura Stevenson, Chief HR Officer at MedVet, remarks:

> When I started at my organization, with the data we had, we could not even calculate turnover accurately. … With my other organization, I could not tell how

many people worked for us across the globe because we only had the United States data in our system. So, I think sometimes analytics get this shininess, but the reality is that in the trenches it is not so shiny.

Given the manual aspect of this process, along with fragmented data stored in various databases and Excel files, data duplication errors and wrong entries are common, which perpetuates the need for HR technology and investment to ensure data are accurate and reliable.

In contrast, organizations operating at the established to advanced levels of WFA capabilities typically implement sophisticated HRIS or HCM systems such as Workday, SAP SuccessFactors, or Oracle PeopleSoft as their primary source for storing workforce data. These systems allow for mass data storage and retrieval of structured data, which is well defined and easily categorized, and unstructured data, which is not defined and typically comprises long strings of text (Leonardi & Contractor, 2019).

For example, when onboarding a new employee, HCM systems collect structured employee data and generate an employee profile, including key information such as age, gender, reporting structure, skills, and direct reports. People with the appropriate permissions can easily access these structured data for reporting and analytics. Beyond these basic features, more advanced HCM systems typically allow for the collection of unstructured data. The Workday Peakon Employee Voice module, for example, enables HR departments to collect unstructured data through intelligent listening and employee sentiment, feedback, and other forms of text or string data (Workday, 2021).

Data governance in HR

Although HRISs and HCM systems allow for the quick and easy collection of data, ensuring processes are in place to consistently maintain data integrity is critical (Green, 2017). As such, HR departments at all levels of the WFA maturity matrix introduce data governance structures to help guarantee that the data fed into the system are reliable, accurate, and credible (Peeters et al., 2020; Shet et al., 2021). According to Green (2017), developing and implementing policies and practices for data maintenance, storage, privacy, and security are "basics" for all organizations embarking on their WFA journey. Echoing this sentiment, Shet et al. (2021) emphasize that setting up data governance systems and establishing data workflows are critical in maintaining and enhancing data quality. Many WFA professionals share this perspective. Tim Haynes states:

> I think [data governance] is essential. There is an element around the structure and organizing the data in the first place, but there is also the more data management or data engineering way to structure your data to ensure you have the best data that is consistent and of good quality.

Alexis Fink, Vice President, People Analytics and Workforce Strategy, offers the following example:

> One thing that will drive people crazy is a data governance problem. Reflecting back on a previous organization, we had seven different fields across our systems labeled start date and they all meant different things. So, your start date at the organization, start date with a company we acquired, calculated start date for a break in service, your calculated start date for a particular acquisition, a start date for training, a start date for a particular job, and all of them meant different things, and if you didn't know what you were doing you would just look for start date, pick the first one you found, and have a completely inaccurate analysis.

In summary, all HR functions must prioritize data governance from the outset to ensure high-quality, reliable, accurate, and credible data.

What are the pull factors?

As discussed earlier in this chapter, building sustainable WFA capabilities necessitates a level of demand for analytics as inputs for business decisions across the broader organization. Following Cascio and Boudreau (2017), we refer to this demand as "pull" factors. These factors may impede the maturity of the WFA function: "No matter how rigorously or completely the HCA are prepared and 'pushed' out to their audiences, the advancement and effectiveness of HCA still depends on the capability, opportunity, and motivation of analytics users" (Cascio & Boudreau, 2017, p. 123). These factors may represent requests from organizational stakeholders actively seeking workforce data to aid in making business decisions. Moreover, pull factors could also represent the organizational context that would enable stakeholders to deploy and utilize the WFA for value creation. We propose that two factors generate various degrees of "pull," resulting in a low, medium, or high level of organizational demand for WFA.

Analytical requests derived from the digitalization of business processes

The first pull factor concerns stakeholder requests derived from data and analytics resulting from the digitalization of business processes. With the arrival of "big data," many organizations have undergone dramatic changes in their business models, centered on how data provides insights into better ways to create and deliver value to customers. Organizations adopt data-oriented approaches across all their business processes (including HR) to create opportunities to gain new knowledge about delivering *information-enriched customer solutions* (Minbaeva, 2021). Although the HR function lags "behind other functional areas of management in the adoption of analytics technology and in the analysis of big data" (Angrave et al., 2016, p. 9), WFA could definitely "ride the wave" of greater use of data and analytics by other business functions within the organization.

Greater use of data-oriented approaches in business functions spurs curiosity among organizational stakeholders, who begin to ask questions like "what do we know about our own people?" or "can we connect our people data with business data?" This curiosity is contingent on organizational stakeholders' buy-in and attitude toward analytical decision-making and will considerably influence how sustainable WFA programs are built. At a low level of stakeholder requests, departments are beginning to evaluate how digitalization may enable workforce data to inform decision-making relevant to their functional challenges. As a result, stakeholders will primarily be curious about questions on "what," "how many," "who," or "what happened" and will aim to evaluate or benchmark the current state of their workforce through descriptive statistics.

For example, business units (BUs) or organizational stakeholders may request from the workforce analyst or WFA function a snapshot of diversity and inclusion metrics, employee engagement, performance, and job satisfaction (Falletta & Combs, 2020; Levenson, 2018; Margherita, 2022; McCartney & Fu, 2022b; Peeters et al., 2020). Other common deliverables for stakeholders would be basic reports or visualizations highlighting key HR metrics, including headcount, number of hires, number of promotions, and turnover (Angrave et al., 2016; Levenson, 2018; Huevel & Bondarouk, 2017).

In contrast, the digitalization of business processes may elicit more modest demands for organizations, raising expectations of the WFA function. At this medium level of requests, stakeholders seek to identify the root cause of challenges exclusive to their function. To achieve this, stakeholders ask the analyst or WFA team for answers to questions such as "why did this happen?" or "is this good or bad?" Levenson and Fink (2017) and Peeters et al. (2020) classified this collaborative process between WFA and stakeholders as "organizational research," where the workforce analyst or WFA team conducts research on specific business issues in line with the demands of their stakeholders.

In such situations, BUs may approach the workforce analyst or WFA function to evaluate predictors of employee engagement, collaboration, team satisfaction, or performance (Peeters et al., 2020). One example is analytics departments critically examining internal collaboration patterns through network analysis, a technique outlined in Chapter 3. Analytics expert Michael Arena, Dean of Crowell School of Business and former Vice President of Talent and Development, states:

> We do a ton of network analysis where we're looking at interaction patterns and then using that to anticipate how to get people better positioned for performance, and how to think about idea flow across an organization … [network

analysis] is a much deeper science than doing the more traditional how do you look at performance management or how do you look at even the flow of talent in an organization? It just requires a different level of thinking.

Finally, building on the previous two levels, organizations committed to completely digitalizing their business processes and integrating data across BUs throughout the organization will focus on making predictions and generating actionable solutions from data. As such, organizational stakeholders will begin to ask questions about "what might happen next." According to Margherita (2022), stakeholders operating at this level of digitalization would ask the WFA team to use statistics and advanced algorithms to examine various data points to create predictions and run alternative scenarios for their business problems. Subsequently, stakeholders ask for prescriptive analytics to determine "what should be done about it" and select the best course of action aligned with the organization's strategy. For instance, Thomas Rasmussen states:

> In my team, our goal this year was to demonstrate five different instances where we have had a significant impact on discussions and the decisions made to improve business outcomes. … If we can bring analytics to the table five times and significantly change the discussion and the decisions that we make, that is our outcome.

Similarly, at these higher levels, stakeholders expect WFA to link to BU objectives and KPIs such as costs and employee experience. Maura Stevenson adds:

> In my previous organization, we had very advanced operational training, and we had ten to twelve thousand courses completed every single day. … So, we could do things like look at how many training courses you took and link course completion to unit performance.

Altogether, the organizations' desire to digitalize business processes and the subsequent requests derived from this digitalization are primary drivers in building organizational demand for WFA. As each stage shows, increased digitalization shifts the demands and types of requests from organizational stakeholders and influences the analysis that the WFA function provides.

Analytical and data-driven culture

The second pull factor that affects the demand for analytics from the WFA function is the degree to which the organization fosters an analytical and data-driven culture. How an organization embeds data and evidence into its values and culture sets the tone for how it uses analytics. Organizations that have little interest in using data to support decision-making will require little analysis from the WFA function. In such cases, although the WFA function may provide reactive analysis, this is not the organization's main priority. In contrast, organizations with a strong analytically-driven culture focus on answering business questions using advanced methodologies and tools (discussed in Chapter 3) to influence strategic decision-making and change management activities (covered in Chapter 5).

In fostering a data-driven culture, the mindset of a senior management team is decisive. Consider one midsize manufacturing company, where the strength of its data-driven culture differed significantly due to the company having three different CEOs over the previous ten years. A WFA specialist explained, "Culture implies a CEO focus. If he or she has a focus on data and repeatedly requests data and evidence from all business-domain experts, then the culture eventually shifts." In this company, the arrival of a new CEO who continuously focused on using data for improving strategic decision-making gradually shifted the attitudes toward evidence-based decisions, creating a culture of inquiry and a habit of making evidence-based decisions throughout the whole company.

Notably, in some established firms where data and analytics are not central to their culture, WFA teams may encounter a traditional mindset rooted in historical practices, marked by mistrust of data and overreliance on managerial intuition. This mindset often masks a general discomfort with analytics and a lack of understanding of how to interpret findings from analytics projects. In such companies, the challenge for WFA functions is to act as effective boundary spanners, gathering, filtering, and delivering a wide range of knowledge across organizational boundaries, ultimately fostering the creation of trust and maximizing organizational buy-in.

Overall, although WFA functions may aspire to be higher in their maturity, it is important to stress that this alone may not warrant an investment in WFA capabilities. Rather, the equilibrium between push and pull factors should determine the investment in furthering or remaining at the desired level of WFA capability. In other words, organizations that significantly invest in WFA maturity but have little organizational demand will see no benefit, and vice versa. Taking this a step further, it is important to note that maturity levels of the WFA function are not idle; rather, organizations and HR departments can evolve and attain higher levels of WFA maturity at their own pace (Margherita, 2022) as long as the demand for such activity aligns with the overall WFA strategic goals and outcomes of the organization while maintaining WFA equilibrium.

Building the WFA function

So far in this chapter, we have offered an overview of WFA maturity as it relates to the ACAI model and have demonstrated how the two competing dimensions of the level of WFA capabilities and organizational demand for WFA influence the formation of WFA capabilities. In addition, we have detailed the individual push and pull factors that constitute each of these dimensions. In the final section of this chapter, we will integrate the application of the logic of demand and supply—the push and pull factors—discussed within the context of progressing the WFA function. We will also illustrate how a point of equilibrium between "push" (supply) and "pull" (demand) defines the structure of WFA functions.

Although limited research exists concerning WFA functions, researchers have begun to illustrate how they may be structured in the industry (Kaur & Fink, 2017; Peeters et al., 2020). According to Peeters et al. (2020), the internal WFA team structure stems from the WFA leader responsible for several specialists or experts. This WFA leader has the autonomy to divide the team into several subspecializations, including reporting, advanced analytics, and visualization, to meet the needs of their stakeholders effectively.

For example, according to Kaur and Fink (2017), organizations may choose to structure their teams around three categories of work which closely align with the ACAI model. First, infrastructure and reporting refer to the individual team members responsible for the administration and maintenance of the human capital system, including maintaining data quality and running specialized reports on business metrics and KPIs. Second, advanced data analysis involves employing individuals who perform tasks beyond reporting on KPIs or basic statistics. Third, organizational research includes team members focused on designing studies or experiments to address particular business challenges.

During our interviews with WFA professionals, many expressed similar views on how they structured their teams based on the various required capabilities and skill profiles. For example, Thomas Rasmussen states:

> We have a relatively small team of five people. We have a person leading it. Then we have a lead senior data scientist who does all the advanced analytics and can also code. So, very much on the data science side of things. There is also a role which is more somewhere in between data manipulation, reporting, and analytics, not on the advanced side, but focused on data extraction, data merging, all that stuff. And then there is a role supporting that role who is a bit more junior, and then there's a person essentially running all of our surveys and so exit surveys onboarding surveys, employees surveys.

Heather Whiteman proposes that, depending on the mindset of the team leader, teams can be divided into or thought of from two perspectives: (a) what team members' roles will offer the business, or (b) what tasks the team members will perform daily. She explains:

> The way I think of it is not how [team members] spend their days but what they do for the organization. Other workforce analytics leaders will structure their

functions more based on how they spend their time. So, they'll tend to bucket them in more of a reporting-type role. More of an analyst-type role. More to a scientist-type role. Maybe even a researcher-type role, and it's just a slightly different mental approach to how we think about the roles.

As can be seen, configuring the WFA function to align with the ACAI model is a critical step for any organization looking to incorporate data and analytics into its decision-making process. However, contrary to existing logic and research outlining how to build effective WFA functions, we argue that each organization and WFA function is dynamic and fluid and, therefore, may have different configurations and numbers of members. As such, when deciding upon the right "mix," the strength of the "push" and "pull" factors will play a significant role in determining the makeup of the team, causing teams to vary considerably in size and roles. We argue that, although in some cases forming a team as the practitioners described may be the right "mix," this might not always be the case for other organizations facing different levels of push and pull factors.

Consider three different scenarios visualized in Figure 7.2. Scenario 1 typifies an organization with a basic setup of the WFA function: usually, one or two employees manage multiple data inputs, often in Excel. The development of the WFA function is "pulled" by business functions other than HR, usually because of the established habits of using data for business decisions. For example, a telecommunication firm heavily relied on data analytics to understand the customer experience. Data analysts from the sales and marketing departments approached HR requesting workforce

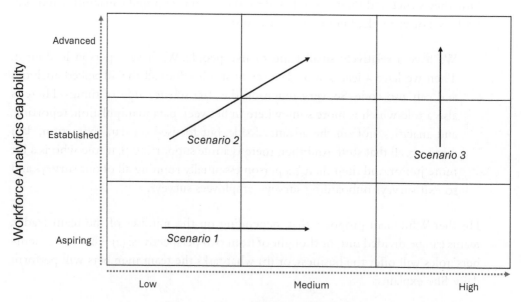

FIGURE 7.2 Workforce analytics maturity matrix: three scenarios.

data to test for correlations between employee engagement and customer net promoter score. The firm was not interested in developing its WFA capabilities. Nonetheless, the use of WFA grew alongside developments in other business areas. Such organizations find themselves at the aspiring level of WFA, with some demand for WFA, a nonexistent data culture, and small business operations. This would warrant a structure of a single analyst (see scenario 1 in Figure 7.3).

A firm in scenario 2 regularly provides the insights generated by advanced operational reporting, has created multiple dashboards for different levels of management, and has developed an understanding of WFA among human resources business partners (HRBPs). Through much closer integration with the business strategy, the WFA function establishes an ongoing dialogue with the executive team regarding the strategic development of the workforce needed to enable strategy implementation. Strategic workforce planning then becomes a must-have tool in the managerial portfolio of team leaders. In this context, WFA functions are usually structured around two main organizational pillars—reporting, including data management, and advanced analytics (see scenario 2 in Figure 7.3).

Scenario 3 describes the advanced development of the WFA function. Such moves are typical for firms undergoing strategic digital transformation. The insights WFA generates are considered inputs for automation, and the WFA function plays a key role in augmentation processes aimed at producing an AI-based, structured ML algorithm.

Given well-established WFA capabilities and strong organizational demand, WFA leaders in such organizations must assemble a WFA team with diverse skills (Fernandez & Gallardo-Gallardo, 2020; Huselid, 2018; Jörden et al., 2021; Peeters et al., 2020). In this scenario, as stakeholder requests increase, more advanced forms of insights linked to BU properties and KPIs to address short-term and long-term business needs are required. Consequently, this demand compels WFA functions to employ different configurations of team roles and capabilities and engage with

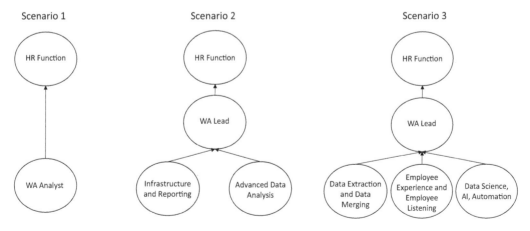

FIGURE 7.3 Examples of WFA function configuration.

external experts to bring in more advanced technical knowledge (see Scenario 3 in Figure 7.3). Low-level reporting tasks are usually outsourced and/or automated as well.

Conclusion

Recent growth in WFA adoption and advancements in HR technology have enabled HR departments to leverage data to make evidence-based decisions. Yet gaps remain regarding the key ingredients required to build effective organizational capabilities in WFA. Accordingly, in this chapter, we have detailed the various "push" and "pull" factors as they relate to the ACAI model to develop organizational capabilities in WFA at each stage of the WFA journey. To fully realize the potential of WFA, these "push" and "pull" factors should be in equilibrium so that WFA capabilities reflect both the maturity of the WFA function and the organizational demand and appetite for WFA.

References

Andersen, M. K. (2017). Human capital analytics: The winding road. *Journal of Organizational Effectiveness, 4*(2), 133–136. https://doi.org/10.1108/JOEPP-03-2017-0024

Angrave, D., Charlwood, A., Kirkpatrick, I., Lawrence, M., & Stuart, M. (2016). HR and analytics: Why HR is set to fail the big data challenge. *Human Resource Management Journal, 26*(1), 1–11. https://doi.org/10.1111/1748-8583.12090

Boudreau, J., & Cascio, W. (2017). Human capital analytics: Why are we not there? *Journal of Organizational Effectiveness: People and Performance, 4*(2), 119–126. https://doi.org/10.1108/JOEPP-03-2016-0029

Buttner, H., & Tullar, W. (2018). A representative organizational diversity metric: A dashboard measure for executive action. *Equality, Diversity and Inclusion: An International Journal, 37*(3), 219–232. https://doi.org/10.1108/GM-12-2013-0140

CIPD. (2019). *People analytics factsheet.* https://www.cipd.ie/knowledge/world-work/analytics/factsheet

Deloitte. (2019). *People analytics solutions.* Deloitte.

Du Plessis, A. J., & Fourie, L. (2015). The use of big data and HRIS by HR practitioners in New Zealand: Empirical evidence from a longitudinal study. In N. J. Delener, L. Fuxman, F. V. Lu, & S. Rodrigues (Eds.), *Proceedings of the global business and technology association 17th annual international conference* (pp. 1–11).

Ellmer, M., & Reichel, A. (2021). Staying close to business: The role of epistemic alignment in rendering HR analytics outputs relevant to decision-makers. *International Journal of Human Resource Management, 32*(12), 2622–2642. https://doi.org/10.1080/09585192.2021.1886148

Falletta, S. V., & Combs, W. L. (2020). The HR analytics cycle: A seven-step process for building evidence-based and ethical HR analytics capabilities. *Journal of Work-Applied Management, 13*(1). https://doi.org/10.1108/JWAM-03-2020-0020

Fernandez, V., & Gallardo-Gallardo, E. (2020). Tackling the HR digitalization challenge: Key factors and barriers to HR analytics adoption. *Competitiveness Review: An International Business Journal, 31*(1). https://doi.org/10.1108/CR-12-2019-0163

Green, D. (2017). The best practices to excel at people analytics. *Journal of Organizational Effectiveness: People and Performance, 4*(2), 137–144. https://doi.org/10.1108/JOEPP-03-2017-0027

Huselid, M. A. (2018). The science and practice of workforce analytics: Introduction to the HRM special issue. *Human Resource Management, 57*(3), 679–684. https://doi.org/10.1002/hrm.21916

Johnson, R. D., Lukaszewski, K. M., & Stone, D. L. (2016). The evolution of the field of human resource information systems: Co-evolution of technology and HR processes. *Communications of the Association for Information Systems, 38*(1), 533–553. https://doi.org/10.17705/1CAIS.03828

Jörden, N. M., Sage, D., & Trusson, C. (2021). "It's so fake": Identity performances and cynicism within a people analytics team. *Human Resource Management Journal, 32*(3), 524–539. https://doi.org/10.1111/1748-8583.12412

Kaur, J., & Fink, A. A. (2017). *Trends and practices in talent analytics* [White paper]. SHRM-SIOP Science of HR White Paper Series. http://www.siop.org/SIOP-SHRM/2017 10_SHRM-SIOP Talent Analytics.pdf

Kavanagh, M. J., Thite, M., & Johnson, R. (2015). *Human resource information systems: Basics, applications, and future directions* (3rd ed.). Sage Publishing.

Kim, S., Wang, Y., & Boon, C. (2021). Sixty years of research on technology and human resource management: Looking back and looking forward. *Human Resource Management, 60*(1), 229–247. https://doi.org/10.1002/hrm.22049

Leonardi, P., & Contractor, N. (2019). Better people analytics. *Harvard Business Review, 96*(6), 70–81.

Levenson, A. (2018). Using workforce analytics to improve strategy execution. *Human Resource Management, 57*(3), 685–700. https://doi.org/10.1002/hrm.21850

Levenson, A., & Fink, A. (2017). Human capital analytics: Too much data and analysis, not enough models and business insights. *Journal of Organizational Effectiveness, 4*(2), 145–156. https://doi.org/10.1108/JOEPP-03-2017-0029

Margherita, A. (2022). Human resources analytics: A systematization of research topics and directions for future research. *Human Resource Management Review, 32*(2), 100795. https://doi.org/10.1016/j.hrmr.2020.100795

Marler, J. H., & Boudreau, J. W. (2017). An evidence-based review of HR analytics. *International Journal of Human Resource Management, 28*(1), 3–26. https://doi.org/10.1080/09585192.2016.1244699

Marler, J. H., & Martin, L. (2021). People analytics maturity and talent management. In S. Wiblen (Ed.), *Digitalised talent management—Navigating the human technology interface* (p. 19). Routledge.

McCartney, S., & Fu, N. (2022a). Bridging the gap: Why, how, and when HR analytics can impact organizational performance. *Management Decision, 60*(13), 25–47.

McCartney, S., & Fu, N. (2022b). Promise versus reality: A systematic review of the ongoing debates in people analytics. *Journal of Organizational Effectiveness: People and Performance, 9*(2). https://doi.org/10.1108/joepp-01-2021-0013

McCartney, S., Murphy, C., & McCarthy, J. (2020). 21st century HR: A competency model for the emerging role of HR analysts. *Personnel Review, 50*(6), 1495–1513.

McIver, D., Lengnick-Hall, M. L., & Lengnick-Hall, C. A. (2018). A strategic approach to workforce analytics: Integrating science and agility. *Business Horizons, 61*(3), 397–407. https://doi.org/10.1016/j.bushor.2018.01.005

Minbaeva, D. (2018). Building credible human capital analytics for organizational competitive advantage. *Human Resource Management, 57*(3), 701–713. https://doi.org/10.1002/hrm.21848

Minbaeva, D. (2021). Disrupted HR? Human Resource Management Review, 31(4), 1–8.

Peeters, T., Paauwe, J., & Van De Voorde, K. (2020). People analytics effectiveness: Developing a framework. *Journal of Organizational Effectiveness*, 7(2), 203–219. https://doi.org/10.1108/JOEPP-04-2020-0071

Pessach, D., Singer, G., Avrahami, D., Chalutz Ben-Gal, H., Shmueli, E., & Ben-Gal, I. (2020). Employees recruitment: A prescriptive analytics approach via machine learning and mathematical programming. *Decision Support Systems*, *134*, 113290. https://doi.org/10.1016/j.dss.2020.113290

Shet, S.V., Poddar, T., Wamba Samuel, F., & Dwivedi, Y. K. (2021). Examining the determinants of successful adoption of data analytics in human resource management—A framework for implications. *Journal of Business Research*, *131*, 311–326. https://doi.org/10.1016/j.jbusres.2021.03.054

SHRM. (2016). *The SHRM competency model.* https://www.shrm.org/learningandcareer/competency-model/publishingimages/pages/default/shrm%20competency%20model_detailed%20report_final_secured.pdf

Sivathanu, B., & Pillai, R. (2020). Technology and talent analytics for talent management—A game changer for organizational performance. *International Journal of Organizational Analysis*, 28(2), 457–473. https://doi.org/10.1108/IJOA-01-2019-1634

van den Heuvel, S., & Bondarouk, T. (2017). The rise (and fall?) of HR analytics. *Journal of Organizational Effectiveness: People and Performance*, 4(2), 157–178. https://doi.org/10.1002/chir

van der Togt, J., & Rasmussen, T. H. (2017). Toward evidence-based HR. *Journal of Organizational Effectiveness*, 4(2), 127–132. https://doi.org/10.1108/JOEPP-02-2017-0013

Workday. (2021). *Workday Peakon employee voice.* https://www.workday.com/en-us/products/employee-voice/overview.html

The future of workforce analytics

Mark A. Huselid, Alec Levenson,
Dana Minbaeva, and Martin R. Edwards

Introduction

Managers face a significant and well-documented list of business challenges: increased competition, shortened strategy lifecycles, resource scarcity, investor demands for productivity and efficiency, globalization, environmental concerns, employee and potential employee expectations, the increasing importance of artificial intelligence (AI) technologies and applications, and stakeholder demands for more effective and transparent governance systems. These factors collectively render a typical organization a very challenging place to manage (McKinsey & Company, 2021, 2022, 2023).

To help address these issues, our book focuses on both the design and implementation of effective workforce analytics (WFA) systems and strategies. For many leaders and managers, the questions quickly become: What does effective WFA look like? What resources are required to implement WFA effectively? Where do we start? Despite the importance of intangible assets such as talent in value creation in all its forms – for example, intangible assets comprise up to 80% of firm value in the global economy (Huselid, 1995, 2018, 2023) – few organizations competently measure or manage the contribution of talent to workforce success.

As a consequence, these data are rarely used to effectively help manage the business. Indeed, the base rate for WFA quality and competence is low in most organizations (Levenson, 2021; Levenson & Fink, 2017). Rather than bemoan this situation, we view it as an opportunity to improve and contribute to business success through more effective talent measurement and management.

In any organization, you can only go as far as your workforce will take you. But, as we have described throughout this book, the workforce is the least measured and managed resource in nearly all organizations. One solution to these problems lies in designing and implementing WFA systems. Indeed, the role of HR management in

DOI: 10.4324/9781003190097-19

executing strategy and the potential for extracting long-term economic rents have been the subject of a tremendous body of literature in recent years (Becker & Huselid, 1998; Combs et al., 2006; Huselid, 1995, 2018, 2023; Storey et al., 2019). And, as we described in Chapter 1, information relevant to talent (and talent management) is increasingly required by investors in publicly-held companies (Zhu et al., 2024).

While the availability of global talent provides many opportunities, it also presents a challenge in maintaining a competitive advantage. In this book, we have advocated for a strategic and focused approach to HR management that aligns closely with the firm's goals, using WFA to optimize both talent acquisition and development. The following sections provide an overview and summary of the material we have covered thus far, followed by a discussion of what we have learned and the future of global WFA.

Chapter 1: Introduction and book overview

In Chapter 1, we began with a description of the recent increase in interest in WFA among leaders as well as academics. We provided an overview of the field, addressing its historical roots, theoretical underpinnings, methodological approaches, and its implications for business success. We emphasized the evolution of WFA, defining it as a crucial practice that extends beyond mere HR metrics to a broader understanding of human capital's impact on organizational outcomes. We stressed the need for a structured, scientific approach to data collection and analysis, as well as the implementation of analytics, to drive business success (in contrast to generic metrics amenable to benchmarking across firms). Our aim has been to clarify the conceptual boundaries of WFA and enhance its application in organizations. Throughout this book, we have advocated for a structured approach to WFA, emphasizing the importance of scientific methods and ethical considerations in analytics practices.

Names like HR analytics, workforce analytics, people analytics, and talent analytics have been used interchangeably in this domain (Edwards & Edwards, 2019). We prefer the term *workforce analytics*, which we believe better captures the focus and intent of this construct. WFA is a broad and diverse field with many complex elements. The field also has a long history – much richer and longer than is typically represented in the current WFA literature. Effectively designing and implementing WFA systems requires appreciating these differences and developing a WFA team capable of capitalizing on various sources of knowledge in the design and implementation of WFA processes. We cover this issue in detail in Chapter 7.

Our key themes in this chapter include the ethical implications of WFA, the strategic importance of asking the right questions, and the practical challenges of aligning WFA with business objectives. In Chapter 1, we also introduce and describe our ACAI model of WFA implementation (**A**sk, **C**ollect, **A**nalyze, **I**nfluence), which is a conceptual framework designed to help managers, consultants, and scholars design and implement effective WFA. As we described, effective WFA systems require us to first **A**sk the right questions; second, **C**ollect the right data; third, **A**nalyze data in the right way; and fourth, **I**nfluence the right decisions and workforce outcomes. In summary:

- Phase 1: **A**sk the right questions
- Phase 2: **C**ollect the right data
- Phase 3: **A**nalyze data in the right way
- Phase 4: **I**nfluence the right decisions

In Chapter 1, we also emphasized the importance of starting WFA processes with strategic questions rather than data accumulation, focusing on obtaining actionable insights that are aligned with business goals and integrating ethical practices into the analytics processes.

Chapter 2: Theoretical frameworks for workforce analytics

In Chapter 2, we focused on the historical development of WFA and its evolution towards focusing on the strategic value of talent for organizational success. We emphasized the significance of shifting from a primary focus on measuring transactions associated with the HR *function* (as this field has historically done) to a broader, more strategic, and *outcome-focused* approach. Making this transition has meant that we need to better understand how talent drives strategic success, as well as the theoretical underpinnings and historical context of WFA, as it is a deeply interdisciplinary field with roots extending back many years. The chapter emphasizes the importance of understanding these roots to effectively implement WFA systems that can tackle contemporary challenges in workforce management.

We then transitioned into a detailed discussion of the interdisciplinary nature of WFA, which draws on various fields, including strategic management, economics, industrial and organizational (I/O) psychology, and more. Each discipline contributes a unique perspective and methodological tools essential for addressing the complex challenges of managing and analyzing workforce data effectively. Furthermore, the chapter discusses the importance of theoretical frameworks in guiding WFA practices. By understanding the theoretical underpinnings, practitioners can ensure that their analytics efforts are not only methodologically sound but also aligned with strategic business objectives. We described the key theoretical domains relevant to WFA, such as:

- Strategic management
- Economics
- Strategic HRM
- I/O psychology
- Organizational behavior

- Psychometrics and econometrics
- Data science
- Organizational development (OD) and change management

Understanding the breadth of these contributions to the field will help professionals ask better questions about identifying strategic positions, roles, talent inventories, and designing measurement systems. It is also necessary to align the sophistication of the analyses with the importance, breadth, and complexity of the problem being addressed (which is the focus of this chapter).

Overall, the chapter serves as a bridge from the introductory concepts discussed in Chapter 1 to more detailed, application-focused discussions in subsequent chapters. It provides a foundational understanding necessary for designing and implementing effective WFA systems, stressing the importance of theoretical frameworks in guiding practical applications.

Chapter 3: Data collection and analysis

In Chapter 3, we emphasized the importance of adopting a comprehensive approach to data analysis, incorporating both quantitative and qualitative data. In particular, Chapter 3 covers a wide range of topics, including:

- The importance of analyzing quantitative and qualitative data and information
- Developing and using Likert scale data
- Prioritizing issues to address
- Going beyond readily available data to collect new data and sources for that new data
- Data limitations
- Preparing the data for analysis, including cleaning and dealing with outliers.
- Building and testing multivariate models based on evidence from social science research
- Addressing correlation versus causation
- Using demographic data appropriately
- Analyzing data statistically
- Data mining versus hypothesis testing
- Analyzing at the appropriate hierarchical level in the organization where the work is done: role, team, business unit/business process, region/geography, and/or enterprise
- Applying the scientific method to balance the role of qualitative and quantitative data in an analysis

Understanding the insights gathered from both numerical and qualitative data is crucial if we hope to fully capture the nuances of organizational dynamics. Likewise, using Likert (survey) scale data appropriately is vital for gathering reliable information on employee perceptions and attitudes, ensuring that these measurements provide accurate, relevant insights into organizational performance. As we described here and in Chapter 4, these data need to be both *reliable* (yielding the same answers with repeated usage) and *valid* (demonstrating meaningful relationships with our constructs of interest).

Prioritizing issues by strategic impact and linking them carefully to firm strategy is essential for achieving the highest possible return on investment in WFA activities. This requires organizations to identify and address areas where interventions will have the most significant impact, maximizing resource allocation and improving decision-making outcomes. Moreover, organizations should go beyond readily available data and actively seek to collect new, transformative data that can reshape their strategic direction. Analyses must also occur at the appropriate hierarchical level, whether that's at the role, team, business unit, regional, or enterprise-wide level, to align strategic decisions with organizational goals. Tailoring analyses to these specific levels generates a clearer understanding of where value is created and helps implement strategies more effectively.

Related themes are explored in other chapters of this book. For example, Chapter 2 highlights the importance of developing accurate models based on existing research and knowledge about business success at individual, team, and organizational levels. Chapter 5 discusses the necessity of early and consistent engagement with stakeholders and senior decision-makers to foster organizational learning and ensure that insights are properly implemented. Collectively, these ideas underscore how a strategic, data-driven approach to human resource management can significantly impact organizational success.

Chapter 4: Considering techniques in workforce analytics

In Chapter 4, the largest in the book due to its series of individual contributions, we highlighted a range of very different analytics techniques. We started with a technique (DAG) that can be used to empirically interrogate or challenge potential causal assumptions made with analytic tools and went on to explore particular techniques that can help answer or provide insight into a variety of distinct questions. If we step back from the chapter, however, the considerable variation in the range of techniques and the potential questions that they could answer reveals the big challenges faced by WFA teams. If a WFA team is aiming to ensure that they conduct the right analyses, the team will need to draw upon a range of statistical and data analytic expertise to ensure this. Notably, the authors in Chapter 4 range from psychologists to general experts in statistical techniques, and the level of expertise required to ensure that a team "conducts the right analyses" is substantial. This underscores that the analytic expertise in a WFA team needs to be broad.

As discussed in Chapter 2, WFA analytic experts may come from different disciplines and are likely to be well-versed in the techniques frequently used in their respective fields. Over the last decade or so, it has become quite common for teams to employ data scientists alongside experts from social science disciplines (e.g., psychology or economics) who bring high-level expertise from their disciplines. It is unlikely that any expert from a single field would have the required expertise to be able to identify the right analysis techniques for all data types to answer all questions.

This necessitates a breadth of expertise within any analytics team – or the ability to draw on external talent when required. However, if expertise is drawn from outside the organization, the WFA team still needs to have enough capability to understand what the external talent is doing and why, to ensure that it is conducting the right analyses. Regarding how to best set up a WFA team, readers can draw on the important knowledge and insights from Chapter 7. Importantly, however, the WFA team must be able to draw on the range of expertise required to ensure that they are able to conduct the right analyses and/or understand whether an external partner is planning to conduct the right analyses.

This points to a problem that WFA teams face when the external analytic environment is changing so quickly. At the time of writing, the growth in large language models and generative AI was developing very quickly. Should a WFA team wish to use such techniques, they must choose between developing and using these tools themselves or drawing on talent and products from external sources. A real danger currently facing teams is that, when relying on external talent or analytic products, their ability to ensure that the right analyses are being conducted may be challenged. This is why the ACAI model as a framework is useful if held up as a key consideration in all activities: it reminds the analytic teams to always ask, "Are we conducting the right analyses?" Similarly, if the team draws on external talent, they should only do so if they can be sure that the external talent is providing the right analytic approach.

Chapter 5: Implementation and change management

Chapter 5 examined why many organizations struggle to translate WFA insights into sustained strategic change. It argued that WFA must be integrated into the organizational sensemaking process to create actionable narratives about how human capital impacts business outcomes within a specific context. Understanding this sensemaking role is vital for increasing the legitimacy and impact of WFA in driving sustainable strategic organizational change.

We also critiqued traditional change models such as Lewin's "unfreeze-change-refreeze" and Kotter's planned change stages, proposing instead that WFA should be integrally embedded in the change management process. We emphasized the importance of sensemaking, a concept popularized by Karl Weick, which highlights the non-linear and iterative nature of interpreting organizational change. We applied our ACAI model (**A**sking, **C**ollecting, **A**nalyzing, **I**nfluencing) as a framework to show how WFA can be used to drive and support strategic change by fostering a shared understanding and facilitating effective decision-making. However, the chapter also acknowledged the challenges organizations face in translating analytical insights into actionable and sustainable changes, suggesting that storytelling and engagement are also crucial for bridging this gap. Specifically, the chapter outlines the stages of sensemaking as they interact with WFA:

- *Envisioning (leadership sensemaking)*: WFA can focus leaders' attention on human capital issues that trigger the need for change.
- *Signaling (leadership sensegiving)*: WFA provides data-driven messages to communicate the vision and need for change to the broader organization.
- *Re-visioning (collective sensemaking)*: WFA gathers additional information to allow broader organizational understanding and interpretation of the change.
- *Energizing (collective sensegiving)*: The WFA team uses storytelling to control the emergence of the new shared schema around the change.

The main points we make and the implications for WFA implementation and change management are highlighted below:

- *Strategic control through sensemaking*: The first segment emphasizes the importance of strategic control via collective sensemaking, which, when achieved, leads to more proactive strategic actions and improved organizational performance. Even if a perfect interpretation cannot be attained, controlling the evolution of new schemas is essential.
- *Unlearning and learning*: To instate a new organizational schema or framework, there's a need to disrupt current understandings. This is a profound observation. Change often demands organizations abandon previously held beliefs and assumptions, leading to the creation of a new shared understanding.
- *Creating sustainable change*: Sustainable change is not just about implementing changes but also measuring and evaluating their impacts. WFA can help track these impacts. Importantly, there's a call to not only focus on individual analytics projects but to view WFA as a continuous cycle, which then fuels further sensemaking and strategic change.
- *Storytelling and engagement*: A core aspect that stands out is the importance of communicating findings in a compelling manner. It's not enough to have insights; it's essential to share them in a way that resonates with the target audience. This emphasizes the skills needed within WFA teams beyond just data analytics.

- *The power of sensemaking*: High-reliability organizations, which operate in volatile and risky contexts, often have strong sensemaking schemas. These organizations are quick to pick up on weak cues and engage in sensemaking. On the flip side, some organizations normalize deviancy, interpreting even adverse events positively. Such organizations need "sensebreaking," which WFA can provide.
- *Overcoming complacency*: The concepts of "immanent sensemaking" and "absorbed coping" are presented as potential pitfalls for organizations that lead to complacency. WFA can serve as a catalyst for continuous organizational learning, ensuring organizations are always ready to adapt to new challenges.

In summary, the relationship between WFA and strategic change is profound. In today's fast-paced business environment, the integration of WFA with sensemaking is not just beneficial – it's essential. It underscores the changing nature of organizational strategy in today's data-driven age and highlights the multifaceted role that WFA teams play in shaping and guiding strategic change.

Chapter 6: Ethics and people analytics

With Chapter 6, perhaps the most dense (and academic) chapter within the book as it draws heavily on literature linked to ethical perspectives, we set out how important it is to take an ethical perspective or lens when considering how an organization approaches WFA. Importantly, ethics need to be considered when carrying out WFA projects as all business decisions have ethical implications. As discussed in this chapter, as WFA as an HR specialization has matured, the field has been awakened to the ethical challenges associated with WFA activities. As discussed, one of the considerations that need to be addressed when deciding the right questions to **A**sk, data to **C**ollect, **A**nalyses to conduct, and decisions to be **I**nfluenced is that an ethical perspective needs to be considered at each stage due to the potential range of ethical challenges in the field. These ethical challenges range from employee personal and data privacy concerns to the dangers of drawing conclusions from analyses that utilize problematic data (the "wrong" data) to the challenges of WFA recommendations being driven by biased data and/or analyses reinforcing bias. A central point made in the chapter is that ethical capabilities and the ability for WFA teams to reflect on planned activities from an ethical perspective are capabilities that all WFA teams need to build as the field matures.

As we look forward into the future, the ethical challenges discussed in Chapter 6 are likely to grow as technological and analytic tools available to WFA teams become more sophisticated. In particular, with the growing use of automated analytic systems and AI, WFA teams will need to be capable of unpicking the implications of automated HR and analytic systems. At the time of writing this book, the rapid development of algorithmic (and AI-based) technologies makes it almost impossible to predict how technological advances are going to impact the field of WFA. Undoubtedly, as technologies, vendors, and analytic service providers become more advanced (potentially beyond the capability of most WFA experts to understand), the potential ethical challenges that come to light will increase. This, therefore, highlights how important it is for WFA teams to ensure that a reflective ethical mindset is a competency as important as any other within the team.

Chapter 7: Building the analytics function

The chapter discusses the evolution and importance of WFA in aiding organizations in making strategic decisions based on workforce data. It uses the ACAI model to highlight the dual nature of WFA maturity, which impacts the development and evolution of WFA functions across different organizations. We argue against the conventional linear view of WFA maturity, proposing instead a maturity matrix that considers both the WFA team capabilities ("push factors") and organizational demand ("pull factors").

The chapter challenges the traditional staircase logic of WFA maturity, where WFA capabilities in organizations are thought to develop in a linear fashion over time. Instead, it stresses the importance of having the right equilibrium between "push" factors (WFA capabilities) and "pull" factors (organizational demand for analytics insights) to build an effective WFA function. It proposes a WFA maturity matrix mapping these dimensions at low, medium, and high levels.

- *WFA maturity*: The chapter begins by reviewing the rise of WFA and how it has been traditionally perceived as evolving from basic operational reporting to sophisticated predictive analytics. We proposed that WFA maturity should instead be viewed as a balance between what WFA teams are capable of producing ("push") and the organizational demand for analytics ("pull").
- *Push factors*: The chapter detailed the internal capabilities needed to develop WFA functions, focusing on three main areas: the skills and competencies required for workforce analysts, the importance of high-quality data processes, and the need for analysts to effectively partner with business units to translate data insights into strategic actions.
- *Pull factors*: This section examined how demand for analytics within the organization influences the development of WFA. We categorized demand into three levels – low, medium, and high – each reflecting the depth of integration and sophistication of analytics requested by stakeholders.
- *Integrating push and pull*: The final section discussed how the interplay between push and pull factors shapes the structure and capabilities of WFA functions. We emphasize that the optimal structure of a WFA function is highly context-dependent, influenced by both internal capabilities and external demands.

The chapter concludes by underscoring the importance of achieving a balance between developing analytical capabilities and fostering organizational demand to create an effective WFA function that can provide strategic insights and support decision-making processes.

Conclusions and key implications

Managing within the ACAI model

The advent of digital technologies compels virtually every company to address digital disruptions such as AI. This necessitates a reassessment of business strategies, focusing on creating information-enriched customer solutions delivered as seamless, personalized experiences (Ross & Beath, 2019; Minbaeva, 2021).

AI comprises a set of technologies that automate tasks previously performed by individuals, effectively transferring human processes to technology. This development obviously has tremendous implications for workers, with two important effects: either replacing them completely or eliminating repetitive or administrative aspects of their job, freeing them up to engage in higher-value activities.

In the context of WFA, many AI applications aim to reduce some of the more repetitive and administrative activities, thereby enabling individuals to focus on higher-level and/or higher-value work. However, such a transition requires employees to develop new skills, both in using AI applications and in performing these higher-value activities.

The prioritization and investment in establishing and formalizing processes and interactions between human and AI agents within WFA functions will vary between companies that are developing generative AI applications and those purchasing them. Companies purchasing applications from developers cannot simply assume that these vendors developed their applications using the same principles the purchasing company intends to incorporate in their use of the application.

However, both employees and managers on the "push" and "pull" sides (see Chapter 7) may exhibit reluctance towards utilizing AI in their work, a phenomenon often termed algorithmic aversion (Dietvorst et al., 2016). This can stem from various factors. Research suggests that people might hesitate to accept suggestions from AI because they view recommendations from humans as fairer, more precise, and more genuine, even if human advice proves to be less effective. Additionally, individuals might be reluctant to embrace AI guidance when they lack information about its past utilization by others. Moreover, the existing organizational culture can make it difficult to implement AI. As previously discussed, many proponents of these technologies argue for their significant cost-saving potential. While estimates differ regarding the number of jobs that might be eliminated due to technological advancements, there is consensus that some jobs are at risk. Thus, companies considering the use of these technologies in WFA may encounter considerable opposition, even from their own teams, as employees might not only resist but also actively attempt to undermine or sabotage the AI implementation.

The push and pull of WFA

Within organizations, the future of WFA is not simply at the top of a linear three- or four-stage maturity model. In Chapter 1, we introduced the ACAI model, which emphasizes the importance of asking the right questions, collecting the right data, analyzing them effectively, and influencing the right decisions. We highlighted that for companies to excel in WFA, they must not only adhere to these four steps but also consciously embrace the feedback loops inherent in the process. These feedback loops entail iteratively moving between collecting pertinent data and refining inquiries, analyzing the data and returning to gather additional information when necessary for more informed analyses, and influencing decisions by delving deeper into the insights gained.

By actively engaging in these feedback loops, the analytical capabilities of WFA functions can undergo continual enhancement, transitioning from aspiring to established and then advanced levels, as depicted in Figure 8.1 (vertical axis).

Within the ACAI model, an additional feedback loop extends from the final step of influencing decisions back to the initial phase of asking questions. As discussed in Chapter 7, by embracing this feedback loop, the WFA team will "educate the market" and foster the formulation of higher-level and more strategic inquiries. This, in turn, reinforces the organizational context, empowering stakeholders to actively seek insights from WFA (resulting in increased organizational demand for WFA, see Figure 8.1, horizontal axis) and rigorously apply them in driving evidence-based decisions and fostering a data-driven culture.

To advance in WFA, organizations must consistently propel this spiral, expanding its reach to encompass a broader spectrum of organizational decision-making in the realm of human capital. This propulsion will generate a few welcome spillovers. One such spillover is linked to the digital transformation of the HR function, which

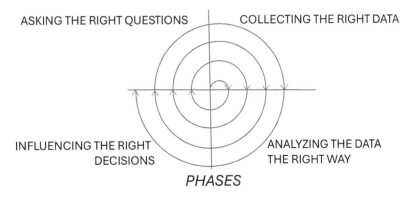

FIGURE 8.1 The ACAI Model.

includes digitizing information, digitalizing processes and roles within the HR operations, and, ultimately, digitally transforming the entire HR function and its strategies. In this scenario, WFA assumes a dual role: firstly, as a driver for automation, often termed as "doing digital," and secondly, as a catalyst for augmentation, signifying the transition to "being digital" (Minbaeva, 2021). By tackling challenges associated with advancing WFA, organizations can navigate the inherent paradoxes of digital transformation, encapsulated in the "duality of digital." This necessitates a holistic approach, integrating the automation of core WFA projects while concurrently prioritizing the enhancement of augmentation through the adoption of digital technologies by organizational stakeholders. Achieving equilibrium between these two facets enables organizations to fully harness the transformative power of digital transformation within HR.

Key points and takeaways from global WFA

Given its broad scope, a book focused on global WFA inevitably covers a wide range of topics and content. In the following sections, we summarize the key learnings from our book, organized by the fundamental elements of our ACAI model, with an eye towards the future and enhancing the quality of WFA. We believe that through this approach, we can ultimately improve workforce performance and, as a consequence, organizational performance.

Phase 1

Ask the right questions

The world of work is changing rapidly; WFA must reflect and support this reality

This is perhaps an obvious point, but it bears emphasizing: the environment is changing on the outside much more quickly than most firms are adapting on the inside. The sources of these changes are many. As an example, Snell et al. (2023) describe both impermanence and adaptation in organizational settings. For them, the nature of work is becoming more project-based and adaptable, reflecting a shift from permanent employment to flexible and temporary engagements. Specifically:

- *Impermanence of work*: A shift towards project-based and flexible work means that employees will need to be reassigned to new and different tasks much more frequently than in the past. This means that WFA systems must increase their focus on monitoring competencies, performance, and availability of employees.
- *Impermanence of workers*: Trends in employee willingness and preferences for freelancing and short-term gigs require firms to increase their emphasis on building

econometric models to match workforce supply and demand, and to develop more nimble recruiting and compensation systems.

■ *Impermanence of organizations*: A movement to more dynamic and temporary organizational structures means that employees can't expect the same level of commitment from employers as in the past, making them less likely to make long-term commitments to the organization.

These trends require HR to manage a more transient workforce that is increasingly employed in short-term engagements and needs to be flexible and adaptable. Workforce measurement and management systems must be equally flexible and responsive to these changing realities.

Developing a world-class WFA system should start with a clear understanding of how talent makes a difference throughout the organization

We often ask our client partners: How would more or better talent make a difference for your organization? How would you know? The field of strategy suggests two primary sources of potential contributions from the workforce: strategy *formulation* (where we decide where and how to compete) and strategy *implementation* (where we focus on implementing our strategy once it has been clarified). Understanding how talent makes a difference in each of these domains is easier said than done and requires a deep understanding of the specific processes involved. As we said in Chapter 2, "Every good regulator of a system must be a model of that system" (Conant & Ashby, 1970).

Developing answers to questions about how talent makes a difference also requires us to think and act much like a social scientist would. As we have argued, the choice of metrics is fundamentally a choice of which questions the firm needs to answer about the workforce. Asking good questions requires us to clearly understand our business's problems and opportunities and to translate them into questions about the workforce. Said differently, one needs to start with a question rather than available data – which is, unfortunately, the approach followed by most organizations.

In *The Differentiated Workforce*, Becker et al. (2009) argued that most organizations fail to capitalize on this because their workforce strategies are too general and not aligned with specific strategic objectives. A differentiated workforce strategy, which focuses specifically on roles and activities critical for success, is essential for sustainable competitive advantage. This requires a shift from broad, one-size-fits-all HR practices to targeted strategies that enhance strategic execution. This approach challenges senior managers and HR professionals to rethink their workforce strategies to focus more on strategic alignment and less on generic best practices.

The Differentiated Workforce elaborates on the importance of linking workforce strategies to the strategic capabilities of a company, arguing that the real strategic value of workforce or talent strategies lies in their ability to significantly improve strategy execution. Strategic capabilities are unique activities that differentiate a firm from its competitors. These capabilities should drive workforce planning and differentiation (Becker, Huselid, & Ulrich, 2001; Huselid, Beatty, & Becker, 2005, 2009; Huselid, Becker, & Beatty, 2005; Minbaeva, 2018). It emphasizes that strategic positions, which can significantly impact one or more of the firm's strategic capabilities, might exist at any level within the organization and are characterized by considerable variability in performance among job holders. This variability highlights the potential for substantial performance improvement, which can drive strategic success.

In the context of WFA, the key implication of a focus on strategic positions is that firms need to have a very clear understanding of *where* meaningful variance can be found in the workforce. For example, if you ask many pundits to identify the most important jobs or roles in any organization, they will likely list C-suite executives, e.g., the CEO, CFO, CMO, etc. Those are certainly highly important jobs, with wide decision latitude and authority. However, if you define "strategic position" or "A position" as an *investment opportunity*, or if you were to ask, "Where can we invest new resources to drive increases in workforce performance?" the answer is likely to be quite different. (Note: the same framing of "strategic position" applies to "strategic team." Sometimes, focusing on the individual is preferred; other times, it's better to focus on the team as an interdependent group.)

By the time an executive occupies a very senior role, they are likely to have had many different types of training and developmental experiences, such that the "low hanging fruit" for training or development will have already been gathered; this includes team-based interventions designed to improve cooperation and collaboration among senior executive teams. The senior leadership teams in many organizations already function at a relatively high level, both individually and collectively, such that large increases in performance will be very difficult to generate. As an example, consider how challenging it would be to dramatically improve the performance of a high-level college or Olympic sports team by, say, 20%. They, too, have already undergone many years of practice and coaching.

In contrast, consider many entry-level positions in organizations (or perhaps in a team of eight-year-olds learning a sport for the first time!). In these examples, large increases in individual and team basic skills are routine and relatively easy to generate (with time and attention). The same is true in organizations. The senior management team may comprise 10 to 30 people, all of whom have extensive years of challenging work experience. The variance in performance from the top to the bottom among these employees is likely to be relatively small, and their knowledge about how to work together effectively is quite high. Now consider a new cohort of accounting recruits, or perhaps program managers in a large corporation. Here, there may be 100 to 300 employees, and the variance from the top to the bottom is likely to be very substantial. For the accountants or program managers, it is not at all unrealistic to expect to be able to increase the average performance of the cohort by 20%.

Therefore, the opportunity for improvement in performance and actual strategic impact is often *greater* at lower levels in the organization. Yet, most organizations spend much more time and money on the development of employees and teams at much *higher* organizational levels. We are not suggesting that firms should discontinue investing in higher-level employees and teams. Rather, we are saying that variance in workforce performance provides an opportunity for potential improvement, and that we are more likely to observe this variance at lower organizational levels.

More effective WFA systems can help firms identify these opportunities and make the requisite investments. Without measurement, most firms will miss this opportunity entirely. Our recommendation here is for firms to focus on identifying and managing the variance in workforce performance, asking, "Where is the variance in workforce performance, and what can we do about it?"

Top talent is a scarce resource; it is critical to have a clear strategy for where you want to "spend" it

We often ask the firms we work with: What if you had to justify the primary activities of each job, role, or team from an economic perspective? Could you do it? In other words, what work would you pay for if you didn't have any work? This line of questioning invariably leads managers and leaders to the conclusion that some jobs and teams (and work) matter more than others. Much like with real estate, location matters (Becker & Huselid, 2006).

We believe it is important to conceptualize investments in the workforce (and WFA) as an investment decision tied to scarce resources. Most firms cannot afford – nor do they need – A performers in all roles, and A teams staffed throughout the organization. It follows, then, that HR policies and practices should not only fit the general strategy but also be specifically tailored to enhance strategic positions. This involves making clear distinctions between roles and teams that are crucial for strategic success and those that are not, ensuring that critical roles and teams are supported by HR practices that drive business objectives.

Developing effective WFA is challenging and takes time and resources. One of our key points has been that it is important to be thoughtful and strategic in where and how these resources are deployed. We believe that the best WFA resources should be deployed to strategic talent in strategic positions and in strategic teams. In short, measures should follow the variance in workforce performance, and firms need to have a strategy for identifying and managing the sources of this variance.

It takes a village (i.e., a broad range of competencies) to build a world-class WFA system

It is important to understand how various disciplines contribute to the design and implementation of a world-class WFA system. We've emphasized the role of behavioral science theory in understanding these questions. The key point we wish to make is that it is important to understand the theoretical frameworks driving firm-level outcomes.

In support of these outcomes, in Chapter 2, we introduced the key theoretical domains we believe to be the most relevant to WFA, such as strategic management, economics, strategic HRM, I/O psychology, organizational behavior, psychometrics and econometrics, data science, and OD and change management. Chapter 2 should be helpful in understanding how to think about designing a WFA system. In Chapter 7, we focused on *who* should be designing these elements and *how* they should be deployed (including WFA team composition at the individual, team, and organizational levels). This was the "push" and "pull" associated with the WFA system that we described in Chapter 7.

Phase 2

Collect the right data

It is critical to match the quality of the data (and the rigor of the data collection processes) with the importance of the questions being asked

Just as some jobs and roles are more important than others, some questions about the workforce are relatively more important, too. Capitalizing on these outcomes will start with reviewing prior research and formulating plausible hypotheses. It also has implications for how to staff the analytics project team.

Carefully plan data collection processes to gather information on the most important elements in the model, as existing data may not suffice

Throughout this book, we have emphasized the importance of developing strategic workforce measures that are aligned with the company's business strategy. We have argued against starting with pre-existing measures or relying solely on benchmarking and stressed the necessity of creating unique metrics that truly reflect the strategic contributions of the workforce to the firm's performance (Huselid, 2018). We also advocate for measures that directly link workforce performance to business outcomes, ensuring that HR functions as a strategic partner rather than just an administrative support.

We also believe it is critical to align the measures that are designed and deployed with the business strategy. The most effective WFA systems craft unique metrics that genuinely reflect the strategic contributions of the workforce to the firm's overall performance. Fundamentally, these are data quality and levels of analysis questions, which must be answered before collecting any data. Otherwise, the risk is starting the analytical process and only later finding it cannot be done properly because of the wrong dataset.

Focus on the HR system, not the HR practice

One of the key conclusions from the HR Strategy literature is the importance of focusing on the HR *system* rather than individual HR *practices* (Becker & Huselid, 1998, 2006; Huselid, 1995). For example, investing significant resources in a new incentive compensation plan will be wasted unless it can be linked with highly effective performance management processes (Huselid, 1995). Many other examples exist in organizations where the returns on one investment (e.g., cross-training) depend on the levels of investment in another element (promotion opportunities). Economists call this form of relationship a *complementarity*, and it is something that smart organizations capitalize on. These relationships can be thwarted, however, when organizations operate in silos and do not coordinate their investments across areas. The ability to conceptualize such ideas and implement them effectively relies on systems thinking, which incorporates the importance of understanding levels of analysis (Levenson, 2011, 2015, 2018).

Speed, cycle times, and refresh rates are much more important in some elements of WFA than in others

Some elements of the workforce that should be considered for measurement are what we would describe as long-cycle measures (e.g., culture), which change relatively slowly over long periods of time. Other measures we would describe as short-cycle measures, which change rapidly and must be monitored more closely. A rough example might be the distinction between climate and weather. A region's climate is relatively stable, but the weather on any given day can be highly variable. If someone is contemplating moving to a new city, we imagine the focus would be on the region's *climate*. If it's more short-term planning, such as having a picnic over the weekend, the focus would be on the *weather*. One of these measures is long-cycle; the other is short-term in nature (although we recognize that climate change has increased the variance in climate substantially, so perhaps we should find another example!). In any case, the key issue is the importance of accounting for these factors in the design of data collection and analytics processes.

Ethical issues in WFA are critical to consider and incorporate

As organizations increasingly rely on AI and machine learning for decision-making, understanding and mitigating potential biases becomes paramount to ensure fairness, equity, and ethical behavior. Ethical issues pervade many elements of the WFA process, but probably none more than data collection, storage, and access. A central point we make is that ethical capabilities and the ability of the WFA team to reflect on planned activities from an ethical perspective are capabilities that all WFA teams need to build as the field matures. In particular, with the growing use of automated analytic systems and AI, WFA teams will need to be capable of unpicking the implications of automated HR and analytic systems.

While WFA offers powerful tools for enhancing organizational effectiveness, it also presents ethical challenges, especially when the validity of the data or metrics is in question. Organizations have a responsibility to ensure the ethical use of data, keeping in mind the profound impacts these decisions can have on individual employees and the broader organization.

In summary, while AI and algorithms can offer transformative advantages in the realm of WFA, the potential for bias, both subtle and overt, remains a significant challenge. Ensuring ethical and fair use of these tools demands continuous vigilance, a thorough understanding of where biases can originate, and a systematic approach to detecting and addressing them. Landers and Behrend's framework, as well as the expanded considerations listed above, can provide a solid foundation for WFA teams to address these challenges head-on. As WFA evolves and becomes increasingly intertwined with AI and big data, the ethical dimensions of these practices grow more critical. While technology provides powerful tools for insight and efficiency, it's up to human actors, particularly those in HR, to ensure these tools are wielded responsibly and ethically.

Phase 3

Analyze data in the right way

We live in a multivariate world: Workforce performance is a function of many different factors; analyses should reflect this reality

Historically, many WFA analyses have been simplistic and bivariate in nature (e.g., focused on the examination of the correlation between two variables). For example, we often hear organizations ask about the correlation between compensation levels and turnover. However, simple bivariate analyses rarely provide significant insight and may indeed be highly misleading. Workforce performance is influenced by multiple determinants.

A common framework suggests that performance is a function of ability, motivation, and opportunity (Huselid, 1995). When diagnosing a workforce performance issue, it is important to consider: Can they do it? That is, do they have the requisite skills? Then ask, Do they want to do it? That is, are they motivated to perform? Finally, ask, Will we let them do it? That is, is the culture and work environment conducive to employees working together to complete their tasks? Breaking down the drivers of workforce performance is important not only to help gain an understanding of "why" an employee or team is or is not performing, but also to help tailor specific interventions. For example, a skills issue might require training, a motivation issue might necessitate performance management, communication, or incentive interventions, while a culture issue might call for a broad-based OD or change management intervention.

In short, our statistical and estimation models need to be as sophisticated and well-developed as the behavior they seek to predict, as outlined in Chapter 4. WFA teams can often find colleagues with sophisticated skills in finance, accounting, marketing, and supply chain functions who, in our experience, are typically happy to help.

Models of workforce success based on the current organization and workforce have the potential to be wildly inaccurate (at best) and biased and illegal (at worst)

Many WFA models are developed and validated based on historical data. For example, a firm may seek to identify the bundle of characteristics associated with leadership performance, or perhaps with the frequency of promotion. Using data from archival records, they might develop a multivariate model of employee performance as a function of age, race, gender, GPA, hours of training, functional expertise, etc. If they find that white men are more likely to be promoted, should we conclude that we ought to focus our hiring and promotional efforts on white males?

Of course not. There are myriad reasons why white males have historically had preferential access to opportunities in organizations (and society in general). However, these conclusions demonstrate the perils of building models of workforce performance using historical data that are not grounded in theory and existing research evidence (Chapter 2). There are many potential solutions – some statistical, some methodological – available based on the specific situation, as described in Chapter 4. However, the key point we wish to emphasize is that the rigor of the analyses must match the importance of the problem.

Phase 4

Influence the right decisions

Don't assume that meaningful empirical findings will create meaningful managerial change: Help is needed to make this happen

Any analytical endeavor is, at its heart, a sensemaking process. WFA systems can create substantial value, but effectively implementing the results requires the comprehensive and holistic approach outlined here. The strategic change process is fundamentally a sensemaking journey in which leaders envision, managers implement, and employees reenact. To successfully navigate this challenging cognitive and emotional terrain, organizations must adopt an approach that leverages WFA as a dynamic, integral component across every phase of transformation.

By embedding WFA into strategic planning, decision-making, and execution, organizations can access critical insights, tools, and platforms that facilitate and accelerate sensemaking throughout the change process. This integration allows WFA to act as a catalyst for meaningful and sustainable strategic change, providing leaders with data-driven frameworks to identify triggers for transformation, communicate change messages, and measure the impact of strategic initiatives. By treating WFA as an embedded capability rather than an on-demand service, organizations can enhance their ability to navigate the complexities of change while building a culture of continuous learning and improvement.

Work to address the academic–practitioner gap in WFA

As discussed, there is much to know and learn in the field of WFA, and as partners in this process, it is important to help practitioners gain a better understanding of the academic (scientific) literature in this area. Likewise, academics must continue to improve their understanding of the challenges and issues faced by practitioners in implementing WFA in their organizations. Bridging this gap can create substantial value, particularly as the performance of HR professionals has an important impact on WFA outcomes (Kryscynski et al., 2017). Key points we have found especially helpful include:

- *WFA as a dynamic capability*: Treat WFA as a dynamic organizational capability that seamlessly integrates with sensemaking, rather than viewing it as an on-demand analytics service. This ensures its continued value in organizational decision-making.
- *Exposing strategic triggers*: Utilize WFA to uncover potential triggers that draw leadership attention to the necessity of strategic change. This proactive identification can shape the direction of transformation efforts.

- *Data-driven change messaging*: Leverage WFA to communicate data-driven, rational change messages when conveying the organizational vision. A clear, evidence-based rationale can help gain stakeholder buy-in and align teams with the intended strategic direction.
- *Facilitating sensemaking*: Involve WFA in gathering and analyzing data to foster collective sensemaking around proposed changes. This collaboration ensures that changes are better understood and accepted throughout the organization.
- *Storytelling with analytics insights*: The WFA team should utilize compelling storytelling techniques to guide how analytics insights are interpreted and embraced by the organization, ensuring that data translates into a shared understanding.
- *Measuring outcomes*: Embed WFA within the organization to measure change outcomes, identify ineffective actions, and generate learning that sustains and refines the change process over time.

These takeaways highlight the critical role WFA plays in strategic change initiatives, emphasizing its value beyond traditional analytics and positioning it as a vital component of organizational transformation.

Think carefully about the supply of (the "push") and demand for (the "pull") WFA

WFA maturity is not just about analytical sophistication. It evolves through the interaction between the WFA team's capabilities ("push") and the organization's demand for actionable insights from WFA ("pull").

- Three key "push" factors enable building sustainable WFA capabilities:
  - Employing workforce analysts with the right knowledge, skills, and abilities (e.g., data analysis, storytelling, business acumen)
  - Implementing high-quality data procedures and governance
  - Developing the ability for analysts to partner effectively with business units
- Two main "pull" factors drive organizational demand for WFA insights:
  - Digitalization of business processes spurring requests for people data/ analytics
  - Cultivating an analytical, data-driven culture where evidence informs decision-making
- The structure and roles of the WFA team should be configured based on the specific equilibrium point (balance) between the "push" and "pull" factors in the organization.
- Aspiring WFA functions may start with just one or two analysts providing basic reporting, while advanced functions have larger teams with specialized roles to enable predictive analytics and a gradual shift towards automation.

- Investing heavily in WFA capabilities without commensurate organizational demand will limit the business value created. Aligning the "push" and "pull" factors is critical.
- Building an effective WFA team requires balancing investments in analytical capabilities with fostering an organizational environment and culture that demands and can absorb data-driven insights.

Build and develop your WFA implementation team carefully

- *Holistic Approach to WFA:* Organizations should view WFA not merely as a tool for data-driven insights but as an integral part of their strategic change process. This implies that WFA teams need to have multifaceted skills, including analytics, storytelling, and business strategy.
- *Training and Development:* Given the emphasis on the multifunctional role of WFA teams, there's a clear indication that ongoing training and development are vital. Teams should be equipped with skills to analyze data, communicate findings compellingly, and align those findings with the broader organizational strategy.
- *Organizational Culture:* For WFA to be effective, the organizational culture must value continuous learning, adaptation, and change. Leadership plays a pivotal role in fostering such a culture.

In closing

The need for WFA represents what economists call a *derived demand*. That is, if talent is an important determinant of firm success, then WFA is likely to be as well. While we believe that effective talent management remains a substantial opportunity for value creation in most firms, we also believe that it is important to invest in workforce management and measurement systems commensurate with their value. This means choosing one's shots carefully.

We believe that the ACAI process we have outlined – which is, in essence, the application of the scientific method to business problems – is central to this solution. Doing this work effectively requires thinking and acting like a social scientist. Be skeptical but purposeful in pursuing building an evidence-based workforce management system (Barends & Rousseau, 2018). But don't underestimate the challenges involved – this may be the most important thing to learn. Managing change with data needs to be designed into the intervention from the outset.

We hope that our efforts have provided a better understanding of the opportunities and challenges associated with designing and implementing effective WFA systems. In some firms – the rare organizations that have already developed a world-class WFA system – we hope our work will provide the motivation to leverage, maintain, and expand the scope and impact of existing efforts. In most other firms, which are at earlier stages of development, we hope that our work can offer the framework, tools, and motivation to build a better WFA system. The challenges are great, but the returns are even greater.

References

Barends, E., & Rousseau, D. M. (2018). *Evidence-Based Management: Making better organizational decisions*. Kogan Page,

Becker, B. E., & Huselid, M. A. (1998). High performance work systems and firm performance: A synthesis of research and managerial implications. *Research in Personnel and Human Resource Management, 16*, 53–101.

Becker, B. E., & Huselid, M. A. (2006). Strategic human resource management: Where do we go from here? *Journal of Management, 32*, 898–925.

Becker, B. E., Huselid, M. A., & Beatty, R. W. (2009). *The differentiated workforce: Translating talent into strategic impact*. Harvard Business Press.

Becker, B. E., Huselid, M. A., & Ulrich, D. (2001). *The HR scorecard: Linking people, strategy, and performance*. Harvard Business Press.

Combs, J., Liu, Y., Hall, A., & Ketchen, D. (2006). How much do high-performance work practices matter? A meta-analysis of their effects on organizational performance. *Personnel Psychology, 59*(3), 501–528.

Conant, R. C., & Ashby, R. W. (1970). Every good regulator of a system must be a model of that system. *International Journal of Systems Science, 1*(2), 89–97. https://doi.org/10.1080/00207727008920220

Dietvorst, B. J., Simmons, J. P., & Massey, C. (2016). Overcoming algorithm aversion: People will use imperfect algorithms if they can (even slightly) modify them. Management Science, 64(3), 1155–1170.

Edwards, M. R., & Edwards, K. (2019). *Predictive HR analytics: Mastering the HR metric*. Kogan Page.

Huselid, M. A. (1995). The impact of human resource management practices on turnover, productivity, and corporate financial performance. *Academy of Management Journal, 38*(3), 635–672.

Huselid, M. A. (2018). The science and practice of workforce analytics: Introduction to the HRM special issue. *Human Resource Management, 57*(3), 679–684. https://doi.org/10.1002/hrm.21916help_outline

Huselid, M. A. (2023). Integrating utility analysis and workforce strategy research: Suggestions for future work. *International Journal of Human Resource Management, 34*(13), 2620–2635. To link to this article: https://doi.org/10.1080/09585192.2023.2225281

Huselid, M. A., Beatty, R. W., & Becker, B. E. (2005). "A" players or "A" positions? The strategic logic of workforce management. *Harvard Business Review, 83*(12), 110–117.

Huselid, M. A., Becker, B. E., & Beatty, D. (2005). *The workforce scorecard: Managing human capital to execute strategy*. Harvard Business Press.

Kryscynski, D., Reeves, C., Stice-Lusvardi, R., Ulrich, M., & Russell, G. (2017). Analytical abilities and the performance of HR professionals. *Human Resource Management, 57*, 715–738 10.1002/hrm.21854.

Levenson, A. (2011). Using targeted analytics to improve talent decisions. *People and strategy, 34*(2), 11.

Levenson, A. (2015). *Strategic analytics: Advancing strategy execution and organizational effectiveness*. Berrett-Koehler.

Levenson, A. (2018). Using workforce analytics to improve strategy execution. *Human Resource Management, 57*(3), 685–700. https://doi.org/10.1002/hrm.21850

Levenson, A. (2021). Competencies in an era of digitalized talent management. In S. Wiblen (Ed.), *Digitalized talent management: Navigating the human-technology interface* (pp. 51–78). Routledge.

Levenson, A., & Fink, A. (2017). Human capital analytics: Too much data and analysis, not enough models and business insights. *Journal of Organizational Effectiveness, 4*(2), 145–156. https://doi.org/10.1108/JOEPP-03-2017-0029

McKinsey & Company. (2021). What matters most? Five priorities for CEOs in the next normal. McKinsey & Company.

McKinsey & Company. (2022). What matters most? Six priorities for CEOs in turbulent times. New York, NY.

McKinsey & Company. (2023). What matters most? Eight priorities for CEOs in 2024. New York, NY.

Minbaeva, D. B. (2018). Building credible human capital analytics for organizational competitive advantage. *Human Resource Management, 57*(3), 701–713. https://doi.org/10.1002/hrm.21848

Minbaeva, D. B. (2021). Disrupted HR? *Human Resource Management Review, 31*(4), 1–8. https7/doi.org/101016/jhrmr.2020ti00820

Ross, J., & Beath, C. (2019). *Designed for digital: How to architect your business for sustainable success.* MIT Press.

Snell, S. A., Swart, J., Morris, S., & Boon, C. (2023). The HR ecosystem: Emerging trends and a future research agenda. *Human Resource Management, 62*(1), 5–14. https://doi.org/10.1002/hrm.22158.

Storey, J., Ulrich, D., & Wright, P. M. (2019). *Strategic human resource management: A research overview* (1st ed.). Routledge. https://doi.org/10.4324/9780429490217

Zhu, D., Ulrich, D., Das, S., & Smallwood, N. (2024). A system for analyzing human capability at scale using AI. In K. Arai (Ed.), *Intelligent systems and applications. IntelliSys 2023.* Lecture Notes in Networks and Systems (Vol. 824, pp 308–324). Springer. https://doi.org/10.1007/978-3-031-47715-7_21

Index